hd

- Are you paying for "junk" insurance?

- Why is buying carpet a "blind" sale?

- Does that beautiful setting conceal a flaw in that precious stone?

- How can you determine if you are buying a real Rolex?

- What causes the big cost variance in cosmetic brands and how much do you *really* need to pay for fine quality and results?

- Is the "fabulous fabric" on that expensive sofa hiding poor quality workmanship?

- Are you reacting to impulse shopping inducements at your food store?

- Is mail-order shopping a safe buy?

- When does that great gray-market deal turn into a service-problem turnoff?

SECRETS FROM THE UNDERGROUND SHOPPER®

answers these questions
and many more.

SECRETS FROM THE UNDERGROUND SHOPPER®

THE ONLY BOOK TO TELL YOU WHAT THE RETAILERS WON'T

SUE GOLDSTEIN

TAYLOR PUBLISHING COMPANY
DALLAS, TEXAS

Library Of Congress Cataloging-in-Publication Data

Goldstein, Sue, 1941–
    Secrets from the underground shopper.

    1. Consumer education. 2. Shopping. I. Title.
TX335.G587   1986   640.73   86-14460
ISBN 0-87833-538-2

Printed in the United States of America
0 9 8 7 6 5 4 3 2 1

Dedication:
It's no secret, I love Josh

Acknowledgements

I always marvel at the lengthy cast of characters that are thanked at the Academy Awards presentations. The list seems endless and I can understand why.

During the past fifteen years of developing *The Underground Shopper®*, I have never been alone. There has always been a dedicated crew to thank and a consumer who appreciates the hard work brought forth in the pages of each book.

Secrets is no exception. But my editor, Christine Caperton, deserves some special recognition for lending the direction and calm that must accompany every frantic rush to meet the deadline. And besides, our friendship has taken on a whole new dimension and that is a real plus in my work.

To Arnie Hanson, the publisher, who took my casual conversation at lunch to heart and offered me an opportunity of a lifetime; to Bobby Frese, who helped in the process by sharing my enthusiasm; and to the researchers who dug into my resources with a vengeance, my sincerest thanks.

Apparel: Judith Putnam
Carpet, Furniture, Antiques, and Auctions: Will Sansom, Kathryn Hayden
Cosmetics: Amanda Youngblood
Food: Kim Goad
Gray-Market Cars, Cameras, and Computers: Beth Ellen Rosenthal

Insurance: Judith Putnam
Jewelry: Beth Ellen Rosenthal
Mail Order: Ron Whittington
Real Estate: Beth Ellen Rosenthal

Of course, the merchants who willingly spilled the beans made this book an invaluable resource guide for most of us unsuspecting consumers and for that effort I am truly appreciative.

And to the readers of this book, cheers—for wanting at last to know what the retailers have never wanted you to know before.

Contents

The fashion industry is filled with ploys that appeal to shopper's emotions rather than their practical judgment. From exploring the true value of high-priced designer fashions to explaining the retailers' markups, *Secrets'* sources guide shoppers through private label garments, designer knockoff fashions, and counterfeits. Are you a smart clothing shopper? *Secrets* discusses the growing alternative for high-quality garments, the off-price merchant, and fashion facts for smart shopping.

These three big-ticket purchases—carpet, furniture, and antiques—are close to "mystery buys" for most shoppers. *Secrets* exposes the "blind-sale" problems of buying carpet and the hidden value or lack of value inside furniture purchases. The auction is one of few marketplaces where the buyer is his own worst enemy. From the antique auction to the liquidation sale, shoppers need to do their homework before they attempt to buy.

Can hope be sold in a bottle? The cosmetics industry comes close to this with its beauty creams. But there is solid research behind the psychology of beauty and its effects on your potential success in business and personal relationships. *Secrets* evaluates these concepts with the facts about what is really in those beautiful little bottles.

Here is some food for thought: thousands of dollars are invested by supermarkets on intense lighting, store design, and research on human behavior in an attempt to capture and control your food dollars. *Secrets* explains the impact of product positioning, FDA labeling requirements, national brands versus store brands, and store and manufacturer specials and promotions on how you spend that coveted dollar—enabling you, the shopper, to control your spending habits to your advantage.

GRAY-MARKET CARS, CAMERAS, AND COMPUTERS 137

Gray deals do not always add up to good prices. Buying a gray-market product saves dollars upfront but can cost in hassles in the end due to problems with warranties (or lack of them), service, and repairs. This is truly a buyer beware area and *Secrets'* sources advise shoppers about what to watch out for when purchasing luxury goods at those underground, overseas discount prices.

INSURANCE 165

This is the one of the few purchases that is sold, not bought. *Secrets* advises on how to avoid "junk policies" and that the single most important decision in this market is selecting an agent, not a policy. Your agent can guide you through the maze of the insurance industry, a challenge to even the most educated among us, or can advise you not to waste hundreds of dollars a year. Which type of agent do you have and when was the last time you reviewed your insurance policies?

JEWELRY 215

From the four C's of diamonds—color, cut, clarity, and carat—to how to determine if it is really 14 karat gold or a Rolex, *Secrets'* sources arm shoppers with gems of information for savvy purchases in the world of jewelry. Is there a flaw in your diamond hidden under the prong of that gorgeous setting? Only your jeweler knows for sure, but shouldn't you?

MAIL-ORDER SHOPPING 237

You can have it all from your armchair—from caviar to vitamins, and at a substantial discount. It is called mail-order shopping and it is an industry that is growing rapidly. *Secrets'* inside sources describe the companies to avoid and steps to take to assure your mail-order purchase is hassle free.

REAL ESTATE AND MORTGAGES   257
The stakes are high when dealing in real estate and your possible future home. This major financial venture is often so confusing the buyer gets lost in the jargon. *Secrets* pulls together the information shoppers need to make wise, clean real estate deals and avoid possible pitfalls and the consequence of buying beyond your means—the dreaded foreclosure.

SECRETS
FROM THE
UNDERGROUND
SHOPPER®

Introduction

I have always loved the story about Frieda Loehmann. In the early twenties, she founded the chain of discount designer stores that bear her name today. Always dressed in black, she would comb New York's Seventh Avenue, sauntering from showroom to showroom, offering to pay cash for designers' out-of-season merchandise.

Although I have never felt the need to saunter from store to store, when I was growing up I was always on the periphery of affluence and had to find other ways to dress the way my wealthier friends did. Indeed, even before I became the Underground Shopper, I knew how to hunt down a bargain. My mother and I would spend many a Saturday afternoon shopping, scanning our favorite stores for markdowns. Her golden rule was "never pay retail." Buy one good thing on sale, she would preach, and wear it to death. And I would.

While shopping had always been something of a pastime, if not a passion, for me, it did not occur to me that I could turn it into the way I earned my living until some sixteen years ago when I found myself out of sorts on a number of counts: new to Dallas and in the midst of a divorce, I was without substantial means of supporting myself and my three-month-old son. I was not sure of much except that I was fearful of being alone and so broke I did not even own a car. Josh was told he would need braces for his teeth (he did) and I dreamed of a Cadillac and an audience with Dick Cavett (almost).

The turning point came when I met my first friend in Dallas, Ann Light. Convinced that every woman in this part of the country was tall, thin, blonde, and had husbands "in-the-business," we felt in order to compete, we would have to learn how to get-for-ourselves-wholesale or resort to the occasional Last Call sales at Neiman-Marcus if we were to survive in Dallas. For a while we pouted about how easy it always seemed for others to have unlimited wardrobes, but then we plotted. We would never be tall or skinny—that much we were willing to concede—which meant our only hope was to affect the look, which was the next best thing.

We put out heads together and came up with a way to look glamorous and well-dressed in spite of our economic woes. We decided to set out in search of bargains in Dallas stores. I must admit we were quite a team: Ann had the car; I, the chutzpah, but together very little money. And when a neighbor told me she had her hair done three times a week at the poshest salon in Highland Park, but instead was discovered at the Beauty College on Tuesday for the $1.99 special, I knew we were on to something.

After several months of scouring the market, we had accrued 124 listings (most of which were factory outlets for clothing). Looking back, I feel certain we could have come up with more but midway through the venture a merchant rather glibly mentioned that another set of shoppers had been in the week before doing research for a similar guide book. Whether he was telling the truth, we will never know. But it spurred us on. Overnight we organized, typed, rated, and went on to the printing presses.

We decided to publish our humble little book ourselves since Random House, Doubleday, and Simon and Schuster rejected it. The one problem we had not anticipated, however, was not being able to find a printer. After countless tries, we resorted to an industrial printer who was located on the outskirts of the city limits. He produced 5,000 copies (his minimum run) which, as it turned out, was just enough for the first day's sales. That first *Underground Shopper®* had almost 100,000 readers in its first year without, I might add, a single cent going toward advertising. It was as if the women of Dallas had never known there were bargains to be had, and their word-of-mouth became our advertising. Thank you to *The Dallas Morning News* and *Dallas Times Herald* for the front page coverage that launched our humble empire of doing what most women do for free.

A year or so later, Ann wanted out of the business and I went solo with the *Underground Shoppers* that followed: my sister compiled the St. Louis and Detroit editions. The next three—Houston, Minneapolis, and Boston—were done by two young couples, one couple quit their job to bargain hunt professionally, and the other to help ease the cost of a Harvard MBA. And then my sister *and* mother teamed up to compile the Miami edition. Still others followed, including Tulsa, Atlanta, New Orleans, New York, and Chicago—each covering fashion, of course, and also listing appliances, gifts, furniture, even cars. (Who was it that said the bad thing about writing a bestseller was that you have to follow it up with another . . . and yet another?)

We eventually began receiving feedback from our readers, many of whom were women complaining the only thing I was not supplying was information on how to get a man (though we did not know since we had never found them to be a bargain)—nevertheless, *The Greatest Little Bachelor Book in Texas* (1980) sold some 50,000 copies but had an even greater readership. That led to my next endeavor, *A Guide to Discount Mail Order Shopping* (Andrews, McMeel and Parker, 1983), which was not nearly as much fun to test shop but proved even more popular, as it is in its second, revised edition. Next on the horizon, *The Underground Shopper's Guide to Fitness & Health* (Ballantine Books, Spring 1987) leads the shopper through the maze of thousands of fitness and health options, from the best videos to the best spas where you can lose weight without losing your shirt.

As the editions have grown, so have the demands on my time. I have a number of researchers staked out across the country. They call the shots, visiting the hideaways, tasting the good life without the hefty price tags.

With *Secrets from The Underground Shopper*, however, we departed from our tried and true format and were excited to explore a new realm of shopping. The off-price industry has changed radically over the years: hunting for bargains is not nearly as black and white as it was in Frieda Loehmann's day, or for that matter, in the early seventies when *The Underground Shopper* debuted. That, coupled with the fact that shopping, I have learned over the years, can be an intimidating experience for some.

With that in mind, rather than listing where to go for the best deals (as we have in the past), we decided the best way for shoppers to arm themselves in the ever-changing world of retail is to know what they are getting into. *Secrets* takes a behind-the-scenes look at some of the most loosely regulated industries—via the experts who reveal the trade secrets of their respective fields.

And another secret is out of the bag—that shoppers *can* have it all, *can* taste the good life and be proud of buying it for less. There are bargains to be had, and the smart shopper will love them without ever having to say I'm sorry for not paying full price.

APPAREL

The good news for apparel shoppers is that sharp competition is yielding many opportunities for good buys on high-quality merchandise. The growth of off-price retailing and such developments as wholesale or membership clubs give shoppers more options than ever.

The bad news is that shoppers continue to be bombarded with tricks, gimmicks, and outright fraud. Consumers must be aware of the pitfalls of the fashion industry and must avoid having the wool (literally) pulled over their eyes. A good start on being a smart shopper is in following these four "by-laws."

1. By looking for high-quality features in garments, shoppers can avoid buying bad merchandise with a well-advertised name.

2. By knowing about deceptive pricing and false sales, shoppers can avoid being suckered by an artificial bargain.

3. By knowing about large clothes with small sizes marked on the tags, shoppers can avoid buying clothes for vanity's sake.

4. By knowing about the massive amounts of counterfeit clothing being pushed by unscrupulous or unaware retailers, shoppers can be wary.

ARE YOU A SMART SHOPPER?

How much do you really know about the dollars you spend on clothing? How much do you know about the garments themselves?

For example, if you buy an article of clothing at full retail price for $200, how much do you believe goes to the retailer who sold you the item, and how much goes for material, workmanship and other costs?

Do you pay $25 for the cost of being sold the garment? How about $50? or $75? Would you believe $100?

Yes, $100 is the very minimum a retailer would take out of the $200 price tag. In many cases, retailers take an even bigger percentage. Furthermore, the percentage taken by the retailer continues to be on an upwardly spiraling trend.

The apparel industry is a fast-paced, competitive business. It is difficult for consumers, who get most of their information from slick advertising, to stay abreast of the industry and cut through the razzle-dazzle that is designed not to educate, but to lure.

Here are some other examples of apparel pitfalls for shoppers:

1. Most "designer" labels have had minimal, if any, input from the designers themselves. The overwhelming trend is to farm out the entire production to a less well-known manufacturer who pays a royalty (about 5 to 10 percent of the manufacturer's cost) for the use of the famous name.

2. Industry insiders consistently report that designer names do not necessarily mean quality. In fact, designer labels have become somewhat of a joke—and the joke is on you if you buy a poor quality garment under the mistaken impression that it is a good item simply because of the name.

3. Private labels, thought of as money-savers when it comes to generic drugs or no-name-brand foodstuffs, can sometimes mask the cost of a garment, allowing prestigious stores to take a walloping markup on clothing manufactured by unknown concerns. This is particularly true of inexpensive imports.

4. Sometimes the "sale" item is not really a sale at all, simply a gimmick to help push the garment. The price is originally placed at an artificially high level, then "slashed" to give the appearance of a sale.

5. Consumers in 1985 purchased almost $20 billion worth of illegal, counterfeit goods including such items as fake designer jeans, copycat "Gucci" bags, and false Izod shirts.

6. More and more consumers are developing the I-ate-too-many-enchiladas-last-month-but-I-still-wear-a-size-6 syndrome. Yes, many of us are all too eager to snap up an item simply because it's a small size, ignoring the fact that it might fit simply because the manufacturer has generously made the garment bigger (on purpose to tempt your vanity).

The fashion industry is filled with ploys such as these that appeal to our emotions, rather than our practical judgment. Consumers can protect themselves by objectively judging quality, by shopping and comparing, and by being aware of the tricks of the rag trade.

Consumers can play an important part in what shows up on America's racks and in its catalogs. The chain-link process among the textile mills, designers, manufacturers, jobbers, contractors, and retailers, is not a one-way street. If the buying public rejects a garment, the message is relayed back through the chain.

On the negative side, if the buying public is willing to accept defects in expensive garments, defective garments will continue to show up on racks. If clothes with well-advertised names are sold simply because of the name's image, then consumers will continue to soak up the cost of paying for that name's image, regardless (and in many cases, in spite of) the quality of the garment.

If a store can add an extra $20 to the regular cost of an item, then reduce the price by $20.01, and it sells like hot cakes, then the practice will continue.

In short, consumers must say "no" to gimmicks, and "yes" to high-quality merchandise at reasonable prices. Consumers do have power. As one longtime retailer put it: "There's an old saying. To the buyer, the dress is diamonds. In the dressing room, the dress is gold. But if it hangs on the rack too long, well, you know what it is."

THE NAME GAME

Why do consumers buy designer clothes? Maybe it is because they like the style, or they like the fit. Or perhaps it is because they feel comfortable with a name they recognize. That way, they know exactly who is making the clothes. Or do they?

The trend among designers is to license their name, turning over the entire manufacturing operation (including the design) to other clothing firms. In essence, most designer companies are marketing firms, selling their name for use by others.

While designers may hang on to control of their top-of-the-line collections, industry observers say most have little or nothing to do with their mainstream line of clothes. "It's an unbelievable trend," said Kurt Barnard, publisher of *Barnard's Retail Marketing Report* in New York City. "There's no way anyone can really have control of the millions of products being sold (under designers' names.)"

Designer John Weitz, chairman of John Weitz, Inc., who licenses his name internationally, told members of the American Marketing Association that creativity has gone out of fashion decisions. "The fact is that it does not matter at this point if the names are French, Italian, English, American or pure fiction," he said. "The fashion decisions are in the hands of sales managers and the marketing is in the hands of media-wise executives."

The designer craze was fueled by the flames of passion for expensive blue jeans that caused millions of Americans to put designer names on the back pocket of their tightly fitting jeans, beginning in the late 1970s.

Firms such as Jordache and Sasson (no relation, by the way, to Vidal Sassoon), began their licensing empires on their name recognition from blue jeans while other names associated with haute couture began marketing lines for middle- to upper-income consumers.

The clothing designers spilled over into other areas as well. Designer names such as Christian Dior (the designer himself died in 1957 but the fashion house bearing his name continues), Oscar de la Renta, Ralph Lauren, and Pierre Cardin began showing up on everything from children's wear to sheets.

Bill Blass, who generates some $300 billion from licensing operations according to *Women's Wear Daily*, even went so far as to lend his name to a line of designer chocolates, while Yves St. Laurent "designed" a brand of cigarettes.

According to industry observers, the designer-craze result has been a distinct reduction of quality. "Don't let yourself be deluded that because a garment has a designer's name that you're familiar with, that it is a quality garment," said Barnard. "Be a wary shopper. Be a sophisticated shopper."

"Consumers should buy what they like and what looks good on them and the rest is conversation," agreed Marvin E. Segal, a Dallas retail consultant and former owner of a chain of up-scale specialty shops. "How enamored can you be with a name? I'm not. There's nothing to get excited about."

If you are a designer-label or name-brand junkie, would you buy underwear from Jodee Bra, Inc., or Albert J. Betesh & Sons? Perhaps not, but those two companies received licenses to produce undergarments from Sasson and Gitano.

Would you buy a man's raincoat from Crown Clothing Co.? If you do not recognize the name, how about Oleg Cassini? Cassini licenses Crown to produce coats for men.

The list goes on and on. Once designers have a marketable image, they are able to turn that name over and over and over. *Women's Wear Daily* carries ads from designers proclaiming they are "available for licensing."

"They don't have control of the product. The only thing they have control of is the bank account," grumbled one New York manufacturer of better garments.

One menswear merchant said he selected fabric and styles from a manufacturer for a line of suits in his discount store, and the same line showed up in a well-known designer's collection. It seems the merchant, Bill Wallace, owner of John Mabry, a Dallas-based store, hired a manufacturer who also had a license to produce suits for the designer. The designer "had nothing to do with" the design—it all came from the licensee who paid a royalty for use of the name.

Does this mean you should not buy designer clothes? Of course not, just do not assume anything based on that name. Do not assume the designer personally sketched the garment, oversaw the production and sent it lovingly on its way with a sense of personal satisfaction and pride. Do not assume you are getting the best value for your money.

And, finally, do not assume that just because the garment carries a familiar label it will not have fabric flaws, frayed seams, or faulty sizing. (This should not happen unless you are buying an item that has been reduced because of imperfections.)

In fact, experts engaged in the business of inspecting clothing for defects say designer-label apparel is no less immune to flaws than garments manufactured by lesser-known names. Just ask the Army.

At the world headquarters of the Army/Air Force Exchange, inspectors look through samples of civilian clothing that is to be sold to military personnel at the Army post exchanges and Air Force base exchanges all over the world. About 10 percent of all garments inspected have defects or flaws, one inspection official estimated. The Army marches the defective clothing right back to the manufacturers. "Designer clothing, as far as I'm concerned, is no different in quality. The quality is about the same as anybody else's," he said.

What you can assume about designer labels is that the designer (unless it is an illegal fake) is collecting a royalty from the sale and that you, the consumer, are absorbing some of the cost that makes that name famous. Name recognition is part of the razzle-dazzle that comes through advertising. And national advertising, particularly television, is a big-bucks ticket item.

And what are the ads telling you? That the seams will not fray? The pockets will not sag? The material is of the finest quality? No. The ads, for the most part, promote image. You will be sexy, tasteful, beautiful, adventurous, whatever, when you pull on this or that brand of clothing.

On the flip side of the name game, do not be fooled by like-sounding names. Do not walk out of a store thinking you got a great deal on a very expensive men's suit, a Hickey Freeman, when you are really buying a somewhat less-pricey H. Freeman. Make sure, for example, that the French-sounding names are truly the designers you are thinking of (if that is your reason for buying the garment).

Like-sounding names have fooled shoppers in years past. One former retailer tells of selling Stetson hats from a company different from the one that made the name "Stetson" famous. The unknown Stetson was required to carry a disclaimer saying it was not related to the original Stetson company. But undaunted salespeople were able to tell customers that the disclaimer was placed in the hat so as to avoid any mix-ups with phony Stetson companies. The joke is on the buyer.

Like-sounding names took a humorous twist a few years ago, only this time the consumer was let in on the gag. The popular Jordache jeans with a horse-head logo were the basis of a take-off by a cheeky group of large women who started selling Lardashe jeans. The Lardashe jeans, sold in hip measurements of 44 to 60 inches, carried a pig's head instead of a horse's. It was cute, but Jordache company officials were not laughing. They sued to stop the ridicule of their name. (A federal judge threw the suit out, but Jordache has appealed.)

The brothers who own Jordache were sued themselves by the brothers who own Guess? Inc., to illustrate a point of how hard it is to figure out who makes what in the apparel name game. Jordache was licensed by Guess to produce Guess jeans which became a very hot-selling garment in the mid-1980s. The owners of Guess charged that Jordache was using inside information from its licensing agreement to copy other Guess lines of apparel in addition to the jeans. So guessing who really makes what is enough to make your head spin.

Another way names may fool you is by an inferior-quality garment being marketed under a famous name. For example, Forbes magazine in 1985 did an article on Sy Syms, a well-known off-price merchandiser. Brioni produces a handmade Italian suit that is one of the priciest in the world, selling retail for about $1,200. Syms' Brioni's sold for $299, the article states, and were not the real McCoy, although made by the same company.

The cheaper Brioni's were put together at another factory, not the one where they were carefully hand sewed. Also, while there are some 15,000 real Brioni's sold annually in this country, Syms had about 5,000 special Brioni's made each year. The less-expensive Brioni's carried a legitimate label but consumers might not be aware they were getting a Syms special Brioni's and not the very expensive, hand-sewed one they had in mind.

PRIVATE LABELS

If it is difficult to figure out who really makes what in a world of designer licensing, there is another emerging trend that adds to the befuddlement: private labels.

There are designer labels, brand-name labels (although some designer labels such as Christian Dior and Anne Klein refer to deceased designers), and private labels. Private labels can be a name developed exclusively for that store (such as Fox for J.C. Penney) or, more simply, the store's name itself.

Celebrity names are also popular private label choices for stores trying to attract higher-income customers. Cheryl Tiegs for Sears was one of the innovators. Sears now has a Stefanie Powers line, and Kmart, Jaclyn Smith. Ironically, the celebrities are well known, not for their work in fashion design, but for their acting and modeling careers. On the other hand, J.C. Penney, in a trade-up move, hired the big designer names of Halston and Mary McFadden to develop private label lines for that store.

Private labels, once a mainstay in the traditional department stores, (stores such as Neiman-Marcus, Bloomingdales, or Saks Fifth Avenue), were put on the back shelves during the days of designer mania, but, since about 1983, have been making a strong comeback. Industry observers attribute their return to the department stores because the designer labels have been losing snob appeal and have become watered down by the proliferation.

In the *Barnard's Retail Marketing Report*, Barnard observed that department stores have become less eager "to submerge their identity" to that of a designer. Another reason that is not likely to warm the cockles of the consumer's heart, private labels make it much harder to price compare. That, in turn, allows for higher markups.

Designer Weitz put it in economic terms when he spoke to the American Marketing Association's meeting in New York in April, 1986: "The stores buy huge quantities of commodity merchandise such as white business shirts or polo shirts or gray suits. They buy them from off-shore suppliers at very low prices and then sell them to the public at a huge margin of profit."

Under designer and name-brand labels, consumers are able to shop and compare quite easily. Private labels allow a retailer to order a garment and put the store's name or a store's brand on the label. There may be other copies of the same garments (made by the same manufacturer) under different labels at different stores.

Two private label manufacturers revealed it is not uncommon to have the same clothing in the same city under different prices. "I know that with some of ours, the same garment might be in three or four different retail stores and may be all at different prices," one manufacturer said.

"We have garments all over the country under different names, different stores and different prices," the other said.

The stores hire contractors to sew the garments. The contractors may do work for several designers or stores.

Another example of private labels garnering higher markups is from a discount merchant who told of a suit he carries for $375 made by Groshire. It is a handmade suit but not a well-known label to consumers. The discounter leaves the label as Groshire. Other stores carry the exact same suit, but with a private store label, and put a higher markup on the garment. For example, the suit sells for $700 at an exclusive menswear store.

Private labels can work in reverse, too. Name-brand manufacturers sometimes supply discounters with their merchandise with the understanding that it is to be sold under a private label. That way, the name brand is not diluted (and conventional department stores which order the name brands are kept happy) by the fact that it is being sold by a discounter.

MARKUPS AND MARKDOWNS

If it is hard to follow the game of musical chairs played by apparel manufacturers when it comes to labeling, markups can be an even more complicated game to observe.

It used to be easy. There was a wholesale cost. By the 1960s, there was a standard retail markup, called a keystone. "We used to say we worked on a keystone," Segal said. "Keystone for years and years was 40 percent. Then it became 50 percent."

But, what is 50 percent to the retailer sounds like 100 percent to the layman. That is because retailers back into markups, viewing them as a percent of the total retail price, not a percent markup over the wholesale cost.

For example, if an item wholesales at $50 and retails at $100, it is a 50 percent markup, not a 100 percent markup, even though it is a doubling of wholesale cost.

Here's how it is figured:

Retail price	$100
Subtract wholesale cost	$ 50
Difference	$ 50
Divided by retail	$100
Equals	.5 or 50 percent

So markups have edged up to 50 percent and beyond. According to Segal, it used to be standard to simply

17

double the cost to arrive at the keystone level. For example, if a wholesale price was $14.75, retail would be $29.50. Then it became standard to round the number to $15 and double it to arrive at a retail price of $30 for the $14.75 wholesale cost.

Keystone today is not a set-in-concrete standard. It is a rule of thumb, or in many full retail stores, a starting point. Segal said brand-name items found in many places, such as well-known labels like Liz Claiborne, will have standard markups. But he said stores using the keystone markup are operating at a bare minimum, and are forced by higher rents, advertising and general operating costs to go beyond it.

"Where you make a little extra in markups is in three places. One, is in imports. Two, is to find an obscure line nobody else has, and three, is private labels," Segal said. What Segal called "a little extra" translates to very high markups in some cases, especially when it comes to the imports mentioned.

Imports, according to Standard & Poor's, a credit analysis firm, officially accounted for about one-third of clothing sold in America in 1983, but this figure was expected to climb to much higher percentages.

In some apparel lines, imports had a greater market than domestic products, especially in sweaters and women's cotton clothing. Imports are bringing much lower wholesale costs chiefly because of cheap foreign labor. In the Far East, for example, labor averages around 60 cents per hour, according to Standard & Poor's.

Perhaps the highest markups of all, some suggest, are at prestigious department stores where Asian-made goods are sold under the store's private label, selling at three or four times the cost of wholesale.

Markups can sometimes be shocking. Many consumers mistakenly believe the major costs of a garment are material and workmanship. For example, in 1984,

Forbes magazine dissected the cost of a $1,345 wool designer coat. The cost of fabric and labor? A paltry $272. The retail markup? A walloping $788. According to *Forbes*, the coat, purchased by a buyer for an up-scale American department store, will triple in price between the runway at the *prêt-à-porter* (Paris fashion show) and the store display.

The cost breakdown:

Manufacturer's price (fabric, labor, $272; designer royalty, $28; overhead, taxes and profit, $107)	$ 407
Landing costs (Customs and duties, $122; packaging and misc., $28)	$ 150
Retailer's markup (includes freight, advertising, sales costs, profit, etc.)	$ 788
Total retail cost	$1,345

In this example, the store (in retailer's terms) used a 59-percent markup.

In contrast to department and specialty stores which use the keystone as a starting point, off-price retailers go below keystone level for markups. Additionally, they use a variety of methods—manufacturer overruns, location in less expensive store space, cash payments to manufacturers, refusal of advertising allowances—to achieve a lower retail cost.

Some discounters also use lower markups, while others sell cheap goods cheaply, retaining a full markup.

The success of the off-price retailer in the early 1980s caused the department stores to become highly promotional to compete. In other words, they stepped up specials and sales. According to industry analysts, this promotional bent has spurred the practice of marking goods higher than they normally would be in order to put them on "sale."

There are, of course, legitimate specials, known as loss leaders. These are used to attract the customer to the stores in hopes that additional purchases (at full markups) will be made. But the trend, undeniably, is toward higher markups followed by price reductions.

"During the past five years, the trend in department store pricing policies has inclined toward taking higher initial markups and then running constant sales—i.e. higher markdowns," according to a 1986 report by Baltimore retail analyst Alex. Brown & Sons Incorporated. "In 1984, department store markdowns hit a historical high—18.8 percent of sales, up from the previous year's 14.9 percent. In spite of these markdown statistics, gross margins did not change significantly."

What this means to the consumer, basically, is that department stores continue to use about the same markup, despite the so-called sales.

Shoppers should think twice about making a decision to buy simply because the item is on sale. Perhaps it is. Perhaps it is not.

The markup-markdown game irritates one retailer so much that he calls it an abuse of the consumer. Bill Wallace, president of John Mabry, said the trend is rampant throughout the entire industry, not just in department stores.

"What it does is totally confuse the consumer," Wallace fumed. "People may recognize the difference between an extremely cheap suit and something that sells for $700 to $800, but the differences say, between a $350 and a $250 suit, are not terribly noticeable. They're subtle."

Sometimes, for example, Wallace said more cheaply tailored suits will not show their flaws until after the garment is dry-cleaned, a problem impossible to detect on the store's rack.

From his knowledge of wholesale costs and retail markups, Wallace said he observes many stores marking a $250 suit at $350, then "slashing" the price to $249.95. "Then there are two kinds of victims. The one that pays more for the suit than it's really worth and the one that buys it on 'sale,' " Wallace said. "I don't think there's a consumer agency in the world that can protect a consumer from that. The only protection is increased awareness by consumers that those kinds of things are going on."

Another deception is false "suggested retail prices," according to Wallace. Some discount stores will take a suit that would normally retail for $300. A "suggested retail price" of $450 will be written on the tag and underneath will be the store's "our price" of $249.95. In this case, the suit is truly discounted by about $50, not the $150 the retailer wants you to think.

Some consumer legislation is aimed at protecting the shopper from false sales. In Massachusetts, for example, a state law forbids a deceptive pricing practice where a sale price is written on a garment's ticket under the original price, unless the item was offered at the former price for at least fifteen days.

In 1985, seven clothing chains paid restitution of $50,000 to the state of Massachusetts and agreed to halt the practice where a fictitious former selling price was placed on the ticket. The seven are the Casual Corner and Caren Charles divisions of U.S. Shoe Corp. of Cincinnati; the Hit or Miss division of Zayre Corp.; the Chess King men's wear division of Melville Corp. of Harrison, New York; Cherry Webb & Tourain; Cummings; and Anderson Little.

Diane Tsoulas, the assistant attorney general who coordinated the investigation, said the stores were unable to show proof, as required by law, that the items were offered for the original selling price. The investigation began after the attorney general's office was tipped off by the United States Custom Service that garments were arriving from overseas, already marked with two prices.

Tsoulas said the violations are not only in the garment industry. "I think it's fairly widespread," she said. "We've especially seen it to be true in furniture and big-ticket items such as appliances."

So what can consumers do? It is a difficult problem. If you are a regular shopper and you discover a store putting an item on "sale" that you know was never offered at that price, contact a local or state consumer agency to see if any consumer protection laws or ordinances have been violated.

The agency will most likely be your state attorney general's office, but many cities and counties have consumer protection offices, too. For a complete listing, write to Handbook, Pueblo, Colorado 81009, for a free copy of the Consumer's Resource Handbook.

Also, you might consider contacting your local Better Business Bureau, telling them you feel the practice is unethical.

Another way to arm yourself against deceptive pricing is to be aware that some markdowns are not markdowns at all, but merely gimmicks to help push sales. This might help curb impulse buying that is spurred by the fact that you just cannot pass up the garment because it is on sale. Again, maybe it is, and maybe it is not.

Legitimate markdowns exist. They might occur at the end of the season, the style is overstocked or a poor style selection was made by the merchant. (Note: Just because the retailers are marking down the cost of clothing does not mean they are not getting a full markup. That is because retailers may be able to re-order a garment near the end of the season at a reduced wholesale cost.)

Markdowns are not only used to get rid of slow-moving merchandise but also to stimulate store sales at certain times of the year, such as back-to-school sales or fur sales in August to promote pre-season shopping.

Markdowns are also called "price reductions," "sales," "special purchases," or "clearances," depending on the demeanor—or the desperation—of the store. They can be a bargain to the consumer who takes advantage of a legitimate markdown and who wisely chooses non-trendy items that will still be in style next season (when buying at end-of-season sales).

KNOCKOFFS AND COUNTERFEIT ITEMS

Knockoffs are a copy of someone else's clothing design, a practice "as common as having breakfast in this business," one attorney told *Forbes* magazine.

Counterfeit items also are copies.

The big difference is that knockoffs are a legal practice while counterfeiting is illegal and may be the ultimate rip-off to the consumer. The fakes are not only copies of the original item, but carry a false label indicating it is the real thing.

The term knockoff, according to *Fairchild's Dictionary of Fashion,* is simply: "Clothing industry slang for a design copied from a more expensive garment."

Some in the industry limit the word knockoff to a stitch-by-stitch copy, usually of a haute couture garment. Other manufacturers and designers prefer to use words like "reinterpretation" or "adaption." In other words, they are watching for all the information they can get on what is going to set this season's trends—hemlines, flowing skirts, wide lapels, color, fabric, etc.—then adapt their own lines accordingly.

Sears, for example, sends representatives to high-fashion Parisian shows, not to order clothes, but to observe. The reinterpretations are not just in the budget garment range. One New York manufacturer shared that an up-scale department store customer brought a $3,000 designer jacket to him and asked his designers to "reinterpret" the jacket to sell for $500 under the store's private label.

The knockoff industry is such an accepted practice that "the quote, unquote original designer is a rare breed. We're an industry of knockoffs," said Segal.

While knockoffs are usually less expensive copies from haute couture lines, the trend toward mass marketing to middle- and upper-income shoppers (especially the career woman) has big-name fashion houses knocking themselves off.

For example, Anne Klein has put out an Anne Klein II line with prices 30 to 60 percent below the designer collection. An Anne Klein II jacket in 1985 sold for about $175, compared to the designer collection where a jacket would draw about $400. (By the way, one business magazine reported that the less expensive collection was expected to bring in three times as much revenue as the designer line.)

Other designers going for the middle market with separate lines are Bill Blass (Bill Blass III), Oscar de la Renta (Miss O), and Geoffrey Beene (Geoffrey Beene, Part Two).

When it comes to knockoffs, the big question is: how can you judge quality? This is a tough one to answer. Some industry insiders suggest that knockoffs at times not only equal but also surpass the quality of the original.

Or, the difference might diminish in comparison to the price differential. For example, Dallas merchant Mitch Smith, owner of P.E. & Co., has a copy of a top-of-the-line trench coat, a Burberry. The Burberry might sell for $575, whereas a knockoff Burberry would start at about $100.

"The basic difference between the real McCoy and the knockoff, number one, would be the label. Number two, would be the fabrication, and number three, the price," Smith said.

The retailer explained that the knockoff would use a cheaper polyester-and-cotton blend while the Burberry uses sea island or combed cotton. But Smith said the knockoff is good looking, wears well, and, obviously, is far cheaper.

How can you judge quality? You may have to trust the word of your merchant, a much safer bet if the merchant has established a track record with you. The knock-off also deserves a thorough eyeballing. Feel the weight of the material. Look for a proper fit. Check for such quality features as finished buttonholes and seams that would indicate the garment is well made and not just a rush job to ride the coattails of a design's popularity.

Where a copycat garment crosses the line from a knockoff to an illegal fake is where an item is deliberately marketed under a false name or image. The problem is a major one for the clothing industry as well as for other industries such as computers and toys. And it is a major problem for consumers who pay extra for something they are not getting. Beyond that, fake goods cut into legitimate jobs and reduce state and federal tax revenue.

Rip-off artists have copied and sold fake Gucci bags, Izod knit shirts, and numerous types of designer jeans, to name a few. Polo by Ralph Lauren, for example, has found more than one thousand cases of fake Polo wear being sold in the last four years, said Milton Springut, a New York attorney who handles trademark cases for Polo.

In one case, Springut said, a Baltimore-area counterfeiter was purchasing imported, plain knit shirts. A fake label and embroidered logo were then attached. The counterfeiter was caught after undercover private investigators in Baltimore and Los Angeles purchased the counterfeit goods.

Springut said the amount of counterfeiting is hard to gauge. "It's a tremendous amount but it's not quantifiable," he said, adding that such factors as loss of brand loyalty are difficult to assess. Counterfeiters operate "in every conceivable way," Springut said. "The labels are put on here, labels are put on abroad. The embroidery's put on here, the embroidery's put on abroad . . . ."

James L. Bikoff is a San Francisco attorney specializing in cases against counterfeiters and is president of the International Anticounterfeiting Coalition, a group of lawyers, manufacturers, private investigators, and trade associations. The coalition backed two major pieces of legislation aimed at stopping the sale of counterfeit goods and the manufacturing of them abroad.

The 1984 Trademark Counterfeiting Act makes the manufacturing or sale of counterfeit goods a criminal offense, drawing first-offense fines of up to $250,000 and imprisonment of five years in jail for individuals. Fines can be assessed up to $1 million for corporations.

To fight the manufacturing of counterfeit goods abroad, Congress also passed a measure in 1984 to allow the President to grant special status (giving liberalized import quotas) based on how well countries are doing at policing counterfeiting within their own borders.

Bikoff said the laws are good but that counterfeiting is a problem that is not going to go away. "The problem is not one that's going to go away because of legislation or because a few people are sent to jail," he said. "The problem is one that's a lot like narcotics—it will always be with us—but efforts like the Trademark Counterfeiting Act will go a long way to bring it under control."

Bikoff said counterfeiters use various methods to

pass off their fakes. Some are counterfeited abroad (Korea, Taiwan, Malaysia, Singapore, India, Argentina, Brazil, Colombia, and Mexico are all counterfeiting hot spots) and smuggled into this country, while others are counterfeited here. Some retailers may not know they are selling fakes while others are "keeping their eyes closed purposely."

One sting operation was set up, according to *Women's Wear Daily* (March 4, 1985), to catch counterfeiters of *chichi* Louis Vuitton bags. The five convicted counterfeiters were given jail terms of six months to five years for their role in a plan capable of turning out 1,000 bogus bags every week from a plant in Haiti. According to court papers, the scheme could have generated up to $38 million a year in sales.

These tips from the coalition will help shoppers avoid buying fake merchandise, from clothing to watches:

1. Pick a store that you can trust, a store that wants to protect its reputation and get your repeat business. Occasionally reputable retailers will find fakes in their inventory, but they will stand behind what they sell.

2. If you find a $60 item for $10, it could be a fake, the coalition warned. Price reductions beyond 40 to 50 percent, combined with a questionable seller, means it could be counterfeit.

3. Look at the label closely. Compare trademarks with ones you know are real. Fakes often are fuzzy, indistinct, off-color, or even misspelled. Or they might be the wrong shape or in the wrong place. If you want a designer label, know what it should look like.

4. Check authentic products to see if other tags are sewn in or attached in certain ways. Then compare these to the suspected fake to see if they are in the right place and firmly attached. Carelessly attached tags can be a strong clue.

5. Look for quality. Look over the garment for cheap materials, shoddy construction, carelessly applied logos, tags, and trademark.

6. Check the packaging. Check for smeared or discolored printing, or messy, uneven wrappings. Watch for bad photo reproduction and broken lettering, especially on records, tapes, toys, watches, and cosmetics.

7. Asking for a refund from the seller sometimes requires verification from the manufacturer that your merchandise is actually fake, according to the coalition. The International Anticounterfeiting Coaltion, 101 California Street, 39th Floor, San Francisco, California 94111-5974, can provide additional help.

HOW TO BE A SMART CONSUMER

It would be nice if we could inject truth serum into those who make the labels for the garments we buy. A label might not say "Made expressly for *(enter name of your favorite department store)*." Instead it might say: "Made by extremely cheap labor in China for incredibly low wholesale costs, but we're marking it way up anyway because it looks good. We're not sure how it will wear."

That is wishful thinking. But a few valuable tidbits of information available on labels as required by law can help shoppers.

The tag on the outside will tell information such as price and size, but the most important explanations are on the inside of the garment. Make sure you read it.

Labels must have country of origin, fiber content, care instructions, and a manufacturer's name and address or a number assigned by the government. The numbers are called R.N. or W.P.L. numbers. Most big-city libraries carry an R.N. and W.P.L. directory that will tell you the name of the manufacturer as listed by the number.

There are three major laws governing the content labeling. The Wool Products Labeling Act of 1939 requires products to list the percentage of wool and the condition of the wool. The conditions are virgin or new wool, made from wool converted into yarn or fabric for the first time. Reprocessed wool is made from samples, cutting table scraps, and mill ends which are collected and made into other fabrics. Such wool has not previously been worn or used. The term "re-used wool" is wool made from old rags and clothes that have been cleaned and recycled into fabric again.

The Fur Products Labeling Act of 1951 requires that fur products correctly identify the type of fur and the country of origin if the fur is imported. It also requires the name, in English, of the animal that produced the fur; whether the fur has been dyed or bleached; and if the fur contains paws, bellies, or other scrap parts.

The Textile Fiber Identification Act of 1960 requires fiber content to be identified on all apparel by type of fiber and by percentage. This law also requires the manufacturer's name and address or the government identification number; country of origin; and identification of fibers by their generic names.

Interestingly, historians note that the push behind these laws was not for consumer protection, but came from the industry. For example, the 1960 law requiring fiber content came after some textile producers tried to represent cheaper synthetics as natural material. Likewise, woolgrowers pushed for an amendment to the 1939 law that would stop the unlabeled use of reused wool.

Perhaps the most important consumer legislation is the flammability acts. In 1953, Congress passed a law banning textiles and wearing apparel with dangerously flammable properties. Later, in 1971, the Federal Trade Commission required flame-resistant materials for children's sleepwear. One of the most effective chemicals found for flame-resistant treatment, Tris, became controversial when it was suspected of causing cancer. It was banned in 1977, and other treatments and materials, such as the generic synthetic, modacrylic, have been used.

The Consumer Products Safety Commission enforces the law. The commission has a hot line (1-800-638-2772) and can answer such questions as whether a pair of old pajamas might contain Tris.

Children's sleepwear must have flame-resistant properties. Consumers must, however, follow the special washing instructions to keep from ruining the flame resistance, and home sewers should look for flame-resistant materials when making children's pajamas or nightgowns.

The federal government also requires all garments to carry permanently attached care instructions. In 1972, the FTC issued regulations governing care instructions. More detailed instructions were required, beginning in 1984.

So the label has important information such as size, fiber, manufacturer, care instructions, and sometimes, performance claims (such as a no-iron fabric or flame-resistant finish). Beyond that, knowledge of fabrics makes us more sophisticated shoppers. Each garment's performance depends on such things as fiber content, dyes and finishes, as well as workmanship and the quality of trims, linings, and fasteners. Most fabrics, according to the American Apparel Manufacturer's Association, are woven, knitted, or bonded and laminated.

Woven materials are sets of yarns interlaced at right angles and can be tightly or loosely woven. Knits are a continuous yarn or set of yarns which form rows of loops. Woven fabrics wrinkle more but tend to hold their shapes better than knits. If you do not want wrinkles in your woven fabric, for example, look for a wrinkle-resistant finish or a blend of synthetic and natural fibers.

Bonded or laminated fabrics are layered fabrics

held together by stitches, adhesive, or foam.

Here is a list of characteristics of different fibers from the AAMA.

Acetate—Used in women's blouses and dresses, and lining fabrics. Luxurious feel, usually dry cleanable or hand washable, needs pressing, less durable than most fibers.

Acrylic—Used in outerwear and knitted apparel. Soft, machine washable. Use low dryer temperatures or dry flat (sweaters).

Cotton—Natural fiber used in all wearing apparel. Absorbent, washable, needs some finish to prevent shrinkage and wrinkling.

Modacrylic—Used in deep pile coating, fleece fabrics and flame-resistant garments. Soft, easy care, warm. Heat sensitive, use low-drying temperatures. Fake furs may require fur-type cleaning and storage. Flame resistant.

Nylon—Apparel, hosiery and lingerie. Strong, abrasion resistant, easy care, low moisture absorbency. Color stains during laundering, therefore proper sorting by color is important, such as whites with whites only.

Polyester—Used in all apparel items, especially durable press items. Easy care, wrinkle resistant, dimensionally stable, oily stains may need pretreatment before laundering.

Rayon—Used in most apparel products. Absorbent, soft. Some rayons have been modified for improved wet strength. Needs to be treated to prevent shrinkage and wrinkling.

Silk—Used in women's and men's outerwear. Natural fiber. Dry clean or hand wash. Needs pressing. Luxurious and absorbent. Do not use a chlorine bleach.

Spandex—Foundation garments, swimwear, support hosiery or other articles requiring stretch properties. Lightweight, strong, resistant to body oils, easy care.

Should not be chlorine bleached or exposed to high heat.

Triacetate—Used in women's wear, men's shirting, and lingerie. Easy care, durable pleats and creases, good drapability. Not as durable as most synthetics.

Wool—Natural fiber used in all outerwear. Warm, absorbent, dry cleanable, wrinkle resistant, needs proper finishing to prevent shrinkage and to be machine washable. Do not use chlorine bleach. Flame resistant.

Beyond the fiber content, a garment deserves a thorough once-over before purchasing. Try to forget the facts that it has a designer label and you love the color. Be objective. Look for a proper fit. Does it hang well in front and back? How well are the extras treated? That is, do the shoulder pads stay in place or do they require constant adjustment? Look for finished seams, working zippers, finished buttonholes, extra buttons, and reinforced stitching at high-stress places such as pockets.

If the material is plaid, do the plaids match at the seams? Are linings tacked down properly? Are there exposed drill holes where the darts are supposed to be? What about the fabric? Are there flaws that cannot be accounted for by variations in natural fibers?

At the Army-Air Force Exchange, inspectors say they find flaws in about 10 percent of the garments they inspect. The Army ships them right back to the manufacturer. Consumers should take a cue.

If there is a problem, reconsider before you buy. If it is the only item in your size and you are still tempted to buy it, at least ask for a price adjustment. The exception is for those "as is" garments that are specially priced due to the flaws.

What if you get home and find the garment has a problem, or worse, it begins to unravel after a few washings or a trip to the dry cleaners? Take it back. It will be easier if you have the tags and sales receipt, so get into the habit of keeping these for awhile after you purchase an item. Be wary of stores with a "no return" policy.

Do not accept the excuse that the manufacturer will not take the garment back, so therefore the retailer cannot refund your money. That is their problem, not yours.

If the merchant does not help, write to the manufacturer. If you are uncertain who that is, look it up by the manufacturer's number in the R.N. and W.P.L. directory (at major libraries).

If there is a problem with dry-cleaning and the dry cleaner says it is a problem with the garment, or something you have done to the article, there is a trade association that arbitrates such disputes. It is the International Fabricare Institute, 12251 Tech Road, Silver Springs, Maryland 20904.

Karen Graber, communications director for the institute, said an analysis (for $10) can be done to determine who is at fault. The analysis must, however, be requested by a member (your dry cleaner is probably a member), a Better Business Bureau, or a consumer group. Despite the fact that it is a group composed mainly of dry cleaners, Graber said the institute strives for objectivity. "We feel it would ruin our reputation if we didn't," she said.

In 1985, Graber said 40,000 such analyses were conducted. Of those, 17 percent were found to be the cleaner's fault while the rest of the problems were caused by the manufacturer or owner.

Another problem with quality to be aware of when shopping is the sizing of the garment. Size standards were set by the Bureau of Standards in 1940 and were followed for years. Gradually, though, manufacturers began to stray as tastes and shapes changed, and they cut clothes more generously. Some manufacturers may cut even more generously than others, hoping to appeal to a certain vanity that comes from wearing a small size.

As a result, clothing sizes have become so discombobulated that the federal government has asked the American Society for Testing and Materials to come up with new size standards. This is not something the industry is likely to welcome with open arms, according to a vice president of a clothes manufacturing concern, because it would require adjustments by pattern makers who would just as soon stick to their own specifications.

Experts generally agree that a key ingredient to smart shopping is to compare garments. If you are shopping at an off-price store for name-brand merchandise, shop a full retail store to compare price as well as quality. Many designers put out several lines of clothing in different price ranges, so make sure you are comparing apples to apples. If you are looking for a particular item, check several stores. The quality may be just as good on a garment without a recognizable name, and the price is likely to be better.

If you are shopping off-price stores, it used to be that you could not expect red-carpet treatment. You also could expect fewer amenities and fewer salespeople so that off-price stores could keep their overhead down. The opposite was supposedly true of better department and specialty stores.

Today, however, there are pluses in shopping in off-price stores besides prices. Grace's Coat & Dress Shop in Red Oak, Texas, and Collage in McKinney, Texas, offer specialty-store labels as well as the ambience and still maintain prices of at least 30 percent off retail.

The Esprit Factory Outlet in San Francisco, California, or the Spiegel Catalog stores in Chicago, Illinois, are other examples of probably the most exciting-looking, fashion-forward outlets around that combine savings and ambience.

Regardless of where you shop these days, you have every right to expect courteous service. After all, you are paying for it. And it may be worth it, if you get a salesperson who can point out an item that is perfect for you but lacks "hanger appeal" or who can point out the item you overlooked that will pull your wardrobe together.

The best shoppers are probably those who shop the better department and specialty stores during sales and promotions as well as the off-price and discount stores.

The best shopperss are those that keep a cool head. To get beyond the razzmatazz of the apparel industry, ask yourself some of these questions:

Would I be as enthused about the piece if I did not know it was a sale or price reduction? (Use your knowledge of price and quality to make sure a sale is a sale and you are not being falsely lured to a purchase.)

Would I be as enthused about the garment if it were not such a small size? (Do not let vanity get in the way.)

Have I taken into consideration the cost of dry cleaning? The time spent ironing?

Does it really fit into my wardrobe?

If it is an end-of-season sale, is the item likely to go out of style by next year, despite the terrific price?

Would I like it as much if it did not have a designer name?

Does it fit? Is the color right for me?

Will I have to make adjustments?

Have I looked for similar items in other stores?

GROWTH OF THE OFF-PRICE INDUSTRY

In 1909 there was Filene's Basement. In 1921, Frieda Loehmann opened her first high-fashion, low-price store in Brooklyn. Today, both Filene's Basement and Loehmann's have chains of off-price stores, and the list is endless of others who have entered the off-price field, appealing to shoppers who like high-quality goods at bargain-basement prices.

Filene's Basement is considered the original off-price store where designer labels at rock-bottom prices are sold, where left-over designer garments from the likes of Neiman-Marcus, I. Magnin, and Saks Fifth Avenue, get their final chance on the sales rack. Filene's Basement, literally the downstairs of the Filene's department store, is known for their tales of proper Bostonians trying on clothes right in the crowded aisles.

But it is Filene's Basement's automatic markdown policy that has made retail history. The already-reduced sale price is marked down to 25 percent off if the item is not sold in 12 days; to 50 percent off after another six days; and finally, 75 percent off after the passing of another six days. If it is not sold after six more days (a total of 30 days in the store), it is given to charity.

Loehmann's fame came from its practice of snipping out designer labels but leaving enough clues for customers to figure out what designer bargain they were getting for their money.

Today, it is not necessary to be in Boston or New York for off-price bargains. Off-price is a trend reaching into every corner of America.

Off-price retailing is not discount retailing. Discount retailers sell inexpensive goods inexpensively, although the trend among today's discounters is to mix in a more up-scale apparel, trying to attract the middle-income shopper. It is also not to be confused with the mass merchandiser chains like J.C. Penney, Sears, and Montgomery Ward.

Off-price refers to the branch of retailing where high-quality, name-brand clothing is sold at prices substantially lower than those of conventional department stores.

Off-price retailers are able to do this by combining smaller markups with advantageous wholesale purchases such as paying cash, rarely returning goods, and refusing the standard advertising allowances (co-op advertising). They also purchase manufacturer overruns, cancelled orders, and out-of-season goods.

Shoppers may have to do with fewer amenities and forgo buying clothes way ahead of the season. Off-price stores often get seasonal merchandise about a month behind conventional department stores and specialty stores, but it still comes in plenty of time for the proper season.

What shoppers can find is the same merchandise that the department stores are carrying, but the prices are reduced by 20 to 50 percent.

At one time, retailers were better able to control the distribution of apparel by manufacturers, pressuring wholesalers into refusing to supply apparel to anyone selling for less than full retail. Before Congress abolished state "fair trade" laws in 1975, discounters in states with fair trade laws even risked jail terms and fines for selling at a lower level than the price set by manufacturers.

One landmark case began in 1974 when a federal grand jury accused Bergdorf Goodman, Inc., Bonwit Teller, and Saks Fifth Avenue of violating the Sherman Antitrust Act by conspiring to fix prices on women's clothing.

The prestigious stores not only fixed prices among themselves, the grand jury charged, but also pressured several manufacturers into forcing other retailers to maintain the same high prices.

The three stores pleaded no contest to the charges and ended up paying $4 million in charge-account credits to 55,000 customers.

With such heavy-handed antics out of the way, off-price stores began to sprout and grow. Analysts said the period of high inflation between 1979 and 1983 provided the medium which nurtured the explosive growth of the off-price industry, when worried shoppers searched for more and more ways to stretch their dollars.

An industry analysis by Standard & Poor's explained the growth: "As major department store retailers cut back on orders from manufacturers to offset weak sales, off-price operators took up the slack by absorbing producer's excess capacity."

Management Horizons, a Columbus, Ohio-based retail consulting firm, has reported that off-price retail grew from $3 billion in sales of apparel and footwear in 1979 to $8.5 billion in 1984, or from 3 percent of all apparel and footwear sold in the United States to 5.9 percent of such sales. The off-price industry is further expected to grow to capture 13 percent of all sales by the year 1990, Management Horizon has projected.

The off-price industry's growth began to slacken in 1983 and 1984, and industry analysts speculate this was caused by a combination of a too-crowded field along with a renewed interest in the conventional department store's high-profile promotions as well as better economic times. Although some off-price chains were troubled, the industry remains strong.

The ten largest off-price chains account for about 40 percent of the total off-price sales. The stores are Marshall's, T.J. Maxx, Burlington Coat Factory, Loehmann's, Hit or Miss, Ross Stores, Sym's, Filene's Basement, Designer Depot, and Clothestime.

Another strong trend in the off-price industry is the outlet mall. By the end of 1986, an estimated 370 such malls opened, up from a mere 60 in 1980.

The malls concentrate factory outlets and give shoppers substantial savings in addition to a growing array of amenities. Some of the largest off-price malls in the United States are Belz Factory Outlet Malls (Orlando, Florida; Memphis, Tennessee; Allen, Texas; St. Louis, Missouri; and Tampa, Florida), Western Development (Potomac Mills), and the towns of Flemington, New Jersey; Secaucus, New Jersey; and Reading, Pennsylvania.

What does this all mean to the consumer? It means

the consumer has a broader range of choices (and prices). It means that increased competition is forcing everyone in the retail industry to offer something more—whether it is better service, wider selection, or a better value for the dollar.

DIRECT MAIL AND WHOLESALE CLUBS

Other ways to avoid paying full retail are direct mail purchases and the emerging wholesale clubs. More and more consumers are choosing the direct mail route. According to an industry survey, $38 billion worth of goods were purchased through direct mail in 1977. By 1985, that number mushroomed to $200 billion.

Direct mail may cut some costs for the consumers, because there is no overhead such as retail sales space and salespeople.

"The advantage of direct mail is selection and opportunity," said Gerald Pike, vice president of Royal Silk Ltd., a mail order silk outlet. "If you live in New York you have a lot to choose from. But what if you live in Laramie, Wyoming?

"What direct mail enables you to do is become more aware of variety and selection, and you can price compare."

Beyond that, Pike said the direct mail operation enables Royal Silk to price garments at 40 to 60 percent less than comparable garments at conventional stores.

Mail order operations also give companies a wealth of information about customers, allowing them to target areas where there would be a large enough concentration of customers to support a retail store.

Another value-oriented trend is the wholesale, or membership, clubs that are popping up from coast to coast. The first such club, the Price Club, began in San Diego, California, in 1976. Now, in addition to the Price Club, there are Sam's Wholesale Clubs (Wal-Mart), Pace membership clubs, and B.J.'s (Zayre's). In 1984, sales at such clubs reached $2.3 billion.

The first of what the owners hope will be a chain, the American Wholesale Club, recently opened in Plano, Texas. Members are employees of the government, hospitals, financial institutions, and transportation companies. The advantage of having specific groups as members is that it is easier to tailor the goods when the customers are a known, fixed group.

Jeffrey Zisk, president and chief executive officer, said the wholesale club offers a variety of goods discounted from 20 to 60 percent. The club takes in 10 percent of the sales price, as opposed to traditional retailers who take at least 50 percent.

"Price is the number one advantage. The quality of merchandise is also an advantage. We carry only first-quality, name-brand merchandise," Zisk said. "The variety of the store's goods can also add to the club's appeal," he said. "You could buy a t.v. set at the same time you buy groceries."

The membership clubs carry a variety of goods, including apparel, and sell at wholesale levels. Usually located in warehouses with few—or no—amenities, the clubs have varying types of memberships. Some are available to owners of small- and medium-sized businesses. Others allow group memberships where members or employees of the organization may shop. Typical types of group memberships are bank employees, government employees, and members of teacher associations. Members usually pay an annual fee.

The wholesale clubs turn over inventory up to fifteen times a year, a phenomenal pace considering the masters of inventory turnover, discount stores, do it five times a year.

In short, consumers can benefit from the mix of options in purchasing apparel. Conventional department stores, off-price retailers, mass merchandisers, discount stores, direct mail operators, and wholesale clubs are all vying for the same dollars. Shoppers can benefit by comparing apparel at all levels.

FASHION FACTS

How much do Americans spend on clothes? Where do the clothes come from? Who makes them?

1. Fashion is not a thread-bare industry. In 1983, for example, the government reported that Americans spent $106.4 billion on clothing and accessories. If you add shoes ($20.5 billion); cleaning, repair and storage of clothes and shoes ($7.3 billion); jewelry ($12.8 billion); and other miscellaneous expenses, the number swells to $150 billion. With a population of 223 million in 1983, that's about $670 for every man, woman, and child.

2. Many work in the apparel and textile industries in the United States, nearly 2 million in 1984, down from 2.3 million a decade earlier. Those numbers continue to be threatened as more and more imported apparel is sold in this country. The official estimate of imports is 30 percent of all apparel sold in 1983, but industry observers say the percentage is growing rapidly. In some types of clothing, such as women's cotton shirts, skirts, and coats, there are more foreign-made goods sold than American-made goods.

3. There are some 15,000 domestic apparel firms, the majority of them in New York, California, Pennsylvania, and New Jersey, according to Standard & Poor's. High-fashion and tailored clothing is produced in the Middle Atlantic States and California while items such as jean-cut casual slacks, which can be mass produced, are usually made in the southern and southwestern states.

4. Textile production, with some 6,000 American companies, is concentrated in the Carolinas and Georgia, but can be found in every state.

5. The International Ladies' Garment Worker Union has blamed the rising tide of imports on the trend toward higher markups and private labels. The growing number of imported goods has spurred "Buy American" campaigns to try to appeal to consumers' patriotism. For example, the Crafted with Pride in the U.S.A. Council launched a $40 million, three-year advertising campaign in late 1985. A nationwide telephone survey by the *Wall Street Journal* and NBC News, in which consumers were asked to name the two most important factors when shopping for clothes, revealed that only 18 percent thought "national origin" was a priority. Fit, price, and style were more important. (Although 60 percent of those polled said they would pay up to 10 percent more for an American-made garment than for a similar garment made abroad.)

6. Foreign labor is far cheaper than domestic. China has an incredibly low wage of 20 cents an hour (1983 statistics), while Asian wages averaged around 60 cents an hour. That compares to $5.48 per hour in the United States for those in manufacturing jobs.

7. Another increasing use of foreign labor is called off-shore sourcing. Fabric is cut in the United States and the garment is assembled in a foreign country, under reduced duty rates. Much of the assembling is being done in the Caribbean.

8. By the time clothing makes it to a store's racks, it has been in the planning stages for months, although the trend is to shorten the time between the designer's concept and the actual purchase. For example, retailers order women's summer clothes in January, for delivery in March. Those same summer clothes were probably designed the previous November—more than six months prior to the time they will be purchased and worn.

9. There are five seasons for women's clothing (summer, early fall, late fall and winter, resort season, and spring); for men there are only two (spring/summer and fall/winter).

10. Off-price retailers do not always work on the same ordering schedule. They will purchase cancelled orders, as an example, that occur when manufacturers fail to meet the full retailer's deadlines.

11. According to the AAMA, in 1984, 24 percent of apparel was sold in department stores; 27 percent was sold in specialty stores; 19 percent in chain stores (such as Sears, Montgomery Ward, and J.C. Penney); 16 percent in discount stores (mainly the large chain discount stores such as Target and Zayre's); and 14 percent in all other categories (including off-price stores, factory outlets, and catalog sales).

12. According to an inspection official at the world headquarters of the Army/Air Force Exchange, the best-quality clothes are usually boy's wear, followed by menswear, and women's and girls' clothing. Children's and infants' clothing are generally the lowest quality.

CARPET, FURNITURE, ANTIQUES, AND AUCTIONS

Ihe price you pay for carpet or furniture is often determined by the number of hands it has passed through and how much you know about your purchase. And most people know less about buying wall-to-wall carpet than any other item they purchase. One employee of a Dallas, Texas, carpet store said buying carpet is often a "blind sale."

Since most people do not buy carpet often enough to be knowledgeable on the subject, they cannot make a wise, informed decision. Instead, they take their chances when the situation of buying carpet arises. "It's not like buying a can of beans at 7-11," he said. "They buy carpet once every eight years." He said everywhere customers go, they are told a different story—regardless of what they want or need to hear. And many salesmen do not bother to find out where the carpet is to be laid. "People think it's a black-and-white decision," the employee said. "The fact is, all carpets are good in certain installations. Any carpet can be bad, too."

To begin with, carpets have all kinds of names, said the employee, trademarks such as Dupont 501 or Antron. But remember, you will be in good shape with a nylon carpet that has Scotchguard. Both 501 and Antron are carpets of this variety, so ask the salesman. Get to the *real* basics instead of buying the perceived quality of a brand name. "If you pretend it's clothing that can't be sent to the cleaners on a regular basis, you will know as much as

I do," the employee said. And use common sense, do not buy soft, fluffy carpet if you are going to put it in an area of heavy traffic that attracts lots of soil.

Probably the hardest problem you will have when buying carpet is simply finding out where it came from. The question of quality, often answered by a check of who made a certain item, can be elusive because, as the employee warned, there are no identification marks on rolls of carpet. Instead, he said, labels and other IDs are on the tag (which easily falls off) or in sample books (which easily get lost).

Robert Elkes, who runs Elkes Carpet Outlet in High Point, North Carolina, along with sons Marty and Robert Jr., said he tells customers which manufacturers (in the carpet industry are called mills) he buys from when they ask. But he downplays the importance of knowing which mill produced which carpet. "I think it used to be that you needed to buy from certain mills, but it's not that way anymore." He said he has more confidence in some mills over others, but he sees overall a parity of quality in what is being produced these days, a consistency that was missing in the past.

However, there are some labeling practices that buyers should be aware of. "It's not unheard of," said the employee, "for a store owner to iron a label off one and put it on another."

The employee said some distributors will sell the same product under several different names, called "blind distribution." The mill, looking for favorable negotiating prices, gives one retail store a so-called "exclusive" on a type of carpet and names the carpet "Brand A." Then it gives another store owner an "exclusive" on the same carpet, this time named "Brand B," and so on. The end result is you do not know whether you bought carpet from a mill in New York City or from one in Yuma, Arizona. And your concept of what the price should be for a certain brand goes right out the window.

There is also the problem of look-alikes. As in the case of most businesses, when one type of carpet is successful, the other mills make their own imitations. However, the employee said buyers who inspect sample books should, in many cases, be able to identify what it is they are buying. "You can take any distributor or any fabric— LD Brinkman, Stevens, etc.—go to any dealer that has samples and find out what the true identity is," he advised. The key is remembering and then taking the time to check and compare.

A Dallas, Texas, carpet dealer whose firm has been in operation for seventy years, said the most prevalent cover-up he has seen is retailers who claim to sell the carpet and make it themselves. "It makes it sound like they have a factory of their own," said the dealer.

An Arlington, Texas, retailer and wholesaler said the most common cover-up he has seen is the "bait and switch." This is the practice of offering a sale item and then persuading customers to choose another item in its place. Sales personnel may tell you the item has gone out of stock, that it has been discontinued, or that "Brand B" is a much better value than the Brand A advertised on sale. The idea of bait and switch, as many marketing texts will attest, is to lure the customer into the store and sell him a higher priced item than previously advertised.

A problem exists with discontinued carpeting in that you may not get to buy more of the same carpeting later to round out your project.

WHERE YOU BUY DOES MAKE A DIFFERENCE

The carpet store employee said he has carpet for $9 per square yard that will sell for $30 per square yard in outlets such as department stores. He said individual stores can buy cheapest if they send buyers directly to the mills. The price they (and you) pay goes up if they buy through a distributor middleman. Retailers, for their part, use credit cards and this inflates prices. The plastic has a high confidence level with customers. And, some retailers finance their inventories with small loan companies, the employee warned. The interest paid on the loan is added to your bill.

The retailer and wholesaler agreed that department stores charge a higher markup. He said Sears & Roebuck, for example, inflates prices 60 to 65 percent, whereas other privately owned carpet stores charge in the neighborhood of a 40-percent markup.

The figure of 40 percent includes 28 percent for operating expenses such as salaries and 5 to 6 percent for advertising. The retailer said 40 percent is needed for a store just to survive. "But most privately owned carpet stores are trying to be competitive in price," he added.

Another charge that may add to your carpet bill is preferred customer treatment. As in probably every line of business, stores bend over backward to accommodate large-volume customers. Unfortunately, this sometimes results in you paying more.

However, Elkes said, "The more you buy, the better off you're going to be; the more we deal with one company, the better our prices are going to be. I don't think it's the buddy system as much as it is the volume you buy."

LOOK BEFORE YOU LEAP

Be wary about making deposits. The Dallas dealer said to never pay cash in advance for carpet. Make a deposit, he advised, but do not pay cash. Many sellers require as much as 50 percent of the bill for a deposit if the carpet is a special order. "If we have it in stock, there's no charge," said the dealer. Remember, if you pay the entirety of your bill ahead of time, and the dealer is someone you have not thoroughly investigated, you could be in for a rude awakening when you find out he has gone Chapter 11.

Carpet is a quantity business that requires, in most cases, installation by someone else. You may not get everything you paid for, either installed or in remnants. "There are schemes of laying out jobs," said the carpet store employee. "There are circumstances where a guy sees how much he can sell and how little he can deliver."

He advised customers to get their installation space measured by someone qualified, most carpet layers do not have much experience in measuring carpet. "Carpet layers know just how to lay carpet, but not measure it," the employee said. Always find someone qualified to do the measuring before you contract for the carpet.

To determine if the carpet you receive in your home is adequate, the Arlington wholesaler said to look for dye streaks (noticeable marks anywhere on the carpet) and dye-lot change (color switches between carpet strips that result from changes in production sequences). One strip may be slightly off in color from another because it was made by the production facility at a different time. "They make it (carpet) twenty-four hours a day," he said. "But there may be a piece that may be installed, but a customer wants it (another piece) two weeks later. The dye lot might be a shade different."

The wholesaler also warned to check the pile height (the deepness of the carpet's strands). This, the Arlington dealer said, depends on how the carpet is cut. Any unevenness in the pile height is a defect in the carpet, and those bad enough to complain about should be fairly noticeable.

As in almost every type of business, carpet sellers have their favorites when it comes to mills. The carpet store employee said the purchase of carpet on the wholesale level is a game of politics, and there is discrimination against those who do not play it well. "It's the buddy system," he said. "I deal with half a dozen mills. These mills I get along with well and they give me a low price." He said he even has favorite salesmen who he will follow when they switch to other mills. These politics lead to high and low prices and explain why you should look elsewhere if you cannot find an item for what you want to pay.

The Dallas dealer said the carpet market has become saturated with new carpet companies—including quite a few that come and go. "I get calls every day from companies that are going out of business." He said these firms ask him to come buy their inventory, and he sometimes gets as many as two or three calls a week. They ask him to buy their whole stock, with cash, for a cheap price. Customers who have done business with these companies are out of luck, he said.

Standards for carpet are few, but the Federal Housing Authority (FHA) does specify that carpets weigh a minimum of twenty-four ounces per square yard. This was referred to as the "actual face weight" by the Arlington retailer/wholesaler. Another standard in the industry is a twelve-foot width on strips of carpet. And, said the Dallas dealer, jute has been replaced by synthetic backing as an industrywide standard substance. No matter what the standard, feel the carpet. "Let your hands do the talking for you," advised the Dallas dealer. "You can feel the difference."

So, what can you do to protect yourself? It all goes back to old-fashioned common sense: get a little help from your friends. Look for a history of repeats and referrals. Ask your neighbor where he bought his carpet. Ask him who installed the carpet. If he had a good experience, consider trying his company, the carpet store employee advised. Remember, too, that all salesmen are not the same. Some are uninformed, unethical, or both, and

some "good," reputable companies have "bad" salesmen. To be on the safe side, ask your neighbor *who* sold
him the carpet, as well. You might even ask who measured the installation space. You could avoid a potential
problem by doing so.

FURNITURE: AN INVESTMENT TO SIT ON

The furniture industry is a complex business made
up of a large number of honest, up-front firms. Yet, there
are also a number of powerful associations between manufacturers, distributors, and the vendors, who, ultimately, sell you the product. Knowing what to look for
and being aware of certain practices can ensure that you
get the better end of the deal.

There are bargains out there, but the buyer needs to
be wary before jumping at the first low-priced item he
sees. Often, after inspection, these items are not bargains
at all.

Take for instance, the materials from which the
product is made. Materials such as fiberboard and particleboard (made of sawdust shavings) are represented as
all-wood products. "You think you're buying solid wood,
but you're not," warned a prominent furniture distributor in the Eastern United States. "It is difficult for a consumer to know the construction, whether it's solid wood,
particleboard, solid veneer, fiberboard, or some combination of mystery woods."

Len Yarbrough, the owner of the Yarbrough Furniture Co. in Denton, Texas, said, "The best way is to take a
drawer out, turn it upside down and see how the side panels are constructed. If it's veneer, you can see the banding
of the veneer. It looks like stripes in the wood." Veneer
pieces usually have five to seven layers of the slices,
whereas solid wood, as you might expect, has one. As
mentioned, look for filler on the bottom panel of a drawer
or on the back of a dresser. Or, get on your hands and

knees and look underneath that table you are thinking about buying.

Yarbrough said you're likely to find that your piece is a veneer. "The vast majority, 95 percent, is a veneer, not solid wood. There is very little solid wood made anymore."

A quality veneer has advantages over solid wood, said Yarbrough: it does not swell in high humidity, it does not crack as badly, and it holds screws better.

Be wary of subtle elements in the sales literature and pitch. The furniture distributor pointed out that sales personnel are taught to use words and phrases that create misleading images of product quality, ingredients, price, and such. The sellers tell consumers they are making an investment when the solid-wood construction is really particleboard.

INFLATED COSTS IN "FABULOUS FABRICS"

The fabric on furniture can also be misleading. According to J. Edgar Broyhill who runs a mail order furniture business, The Edgar B. Furniture Plantation in Clemens, North Carolina, many manufacturers of sofas, chairs, loveseats, and other items are "men of cloth" who mark up the price for fabric. "There's been a shift from wood-cased goods to upholstered. Why? You're able to hide and mask inferior products for more money," he said.

One of the advantages of using fabrics is that they can make almost any piece look good. "You can't tell unless you take the upholstery off what the furniture is made of," explained Broyhill. In fact, there have been some pretty interesting materials used in the past. "Years ago, some manufacturers were going to the East Coast and getting Spanish moss to stuff the sofa with," he said. "It was all an effort to look for free raw materials."

Fabrics have also been used to sell a piece of furniture for more than its worth. According to the furniture distributor, inexpensive fabrics ($2-$4 per yard) are used on sofas or other items that retail for $1,000; $1,500; and up. In reality, he explained, these items have a wholesale cost of only $300 to $400, the difference in price is attributed to the "fabulous fabric."

"Most consumers pay extraordinarily high prices for upholstered furniture," said the distributor. So upholstery serves price fixers as an excuse to inflate the markup.

Discontinued merchandise can be another source of regret after a purchase. An example is the purchase of part of a set—maybe chairs, but not the table. Will you know that the set is a discontinued item? Maybe. Some retailers get discontinued items at special prices, then promote the price as regular brand-name furniture, said Broyhill. Six months later, when you come back for the table, you cannot get it—and you will have to settle for just the chairs. When buying, ask about the status of the item.

Private labels, which are simply the retailer's house offerings, can give you a chance to buy quality for less. The brand-name labels on a manufacturer's product are lifted by the retailer and replaced by the house brand, especially if the items are not moving (selling) at a certain price level. You can then buy it for less. While you are sometimes taking your chances with the private brand, you often are taking home a better piece of furniture than you could have otherwise bought at that price. One of the reasons that these labels are "lifted off," is that some of the prestigious outfits (Ethan Allen, for example) would not want their product considered a discount item. However, if the label is removed, then they will consent to selling at a lower price.

Unfortunately, labels can also be a way of falsifying information. Retailers prevent comparative shopping by falsifying manufacturers' numbers and labels. "Unlike the auto industry," said the distributor, "which clearly identifies the retail price of products and accessories, no clear identification is possible when shopping for furniture."

UNDERSTANDING THE MARKUPS

Like many other products, furniture will usually go through a series of markups. Broyhill said there is a standard furniture retailer's rule: fifty and ten.

Fifty and ten means, literally, a markup of $55 on each $100 of the suggested retail price. Fifty percent of $100 is $50. To find the *wholesale* of your item, take 10 percent of that $50 remainder away, reducing the original $100 to $45. If you are buying a $200 piece and the retailer is using the fifty and ten rule, the wholesale price should have been $90. For a $300 piece, the answer is $135, and so on. This is a common markup system, Broyhill indicated.

The Eastern United States furniture distributor said, however, that manufacturers set inflated suggested retail prices at approximately 40 percent above actual manufacturing cost. The dealer sometimes will add another 10 to 15 percent onto that. This latter markup is based on the appearance of the product, not on the manufacturer's suggested list price, the distributor warned.

Rose Blumkin of Nebraska Furniture Mart in Omaha, Nebraska, has been in the retail business for fifty-five years. She said she charges only 10 to 12 percent markup and survives and wonders why others cannot do the same. "You can't take vacations, go to Hawaii, and gamble. You can't neglect the business and survive."

Other retailers, she said, are in debt when they start, borrow money to buy merchandise, and, inevitably, go bankrupt. They charge a big markup trying to recoup their losses, if they stay in business long enough to sell something. The markup sometimes is as much as 60 percent, although expenses still keep the business from making a profit. Blumkin pointed out one expense she no longer has to worry about. "We own the buildings, so we pay no rent. That helps." The moral: who owns the building might be as important as who owns the inventory.

In fact, many of the markups are nothing more than a way for a retailer to cover costs. Sometimes, there is a credit hold on him, which means he cannot get your order to you on time. Or maybe there is no more room in the warehouse. Of course, the high price may be caused by other problems. In what part of town is the showroom located? This could be an indication of the high rent paid by the retailer, and, of course, high prices paid by you. Some stores pay astronomical rents ($20 or $30 per square foot) for their store and warehouse space, Broyhill said. Both Broyhill and the distributor said the common markup for these costs is usually 40 to 45 percent and include: 7 to 8 percent for rent; 15 to 18 percent for personnel; 10 percent for advertising and public relations; and 1 to 2 percent for utilities.

Volume also determines the price you will pay. Broyhill said he treats all customers the same, but he warned that many businesses do not. Instead of trying to work big-volume customers into an established ordering system, these companies bend over backward for big clients. Preferential treatment may include faster delivery and lower prices. "It's very tempting," said Broyhill, "to go to a large office building and bid on a $100,000 job in an effort to get a quick buck." But he said he does not bow to this temptation; his average sale is $2,600 to a married couple with a single-family home.

The practice of rewarding big orderers goes beyond the retail level, all the way back to wholesale. Retail buyers go to four markets (furniture expositions) per year, said Broyhill. Only four trips are needed to find all the manufacturers they want. Also, it takes three months to get the furniture as a rule. "If he stopped buying today," said Broyhill, "he'd have three months of stuff left."

Big retailers however, go to *pre*-markets, which are private meetings which yield better deals for these big outfits who have an opportunity to select merchandise before the smaller operations do.

Large retail chains are dominant over smaller entities in the field, said the distributor. "There's a close relationship between the manufacturer and these large chains," which creates a certain intimidation factor in transactions, he said. Often, the only reprieve for small sellers is to stock more imports.

Although the distributor said he believed you could get a better value from imports than from some of the American products, Broyhill disagreed.

"All imported furniture is a cover-up to get a better price," he said. "It's inferior quality and is sold at ten times what it is worth. This is why the import business has grown so dramatically. It's cheap to get and is easy to pass off as better quality."

Once you have picked out something you like, be careful of paying deposits. Broyhill said that some sellers try to use deposits to commit customers to their orders. There is no going back once you are in this deal. In some cases, as much as the whole bill is sought by a mail-order seller, said Broyhill.

He related the story of a phone-order firm that five years ago was growing and spent the deposits it required from customers on expansion of its facilities and inventory. The firm's accounting system could not keep up with these maneuvers, and it went into Chapter 11 bankruptcy. Customers were out $3 million in deposits.

Broyhill said he instituted a surety bond for his customers shortly after this incident and other similar ventures. Set up with his bank, it was a way to insure customer's deposits. The only catch is the bond agreement must be signed by the customer and himself, but not many customers believe they need such a bond. "Customers are carefree," Broyhill said. "A lot of customers order by the phone. They don't read the contract, they don't read the catalogue—they are concerned only afterward. Then they know they are in something they didn't want to get into."

SHOPPING FOR ANTIQUES

When purchasing antiques, jointery is the key, according to the owner of a furniture repair and restoration shop in a south Texas town. He said to look for the "dovetailed" variety, which features interlocking pieces of wood. This type of jointery is easy to recognize, although you might have to get the salesman's permission to look under the chair. Many old and new pieces are dovetailed, he said. Although it may be hard to discern the age of the piece—the newer ones are mechanically made, whereas older pieces are done by hand—it is a good piece either way, said the owner.

In antiques, as in any piece, you should be able to tell the identity of the material by the tightness of the wood's grain—a distinguishing characteristic even the novice can find. If you have forgotten, for example, that walnut is a brown wood tinged with red, you might still recall that it has a tight grain. Other woods, such as gum, have virtually no grain. Oak is a common wood with an open grain.

The owner advised customers looking for antique pieces to take out desk or dresser drawers and examine them for repair marks. If a piece has a noticeable line or looks like a different color, it is probably a reconstruction job. The wood used may be warped, so you need to see if drawers sit straight and easily slide in and out. Actually feel the slides, he said, to determine how worn they are.

Look past the aesthetics of the piece, then determine whether it will be functional or not. After all, "What good is a piece of furniture, even an old one, if you can't use it in the house?" the owner asked.

Look for gaps, the owner said, on the piece's underside that appear to be filled with some kind of filler material—it is a slipshod method of making furniture that, in most cases, should lead you to select *another* piece instead of the one you saw with the filler. "If you go to a top-of-the-line furniture store," he said, "it'll give you an idea of what to look for in antique or second-hand furniture."

As in new furniture, watch for the veneer covering. However, in an antique, the modern variety is not as good as the old, so veneer on an antique piece might hold up nicely and need not be discounted—it is probably a better piece than a new one.

Any damage in an antique or second-hand furniture, the owner warned, is probably harder to fix than you think. On sofas and other items, upholstery and other coverings effectively hide potential problems that might mean a hefty reduction in your bank balance. And, if it is already your piece, catch those problems when you decide it is time to reupholster. Inspect the frame while your prospective piece has its clothes off. Otherwise, you may have sunk your own ship. "I had one set we did a couple of years ago—a seat and chair frame," the owner recalled. "They took the upholstery off and realized the frame was shot. It cost $1,000 to fix."

AUCTIONS: YOU SET THE PRICE

The major avenue for selling antiques is the auction. An auction is a contrived meeting of buyers for bidding on merchandise. It is also the one buying situation where the shopper is more likely to do harm to his pocketbook than he is to be ripped off by someone else's deed. Unlike

60

other buying situations, a bad decision often comes from the shopper with little help from anyone else. Items at an auction are sold quickly, for the highest price obtainable for the seller (the highest bid), and no one forces a shopper to bid. The result is the seller gets market value for his items. Of course, if a shopper wants to pay more, well. . . .

Remember, when you bid at an auction, someone is bound to top it. Do not expect the auctioneer to stop you if a bidding war starts. After all, he is trying to get the highest amount possible for an item because he works on a commission basis or is taking a percentage of the proceeds. The relationship of the auctioneer and the buyer is, of necessity, that of two adversaries. The auctioneer works to get you to bid because he is paid to do so. Do not expect him to say, "Oh, I'm sorry, those poor people do not realize they have overbid on this." It simply will not happen.

HOW AN AUCTION IS SET UP

The auctioneer works on a commission basis. He may take home 10 percent of $100,000 in proceeds or 1 percent of $1 million in proceeds. The commission is based on what the seller expects the auction to generate in liquid cash and is often preset. It is usual for the seller who hired the auctioneer to pay for advertising, security at the auction, rent, and repair and cleanup of items. However, sometimes the auctioneer is responsible for these expenses. One operation, Southco Auctioneers, Inc., of Denton, Texas, prefers to arrange its own advertising because it wants to establish name recognition for the company. The smaller the sale, the greater the percentage taken by Southco since they usually handle the advertising.

When Southco begins organizing an auction, they line up the merchandise, verifying that everything to be sold is on hand. They inventory the merchandise and, finally, advertise the upcoming event. Much of the advertising is done in the form of mailings sent to regular clients. Between 10,000 and 60,000 brochures are sent out, depending on the merchandise to be sold. There are numerous auctions that involve specialized inventories, and the nature of inventories varies greatly. Southco specializes in auctioning construction equipment and complete liquidation of all types of companies, and also handles city auctions periodically.

Virtually any type of merchandise can be sold at an auction. Jerry McClellan, an auctioneer in Houston, Texas, said he has sold everything from livestock to china. The items to be sold at an auction can come from a wide variety of sources, from moving an inventory out of a Chapter 11 situation for a cash liquidation to selling goods from an estate, imports from overseas suppliers, or items brought to the area by haulers from other parts of the United States. McClellan explained that it is an industry of trading, and the idea is to get products to an area where they can sell for more money. Shoppers may find that there are areas nearby where a product they want sells for less than in their area. Goods move around fast, and they sell for different prices in different places. So, keep up with prices elsewhere. If it is a type of item you see all the time, do not be too "trigger-happy," advised McClellan. Chances are something identical or at least very similar will turn up somewhere else in your area.

Auctioneers may take title of the item to be sold for a short time. Acting as a product broker, they take possession of the item before the auction and then sell it. There is very little else done. As a result, they do not guarantee that the chair does not have a broken leg or that the lawn mower will start. The auctioneer sometimes knows less about the condition of an item than the previous owner, and, therefore, usually sells everything "as is." McClellan asked, "How are you going to guarantee something you don't know anything about?"

According to McClellan, 99 percent of auction items are sold without warranties. This makes it critical that shoppers check out the merchandise—do their homework—and investigate an item thoroughly before they bid on it. Items can be viewed prior to the auction, and the viewing period usually is from three days to a week, depending on the inventory to be sold.

DO YOUR HOMEWORK BEFORE YOU BID

Since the auction sale is usually on an "as is" basis, the responsibility for making a smart bid falls on the shopper. Knowledge of the products being auctioned and a thorough inspection of the inventory is the shopper's best preparation going into the bidding process. Knowledge of the product is especially critical when the auction is for antiques. "Lots of places sell reproductions along with the antiques. We announce that, but a lot of places don't," shared one auctioneer.

"Price ignorance," as the Southco auctioneer called it, is the biggest pitfall for shoppers at an auction. "The people aren't aware of what the prices of some things are. . . . They get caught up in the excitement of it (the auction)."

If the item you are intending to purchase is worth a large sum of money, consider taking an appraiser with you to the auction. An appraiser is especially useful if you are thinking on bidding on antiques, according to the Southco auctioneer. "On any of it, I think it's a good idea to know what something's worth," he advised. An appraiser can help you do just that.

Most auctioneers help shoppers who have not done their homework. That is, they do not misrepresent anything they are selling in an effort to inflate the value, the Southco auctioneer said. But he added, "Their job is to promote." In most cases, however, the auctioneer is knowledgeable about what items are worth, and he might even tell you before and after the auction. "Any auction company that's any good knows what stuff is worth. They do an appraisal," he said. But the auctioneer is in a difficult position. On one hand, he is working for the seller, but on the other, he has bidders who want to be treated fairly. This dilemma becomes especially troublesome if the audience is made up of loyal followers. "If you're a loyal buyer," said the Southco auctioneer, "they'll (the auctioneers) make recommendations as to not overpay on certain items."

These loyal buyers or regulars are knowledgeable auction shoppers who do their homework on the items involved. Regular customers may be notified in advance of an auction and may follow the auctioneer wherever he conducts auctions. Novices should watch for them because they are knowledgeable bidders. These are people the auctioneer may know personally, and they may or may not get a better deal because of that connection. Of course, it takes a long time to develop that kind of rapport with an auctioneer. And the more people he feels obligated to, the more pressure he will be under. But if you can become known as a "regular," you may receive some good advice on buys before an auction.

WATCH OUT FOR THESE SITUATIONS

However, there have been cases when the auctioneer is in cahoots with someone bidding in the audience. This suggestion conjures up thoughts of the auctioneer awarding an item to someone for one price and then privately selling it to the conspirator for a lower price. This person could be a longtime friend or business associate. The bidder in this scenario might instead be a friend of the seller—a relationship that could influence the auctioneer. Such relationships are very difficult to find or prove.

Max Slaughter, an auctioneer with Mid-South Auctioneers, Inc., in Irving, Texas, explained how "shills" operate. A shill is a bidder planted in the audience and who is told by the auctioneer to inflate the bidding. Although Slaughter has heard of such tactics, he said "I personally do not (use them). You do understand that's against the law."

Laws, with such situations in mind, were written to protect the consumer, advised Sara Bogan, former secretary of the Department of Labor and Standards which oversees the regulation of auctions in Texas. For example, if the auctioneer is going to have someone bid on an item for him, this arrangement must be announced beforehand. If the owner has a bidder, this must also be announced. These announcements theoretically prevent the auctioneer from awarding an item unfairly, such as ignoring a bid.

If items are to be kept *on reserve* (which means bidding must start at a certain level), it must be announced beforehand. This way shoppers will not be surprised where the bidding begins. It is important bidders pay as much attention as possible and not jump into bidding without knowing what amount is being tossed around.

And what about the danger of someone coughing and accidentally bidding on an item, and then having to buy it as a result? Stories such as this are myths and only happen in the movies, according to the Southco auctioneer. "An experienced auctioneer can tell whether a person has bid or not. There's no particular sign." However, he listed the most common bid signs: winks, raising of buyer cards (given to you at the auction), and raising of hands.

It seems incredible that an auctioneer can tell a bid versus a non-bid, but they can, assured the Southco auctioneer. "If a man is waving at someone else in the crowd, the auctioneer can tell that. That's a big myth that if you bat an eye the auctioneer will take you. . . . He *can* distinguish the difference."

IS THERE HELP IF SOMETHING GOES WRONG?

What if you have done your homework, even brought an appraiser with you, and when you go to pick up the item you bid on and was awarded, it does not look like it is in the same condition or even the same item you viewed before the auction? If something you bought does not look like the same thing you saw previously, you can usually squelch the deal, according to Marilyn Burgess, vice president of Lone Star Auctioneers in Fort Worth, Texas. "If someone goes to pick up merchandise and it's not as the auctioneer represented it to be (chipped, etc.), that customer is not obligated to pay at our auctions." She added that the misrepresentation must make a noticeable difference in the product and must be something that is provable. However, Lone Star is fairly lenient on this "proof," she said.

And despite the lack of warranties, the auction transaction is similar to a customary retail transaction in other ways. Usually a receipt is given for each item purchased, McClellan explained. And the traditional consumer pressure that can be applied to retailers can be used on the auctioneers as well. Because contemporary communication and regulation systems are efficient and thorough, auctions today are organized and the fly-by-night operations cannot slip through, mused McClellan.

Although there is no federal regulating force for auctions, most states govern the operations through various levels of departments or commissions. For an example, in Texas, the Department of Labor and Standards requires that all auctioneers are licensed. The auctioneer or auction company owner's license number and name must be stated in all advertising matter. Thus, consumers have an outlet (the department) for recourse should something go wrong.

The registration of the auctioneer's license assures consumers that the source of the auction items is known. Should you go to an auction that is not regulated, there is the possibility that the merchandise is stolen or that it has claims against it by some other party (a lien). This legally jeopardizes your acquisition of the property. Before you buy, ask to see the auctioneer's license registration card (all auctioneers, including their associate auctioneers, are required to carry these during the auction process) and ask about the origin of the collection being sold.

The auctioneer is also required to process the necessary paperwork for the auction sale. This includes sending the sales tax to the state comptroller's office, seeing that the buyers receive the title to their merchandise, and that the seller (who pays his commission) receives the proceeds from the sale. According to Bogan, the auctioneer is entirely responsible for seeing the transaction is completed correctly. To help ensure this, auctioneers in Texas must buy a $5,000 surety bond and file it with the state. It is a matter of public record that can be checked. The bond is a form of insurance coverage that the auctioneer is on the level. However, the amount of coverage is very small compared with what an auctioneer makes on even one sale.

Another provision concerns associate auctioneers, or helpers, who fill in for auctioneers under various circumstances. The associate auctioneer must be under the direct on-premises supervision of a licensed auctioneer. There must be a legitimate employee-employer relationship between the two for it to be sanctioned by the state.

Any violation of the rules by an auctioneer can result in a fine or jail sentence. In Texas, an auctioneer who conducts an auction without a license commits a

Class B misdemeanor. Other violations, such as misrepresentations of merchandise, are Class C misdemeanors. Since the Texas license must be obtained each year, this assures the auctioneer adheres to the state regulations. Rules vary from state to state, and there are some variations even within the same state based on the merchandise being auctioned, such as livestock or automobiles.

Actually, the auctioneer has little recourse against his customers should a buyer "overspend" in the excitement of bidding or lose track of how many items he has bought and the total amount owed. What happens if you cannot pay the total bill you have accumulated? According to Burgess, you just do not get to remove your purchase from the premises. The auctioneer holds the merchandise and simply has to determine what to do with it. "The buyer is committing a trust, an agreement, every time they hold up their card. They are saying 'Yes, I'll buy.'" Lone Star Auctioneers, like most auctioneers, keep a "walk list" of buyers who did not pay for items at an auction and those buyers are not allowed to participate in future auctions, Burgess warned.

GOVERNMENT AND POLICE DEPARTMENT AUCTIONS

Shoppers can find some very good buys at government or police department auctions where abandoned vehicles, stolen property such as televisions and jewelry items that has been released by court order, and used government equipment is sold. But remember, like any other auction, there are no guarantees about the condition of the goods and it is the buyer's responsibility to inspect all items carefully before bidding. And again, knowledge about the appraised value of the item is up to the buyer. Just because it is a government sponsored auction does not mean that a buyer does not have to be very careful. And like other types of auctions, the buyer is most likely to damage his pocketbook himself. The same advice applies: do your homework.

LIQUIDATION SALES

Auctions are a form of liquidation, an operation where merchandise is sold and cash is generated quickly. Liquidators, like auctioneers, may work on a commission basis and may or may not take title to the inventory. The liquidator who manages the quick disposal of a merchant's unwanted inventory serves a very special purpose for the merchant. When the merchant has to vacate the premises by the end of the month, sometimes the auction is the best alternative in handling the unwanted inventory.

The liquidation sale, often called the "going-out-of-business sale," frequently must be moved to a location other than the merchant's premises because the landlord will not allow an auction at his store property or mall on the basis it does not look good for the other businesses. Thus, many liquidation sales are held at hotels, coliseums, and such, and this is where a great deal of confusion sets in and consumers get hurt. Because a lot of fly-by-night operators also advertise as "liquidating" goods for sale at the same type of locations, it is very difficult for a shopper to determine which ones are legitimate liquidators.

Industry sources said the majority of liquidators are good and try to stay out of the picture so the disposal of the merchandise seems as normal as possible. But, unfortunately, there are few legitimate liquidators. Colonel Ralph Segars, a liquidator for twenty-three years and owner of Colonel Ralph Segars and Associates in Dallas, Texas, said he had seen more than his share of the other type of so-called liquidators. "There are some fly-by-nighters who come from other states, other parts of the country. They say they're liquidators, but it's their *own* merchandise." He continued, explaining that most of this merchandise is bought from other liquidators or is discontinued or damaged.

Segars described the "traveling salesman" type of liquidator who frequents hotels and other haunts: "Just this week I heard of a deal where they pulled up in a truck selling merchandise that came from such and such a state." He warned that the less consumers know about the seller, the less they are protected. "They (consumers) really need to buy from people who are established. A lot of people advertise and don't even put a phone number or say where they're from. You can probably go to a store and pay less."

Segars said that taking home a box of goods from a liquidation sale is sometimes a risky proposition, especially if you are dealing with a shady operator. Liquidators selling you a box of something might stuff it with something else, and if you do not check the contents before you leave, the box might not be full of what you thought. He compared this practice to a similar practice perpetrated at some farmers' markets, where you might "get the good apples on top." That is, the crate you take home may have big, red, juicy apples on top, but on the layer beneath there are rotten ones.

How can a shopper protect himself and determine if he is dealing with one of the few "real" liquidators? First, ask the store manager how long the going-out-of-business sale has been in progress. Second, check your local telephone directory to see if the liquidator has been in business long enough to have a listing. Another tipoff would be if when you arrive at the sale, the merchandise advertised is not available and more expensive merchandise has been substituted. This is the old bait-and-switch scheme, and it is also the warning that you do not want to do business with this operator. The one positive clue is an original price tag attached to the merchandise. This also allows the shopper to compare the original retail price with the liquidator's price. But just because the original price tag is attached does not mean the manufacturer will honor the warranty for product. Although warranties depend on the parties involved, they are often not part of the deal since the consumer is getting a great discount on the merchandise.

There is another type of liquidation: the merchant sells his unwanted inventory out right to a liquidation firm that specializes in salvage. What sets the salvage operator apart from the other types of liquidators is he buys the inventory rather than just handling the sale. The merchandise is put up for sale in the salvager's store or location rather than at a neutral location.

Auctions and liquidation sales provide excellent opportunities to purchase a wide variety of merchandise at below-retail prices. However, this same environment can induce a buyer into paying above-retail prices on the very same merchandise if he is not careful and has not done his homework. Get smart *before* you shop.

COSMETICS

Flip through any fashion magazine and look for the glossiest, most sensual ads—invariably the ads sell beauty. If a woman used everything advertised in one magazine, she could have silky-smooth, blemish-free, firm, perfectly "textured," youthful skin devoid of lines and wrinkles; a natural-looking glow, with a healthy-looking, natural, glowing blush; huge, expressive eyes; long, dark, thick, yet soft and natural eyelashes; soft and smooth, kissable lips in a frankly fabulous color; shiny, shimmery, soft, sexy hair full of body that glows with health; strong, moisturized fingernails covered with a shimmery sheen; and a bronze and beautiful "tan," rich, deep, and long-lasting.

Sounds pretty beautiful. Shoppers can have all this and more thanks to one empire, the empire of cosmetics. Just by buying all this stuff, a person can be beautiful. Yet not everyone is beautiful.

How can one industry wrest $16 billion a year from a supposedly enlightened public that should know by now that beauty is only skin deep?

Think of the cosmetics industry as a castle, a lovely castle off in the distance. It is a fanciful image. In fact, cosmetics companies rely on fantasy, for it is part of what they sell to make money—lots of money.

The cosmetics empire is built on a quagmire of vanity, hope, and customers' personal preferences. And with close inspection, this empire has some facets that are a mirage and some that are distorted. Somehow this empire has survived for centuries on this shifty foundation because, in fact, it is responding to our desires and demands, and because it is simply fun.

THE PREOCCUPATION WITH BEAUTY

It seems only fair to exonerate the cosmetics industry first. Despite the hyper hype and glitz and promises upon promises, the entire industry is only responding to our demands. It is not entirely the fault of cosmetics gurus that we put so much emphasis on personal beauty. Even in 1887, Finck wrote in *Romantic Love and Personal Beauty:* "Inasmuch as personal beauty is the flower and symbol of perfect health, it might be shown, by following this argument, that ugliness is a sin, and man's first duty is the cultivation of beauty."

Even psychologists, with their reputation for ignoring the surface and probing deeper to find the real person, know that beauty is only skin deep, but they are catching on to the notion that perceived beauty goes all the way to the bone. Cosmetic psychology, almost unheard-of twenty years ago, is a hot topic today.

In a landmark 1972 study, social psychologists asked college students to examine photographs of people and evaluate their personalities. The students consistently rated the physically attractive people to be kind, sociable, interesting, sexually warm, poised, and self-assertive. (The attractive people were also rated more self-centered than the unattractive ones, but the positive attributes far outweighed the negative ones.) The psychologists called this a "positive halo effect," meaning one positive attribute (good looks in this case) is likely to generate a more favorable general impression of a person.

Drs. Jean Ann Graham and A. Jan Jouhar have found that "people make inferences about what a person is like on the basis of his/her facial features and appearance and the presence or absence of certain cosmetics." For example, people with coarse textured skin (acne, large pores) may be judged to be coarse people, and those with thin lips may be viewed as less talkative.

These are just two examples of the unfairness of first impressions. But keep in mind what was judged in the studies can be manipulated. That is where cosmetics and cosmetic psychology comes in.

Drs. Graham and Jouhar presented a study focusing specifically on the use of cosmetics. Their conclusions:

". . . Both males and females in this kind of population (professional working people in the age range of 24 to 41 years) judge people whom they do not know to look better and have better personalities when using cosmetics compared with when not.

"So it seems that a positive stereotype of the kind, 'what is beautiful is good,' exists for cosmetic appearance in the same sort of way that the physical attractiveness stereotype exists, but it seems likely now that we can extend our conception of this stereotype to include 'what has been made beautiful is good' or 'what is cared for is good.'

"It appears therefore that not only do those who are physically attractive to begin with have the advantages of positive personality attributions but so, too, can those of average attractiveness and who make the effort to use cosmetics, gain these advantages."

"Attractive people do better in job interview situations, people are likely to help them more, and, of course, the physically attractive are preferred over the unattractive in terms of interpersonal relationships," wrote Dr. Graham in a 1983 paper (presented at the First International Symposium of the Psychology of Cosmetic Treatments).

Dr. Tom Cash conducted a study on physical attractiveness in the job market. "This study and others indicate that, in general, the unattractive are less likely to be hired, are offered smaller salaries, and are not expected to be very competent if, in fact, they are hired."

This is unfair, but true: if you want to play the career game, cosmetics are a part of the rules.

Trying to decide if the existence of cosmetics invented these rules or vice versa is probably a futile exercise. But the fact is cosmetics as a whole are not a rip-off, but the opportunities for being ripped off during a cosmetics purchase are great.

In exploring the industry castle, it is important to know that we are essentially on our own.

THE INDUSTRY WATCHDOG IS ON A SHORT LEASH

With all its regulating (and overregulating) capacities, our national government is severely restrained in protecting the public from the cosmetics industry.

The Food and Drug Administration, which oversees the cosmetics industry, cannot approve or prohibit the sale of a cosmetic in advance. Only after a product has been on the market and found harmful or misbranded can it take action.

Even then, the burden of proof is on the FDA to show that a product is dangerous or misbranded. Confounding the situation further, the FDA makes cosmetic-safety surveillance its lowest priority. The agency spends less than 1 percent of its budget on cosmetic-safety surveillance. In 1986, that meant the FDA had a $2.6 million budget to oversee an industry that was worth $15.5 billion in 1984.

So if a product is to be free of intense government scrutiny, it cannot promise to alter the body chemistry in any way. The moment it does, or claims to, it is classified a drug, and the burden of proof of effectiveness falls on the manufacturer.

Manufacturers are required to list ingredients on labels, but to report only fragrances and "secret ingredients" to the FDA. Some voluntarily report all ingredients (even then, updating is not required), but the amount of each ingredient is not required. That can be dangerous in itself.

The current hassle over methylene chloride is a case in point. Methylene chloride is a carcinogenic ingredient used in both hair sprays and the coffee decaffeination process. The FDA has proposed to ban this chemical in cosmetics, but to allow the coffee decaffeinators to continue to use it, because the amount used in the process poses only a one in a billion risk.

If the FDA does not succeed, and a manufacturer reports only that methylene chloride is used, there is no way for anyone but the manufacturer to know if a harmless or dangerous amount is used.

The FDA has recorded some successes in getting dangerous or ineffective products off the market. It persuaded Roux Laboratories to recall its lash and brow tint because of its unsafe ingredients. It has required the Listerine manufacturers to quit touting their mouthwash as effective against colds. Back in the 1920s, it finally stopped production of Koremlu depilatory cream, which contained rat poison.

Those victories can be hard-won and long battles.

Remember the hexachlorophene story of the early '70s? Remember pHisoHex, the darling of hospital nurseries and pimply teenagers, which was loaded with it? Hexachlorophene is a first cousin to an herbicide called 2,4,5-T. The manufacturers claimed it killed staph germs, and it did. But it also caused brain damage in rats and convulsions, burns, and death to infants who were bathed in it, and abnormalities in animal offspring.

Evidence of the dangers of hexachlorophene first appeared in the late 1950s. But it was not until 1972 that the FDA announced that restrictions would be imposed on the chemical. In that span of time, hexachlorophene was proudly touted on product labels. Manufacturers churned out reams of copy singing its praises, ignoring dead rats and burned babies in convulsions. Yale University even released a statement that the presence of staph germs went up when Yale University nursery workers quit using hexachlorophene. What went almost unnoticed was that Yale was the first to report that the chemical was effective, so it had some proprietary interest in keeping the chemical on the market.

The FDA was stymied by the cumbersome process of assembling evidence, appraising it, drawing conclusions, and taking action, perhaps only to have its case not hold up in court. All it could do for a while was issue feeble warnings and announce "continuing studies." Finally, a combination of FDA pressure and continuing bad publicity forced hexachlorophene out of the market forever.

The FDA essentially must depend on the threat of publicity about a dangerous or ineffective product. Fortunately, this process works very well in bringing about a "voluntary" withdrawal of a product.

The manufacturers themselves exhaustively test their products for allergic reactions. It is an industry standard that no product can be marketed unless the test incidence of sensitization (allergic reaction) is less than 1 in 10,000. This standard applies to every cosmetic, from the most elegant preparation to the cheapest dime store goop.

The Public Information Office has a list of the newest carcinogens. You can get information by writing: Public Information Office, National Toxicology Program, P.O. Box 12233, Research Triangle Park, North Carolina 22709.

Also available to dermatologists and poison control

centers around the country is the booklet, "Cosmetics Industry on Call." It lists a contact person and telephone number for each company that belongs to the Cosmetic, Toiletry and Fragrance Association (CTFA) to call for product information.

The CTFA claims that its active members are responsible for manufacturing and distributing more than 90 percent of all the cosmetic products made in the United States. The association has a panel of seven scientists that conducts independent reviews to assess product safety.

The February 1986 issue of Cosmetics and Toiletries featured a story on product testing titled, "Alleged Adverse Reactions: Cooperating with the Dermatologist," by Edward M. Jackson, M.D.

According to Jackson, testing is done in four stages: (1) animal models, (2) human patch testing, (3) test market introduction, then (4) national introduction. "Supplying patch test samples is a service that most companies in the cosmetics industry willingly perform," the article states. ". . . The best source of cosmetic ingredient patch test concentrations and vehicles is available directly from the cosmetic company."

Jackson also soothes a lot of rattled nerves with this statement on the ever-depressing news about colors:

"While irritation, sensitization, and photosensitization reactions can occur from exposure to any chemical, including colors, it is also true that no other cosmetic product ingredient class has more safety testing supporting it or has a longer safety record than colors. This is just another way to say that idiosyncratic reactions can always occur no matter how much safety testing has been done."

Probably the most powerful regulating body the cosmetic industry contends with is the public.

"Product safety can depend on the integrity of the

company. All you need is one or two scares, and a company can go right down the toilet," a former manager for Revlon pointed out. "A product may not do anything for you, but it shouldn't hurt you."

"Elizabeth Arden is dedicated to the finest quality and finest service it can offer," stated one spokesperson. "You can't be around for years and not be a good company."

Speakers for many cosmetics manufacturers echoed this theme that the company reputation was the biggest concern in regulation. The conclusion can be safely drawn that the industry is regulated by itself.

Public opinion, public spending habits, negative publicity about a product determine most what is found on store shelves. In the end, it is the consumer who decides what will stay and what will go.

So much for safety. How about *effectiveness?* It isn't too much to ask that a product be more than simply harmless.

The government definition of "cosmetic" is "(1) articles intended to be rubbed, poured, sprinkled, or sprayed on, introduced into, or otherwise applied to the human body or any part thereof for cleansing, beautifying, promoting attractiveness, or altering the appearance, and (2) articles intended for use as a component of any such articles; except that such term shall not include soap."

Notice there's no mention of effectiveness.

NONSENSE HAS MANY SYNONYMS

The cosmetics companies face the frustration of trying to make customers believe their products are better than any other, without making claims the FDA could swoop down on. So they invent new words, new needs, new claims. What they would rather the customer did not know is that all these terms listed are essentially synonyms for nonsense.

1. Hypoallergenic—It sounds so pure, so scientifically correct. It must mean there is practically no chance a person can get an allergic reaction.

There is no standard definition of "hypoallergenic."

"What 'hypoallergenic' tends to signify is that the product contains no known allergens," stated Paige Blankenship, manager of communications for the Cosmetic, Toiletry and Fragrance Association.

Allergens are ingredients that can cause an allergic reaction. A handful of ingredients have been shown to cause a reaction in some people, and all hypoallergenic means is that those few allergens are not in the product.

But allergic reactions are something with which no manufacturer wants to be associated. So each product is rigorously tested before it hits the market. Remember, the standard is that a product will not be sold unless the test incidence of sensitization (allergic reaction) is *less* than 1 in 10,000.

Paying more for hypoallergenic means paying more for a product that does not have oil of Peru, cinnamic aldehyde, costus oil, or any other known allergen in it. Chances are the consumer will not be allergic to these ingredients anyway.

So hypoallergenic is an imaginary bulwark against allergic reactions. So is the next synonym:

2. Organic—It sounds so healthy, so in tune with Mother Earth. It could not possibly hurt another living thing.

"There's no pat definition of 'organic,'" said Blankenship. "What that tends to signify is that one or more of the ingredients is something that comes from the ground."

Aloe and cocoa butter come from things that grow in the ground. And many people are allergic to them.

The image the industry wants the customer to conjure up is one of purity, of a product with no nasty synthetic ingredients that could pollute our nation's rivers and streams. Somehow a pure product with only a few ingredients is supposed to be more effective. The logic in this is elusive.

The oatmeal and bran touted in a soap have no cleansing value. Neither does skim milk in a skin cleanser, or honey in a shampoo. Whatever these ingredients contribute to the product is simply overwhelmed by the other, effective ingredients.

Consider also that organic ingredients need an army of unnatural preservatives to keep the product from going rancid in a week.

3. Dermatologist Tested—If a dermatologist tested it, it must be safe. After all, what dermatologist would want to be associated with something that is irritating?

Dermatologists are paid to test products so manufacturers can proudly claim it on their packages. But they cannot test much more extensively than the aforementioned 1-in-10,000 standard. And nowhere does it state that because a product is dermatologist-tested, it is effective.

4. Nourishing—This one is usually used in conjunction with hair and fingernails. The implication is that the addition of moisturizers, vitamins, etc. will improve the overall condition of these body parts. Hair and fingernails are dead. The best one can hope for is a good-looking corpse.

Nail polish is paint made of plasticizers, polymers, and a slew of other synthetic ingredients. A claim that a polish will strengthen nails is true only because painting any hard coating on nails will strengthen them. Any conditioner thrown in is going to be overwhelmed by the plastic ingredients. The only thing that can permanently improve the condition of fingernails is general physical health.

The same goes for hair. Shampoo makers crow about vitamins and repairing qualities. Hair cannot starve to death: it is already dead. And all shampoo can do is clean the grime and oil off hair. Extra ingredients, such as conditioners, are overwhelmed by the soap in the shampoo and go right down the drain with the lather.

Also associated with hair and skin is this doozy:

5. PH-Balanced—Skin on the human body registers about 6.8 on the acid-alkaline scale of 1 to 14. The idea is that this near-balance should be jealously protected, and any threat means instant irritation.

Human skin can tolerate a little acidity or alkalinity. It is made to rebalance itself after being subjected to products that register higher or lower on the scale. Alkaline shampoos temporarily open hair's imbrications (the spaces between the shingle-like cuticles on the shaft), making hair feel rough for a short time. Oil smooths hair again, and oil cannot clean off oil nearly as well as soap can.

Soap is alkaline, therefore under attack. Because it is alkaline, it removes natural oils and the grime entrapped in them. But soap has to do that in order to do its job of cleaning. The body understands this and adjusts accordingly; how come the manufacturers don't seem to?

Instead the ads feature litmus papers dipped in the product, then register "balanced." That's done by mixing a few acid ingredients with the alkaline ones.

The lather is never tested in the ads, because the alkaline ingredients take over when the product is mixed with water.

6. Natural Cell Renewal—This one is a favorite in

the current trend toward scientific claims. It also is based on fact, that new skin cells look better than dry old dead ones.

"Natural cell renewal" is a cosmetic term for "epibrasion," which means scrubbing the skin surface. Epibrasion encourages the skin's process of shedding its upper layer, discourages acne by removing oil, and improves circulation. It also irritates enough to create a little harmless fluid collection that puffs up skin, minimizing wrinkles.

The cosmetics industry would rather the public did not know that all of epibrasion's advantages can be attained by gently scrubbing the skin with the rough side of a washcloth. After all, it is not in the business of selling washcloths. Instead, potion after potion is produced, each implying that under that nasty upper crust is a fresh new skin that can only be uncovered with this unique formula.

Cleansing grains are the most notorious, never mind that they are about as abrasive as a Brillo pad made of spaghetti. Masks come in second, some facial grime comes off with a mask, but not as much as would with soap and washcloth. The logic of a moisturizer claiming "skin renewal" while seeping into the skin is elusive.

These are only a few examples of the freedom the cosmetics industry has to advertise its products. Unless a product is outright dangerous (carcinogenic) or has been shown to irritate too many people or makes promises it cannot keep, anything can and *is* said about cosmetics. In this the enormous realm of what is safe and what is not illegal, the cosmetic companies do not promise the moon, but imply that the moon is there for the grabbing.

They may say their product will make skin look younger, but not, "This gets rid of wrinkles." An ad for an eye cream says, "restrain the aging process," but not "reverse aging." Advertising for shampoos promise a "healthy shine," not healthy hair. Using a bar of soap may "improve the appearance," but not outright make a person beautiful. Foundations "improve the look and feel," but their use does not guarantee silky, even-toned skin.

Most products can live up to their most basic claims. Every mascara can darken and thicken eyelashes. Blush definitely does put a spot of color on cheeks. Moisturizer can seal in moisture. Shampoos and conditioners can make hair shiny and fluffy. But "legendary" lashes? "Natural" blush? "Rejuvenating" moisturizer? "Full and beautiful" hair? By whose definition? Not the government's, and maybe not yours. Since these claims are a matter of opinion, they do not have to be proved by the manufacturer.

As hard as the advertising copywriters push the limit, they cannot and do not promise permanent changes. A consumer can save lots of time and money by simply ignoring the copy in advertising.

Also worth ignoring is the chatter from sales representatives. Their job is to convince you that their particular brand is exactly the right one for you. Ever notice that whatever product you tell a salesperson you use, she will retort that it is wrong for you? Such black-and-white sales talk in such a gray empire should be very suspicious.

But when you listen closely to a sales spiel, you can pick up the same words in each pitch: clean skin, unclog pores, protect, moisturize, apply makeup lightly, feel good and smell good!

Hair can build up a tolerance to one shampoo over a period of time. Have you ever noticed a change in your hair after switching shampoos? Hair tends to react differently for a while to new products. A case in point is Neutrogena's current ad: it "actually promises results." It urges the reader to take a 14-day vacation from your regular shampoo." Of course, what it does not say is that just about any shampoo will make hair seem different if used for fourteen days.

MOISTURIZERS: FACTS LOST IN THE FOG

Moisturizers and other facial cleansers were responsible for $1.2 billion in sales in 1985 and, according to Standard and Poor's Industry Surveys, see above-average growth prospects.

Demographics are one factor according to S&P: "the 35-to-54-year-old segment is expected to rise by about 54 percent over the next twenty-five years, providing the basis for an expanding market for wrinkle treatments and makeup for older skin."

That means the group with that old, tired-out label "baby boomers" is getting old and tired out, but still in the work force. The result is more disposable income and therefore more impulse buying, which, according to S&P, accounts for roughly two-thirds of all cosmetics and personal-care purchases.

"(Women) just want to look as young as they feel," says Sandy Burroughs, vice president of marketing at Germaine Monteil (in *Adweek*, February 25, 1986). And the plethora of moisturizers all promise exactly that—youthful looks.

But overriding those reasons is another fact: it is easy to make a moisturizer and easy to make one a tiny bit different, but just as effective.

Jonathon Zizmor, M.D., in his common-sense book with the delightfully cumbersome title, *Dr. Zizmor's Brand-Name Guide to Beauty Aids and Everything You Want to Know About Them and Whether There's Anything There That'll Hurt You and Most of All Whether They Really Do All (or Even Some) of the Things For You That the Labels Say They Do* (1978, Harper & Row), cuts through all the moisturizer mania with a very simple explanation.

"Moisturization of any kind is a matter of getting *water* (not oil) into the skin," according to Zizmor. "Once the skin is hydrated, the oil in the moisturizer locks the water in and prevents the symptoms of dehydration— flaking, fissuring, and uncomfortable tautness. This basic principle is the key to moisturizers."

Water first, then oil, it's that simple. But cosmetics advertising and simple truth usually mix like—well, like oil and water. Oil is bad, shouts one ad, use our products with emollients! ("Emollients" is a synonym for oil.) Or instead use collagen, or lanolin (wool wax—oil). Check the ingredients of "oil free" products; most of them contain one or more of these ingredients: stearic acid—a waxy substance found in animal fats and *oils*, petrolatum—most commonly known as Vaseline Petroleum Jelly, isopropyl palmitate—an acid that feels waxy to the touch, and cetyl alcohol—derived from whale *oil*.

Sound greasy, don't they? Merle Norman's Protective Veil ("a light, *oil free* moisturizing lotion that helps lock in skins' natural moisture and protects skin from soil and environmental pollution") contains stearic acid and isopropyl palmitate. Another place to save money is not to buy the notion that oil is bad for your skin. It's the *only* way to lock in moisture.

Zizmor continued his explanation of how to get the water-oil combination. Water is attained by keeping your environment humidified, cutting down on the use of dehydrating hot water for showers and baths, and— surprise!—patting it on your skin. Then for the oil, he convincingly explains his number one choice for effectiveness (and price) is Vaseline Petroleum Jelly. Vaseline? Dab it on and rub it in well, he said, and it is all your skin needs.

Do not laugh yet. Petrolatum is touted as among the best products to seal in water. Check the ingredients of pricey brands, such as Shiseido Facial Soothing Lotion (9 ounces for $18) and Merle Norman's Super Lube. There it is on the box—"Petrolatum." Mid-priced products, such as Allercreme Special Help Eye Cream with Collagen (discount priced $4.20 for 0.5 ounce) lists petrolatum second on the sixteen-item ingredients list, and collagen thirteenth.

The authors of *The Buyer's Guide to Cosmetics* (1981, Random House) conducted a survey of more than five hundred women, using Vaseline as a control product, marked simply "Eye Cream." It was rated above a much pricier cream (Helena Rubenstein Eye Creme Special), and tied with another, much more expensive cream (Orlane Baume à la Gelée Royale). And of the group, only one tester actually recognized the product.

This book does not recommend Vaseline or any other specific product. This is merely to demonstrate that price and fancy-sounding ingredients do not a better product make in the case of moisturizers.

"Generally I would not use Vaseline on the face, because I feel that it is heavy, greasy, and that it suffocates the skin, not allowing it proper 'space' to breathe," said esthetician Regina Lynch Worthy, a specialist in skin care, facial massage, and makeup application. "I would use Vaseline on the hands or feet, elbows, or rough areas of the body."

Many people would never consider Vaseline as a moisturizer anywhere on their bodies. They may cite its greasiness, its unpleasant odor, its lack of glamour. There is the tough question a person who wants to save money on moisturizer must answer: how much is fragrance, feel, and glamour worth?

"Exotic ingredients in a moisturizer are no more beneficial than common-sense ingredients," according to

Worthy. "Some natural moisturizers are almond oil, honey, cocoa butter, mashed papaya, aloe vera, sesame seed oil, or the high protein and fat content of strained corn kernels . . . .

"In other words, a good moisturizer does not have to contain the placenta of an exotic African bird in order to work."

The oil-water combination is the same in every kind of moisturizer, be it day cream, night cream, eye cream, body lotion, hand lotion, foot lotion, cuticle cream, neck cream or elbow and knee cream. The difference may be in concentrations, fragrances, or simply packaging (therefore price). But Zizmor said, "All this diversification is utter nonsense. The products are all so similar that they are literally interchangeable."

Salespeople love to push day and night creams (cremes) on customers. Their reasoning is based on fact: your skin, like the rest of your body, repairs itself at night. But look at the ingredient lists. The only difference is in concentration.

Wrinkle creams are a slightly different story. Wrinkle creams work by smoothing the skin with oil first, of course. But then they cause a slight harmless irritation, which makes the skin swell up just enough to smooth out the wrinkle for a while. That fact makes the ads for soothing wrinkle creams that actually, deliberately irritate the skin amusing. But they do work, as far as they go. The irritant is most commonly estrogen, which has caused much controversy lately. The facts are not in whether estrogen applied on skin can seep into the body. Too much estrogen may be carcinogenic.

Anyway, wrinkle creams will not go so far as to eliminate wrinkles. Wrinkles are a result of sun exposure and the skin's natural aging process. To get rid of them means to reverse those effects, and that would mean altering the skin structure. The cream would then be classified a drug, requiring the manufacturer to prove that it works. So far, no one since time began has developed a cream that has been proven to eliminate wrinkles permanently.

The cosmetics people are wise to this. Read any advertisement closely and you will find terms like: "reduce the lined appearance," "on its way to looking younger," and other phrases that imply but do not state that wrinkles disappear forever. Just about every moisturizer claims to smooth away "tiny dry lines." This claim is true, only because plumping skin with moisture will smooth very tiny lines. Unfortunately, not all facial lines are "tiny dry lines."

The good news remains that any moisturizer will work as long as it has oil in it and water between it and the skin. That is all a consumer needs to look for. All of this may sound like nonsense to the consumer who is convinced that her moisturizer is the key to her youth and happiness.

THE FOUNTAIN OF YOUTH IS FILLED WITH PLAIN OLD WATER

Technology is a wonderful thing in the cosmetics industry. In the past, it has made lipstick last longer, mascara thicker, foundation lighter, and a plethora of products to eliminate the drying effect of plain soap.

Aging has always been an obsession with the cosmetics gurus. But now the manufacturers have started leapfrogging in earnest to capture more of the anti-aging market. And the game has started to head in dangerous directions. Keep in mind that these products, as far as anyone can tell yet, are harmless to humans. The danger lies in more and more extravagant claims, claims that teeter on the edge of therapeutic (which make the products drugs). If the trend continues, some company may actually fall into the drug category and devastate the credibility of the harmless, immensely profitable moisturizer industry.

Perhaps more importantly, customers will not repeat purchases of pricey items if they find a bargain brand does just as well. If these products fail to hold clients, empires just may collapse.

The current rage in the skin game is to include elements already found in human skin, that age and sun exposure deteriorate over time. Examples are collagen, elastin, and glycosphingolipids (GSL, found in Glycel).

These ingredients are being pushed in huge advertising campaigns, with prices to match. Glycel, promoted by heart surgeon Christiaan Barnard, M.D., topped $5 million in sales in its first month. The introductory kit, boasting six GSL-laced potions totalling 11.2 ounces, sold (and sold out) for $195 each.

The promoters of the products insist that rubbing these ingredients on the skin will replenish the skin's natural supply. That notion has been compared to giving someone a blood transfusion by rubbing blood into the skin. (Dermatologist Vincent DeLeo of Columbia-Presbyterian Medical Center in NYC, *Time*, March 31, 1986).

Other skin experts' comments include: "Extremely suspicious," "a great moisturizer," "could just be some fancy moisturizing cream," "(the GSL) molecule that size has as much chance of getting into your skin as an elephant has of getting into your office."

Barnard himself wavers between defending and protesting the claims. He said his contribution was mere research on the regenerative powers of GSL, not on proof that rubbing it on the skin will help. When complimented on his skin, which looks much younger than his sixty-three years, he suggested that it is a result of fetal-lamb-cell injections.

But he is the star of the huge advertising campaign. By his own admission, he gets 5 percent of 3 ½ percent of the royalties, plus fees for consulting and promotion, and a share of the $3.5 million Alfin Laboratories paid for worldwide rights. It is speculated that Barnard will make $400,000 from Glycel in 1986 alone.

Confounding the picture is Barnard's reputation as an ace surgeon. A Glycel devotee defended her purchase of the pricey product with the dubious promises, saying, "After all, who ever thought you could put a heart back into somebody else's body?" (*Time,* March 31, 1986) Albert Kligman, M.D., professor of dermatology at the University of Pennsylvania medical school, summed up the other side: "I wouldn't give the slightest goddamn if Estee Lauder said what Barnard is saying. But when a world-famous surgeon makes medical claims, people are going to pay attention." (*People,* April 1986)

Denounced by some doctors and defended by seekers of hope, Glycel has created quite a controversy—and a lot of publicity. But Alfin President Irwin Alfin foresees the future with his statement: "The burden of proof will rest with the consumer. If they like the product, they'll continue to buy it. If they don't like it, we won't have a business."

Collagen and elastin do deteriorate as part of the aging process. The implication is that rubbing them on the skin will replenish natural supplies.

Russell Griffith, M.D., a Dallas dermatologist, said, "The molecules (of collagen and elastin) are so big, it's inconceivable that they could permeate the dermis (skin)."

So why are they pushed so hard, touted as anti-agers? Because they both are substances that have a great capacity for holding water.

But so does urea, derived from uric acid, found naturally in the body—urine. Urea's moisturizing qualities have been known since Babylonian times, when women drenched towels with urine to wrap around their legs. Today's urea is not derived from organic sources, but it is still immensely effective in sealing in moisture. Urea is the main ingredient in such products as Moon Drops Moisture-Enriched Skin Freshener.

The bottom line is that no product has yet been developed to slow the natural aging process. If there were, the publicity would come from the Nobel prize the inventor would undoubtably receive, not from magazine advertisements. As for the claims these products make, Barnard summed it up:

"Anti-aging is a very loose term." (*People*, April 1986)

So all this anti-aging mania is a myth. In myths one finds castles. In castles one finds towers.

PACKAGING THE FANTASY

It is not true that you get what you pay for when you buy a cosmetic, you get a whole lot more. On average, the cost of ingredients amounts to *seven* cents out of every dollar. Add the cost of the container, and what a customer actually takes home amounts to one-quarter of the price paid. The other three-quarters of the dollar go to packaging, which is more than the container and includes the fantasy, reputation, and prestige of the product and the cosmetics company. These elements are ferociously guarded because without them, the cosmetics castle would look like a barn.

Ask a company why its prices are high, and expect a lot of mumbling about reputation and research. Famous companies are not about to give away their defense strategies. Fortunately, some other industries have spied enough to unravel the secrets.

Knockoff companies produce imitations of prestige items and offer them at a fraction of the prestige price.

They are not to be confused with counterfeiters, who illegally try to palm off their knockoffs as the original.

Private-label manufacturers try to duplicate name-brand products, which stores buy and market under their own name. The price difference can be staggering.

Diverters buy products in quantities and divert them to stores who normally would not pay the usual factory prices or are not allowed to buy the product at all.

Packaging is cited over and over as a major factor in the cosmetics industry. It is much more than the shape of the bottle. It is the shape of many, many bottles of almost the same stuff. It is the color and shine of the box. It is the pump bottle versus the spray bottle. It is the mock-turtle case with the nail-breaking clasp. It has nothing to do with what is in the package, everything to do with sales.

"The container holds the visual appeal, because the product functions the same, whether it's in a brown paper bag or a shiny box," said the former Revlon manager. "The challenge is to make packaging that will knock someone's socks off.

"The efficacy of packaging material is established by tests. If it does well, if it extends shelf life, it works," he said.

"There is more effort in marketing and the visual appeal than there is in research," he continued, "because the products are easier and more straightforward. There are very, very minor differences in products."

Tom Conry cites "misery of choice" in his book, *Consumer's Guide to Cosmetics* (1980, Anchor Books). Faced with so many brands of essentially the same stuff, customers may ease their dilemma by choosing a pretty package. "Since package design may well clinch a cosmetic sale, the cost of the container often exceeds that of production," he writes.

So if a company makes a new product and markets

it and it does not sell, instead of revising the product it-self, it can simply revise the packaging.

The fragrance industry knows this. Stuck in an over-saturated market with a fickle clientele, major compa-nies have shifted to repositioning and extending old lines. That can mean "extending the line," adding soaps and lotions to a perfume line—repackaging. Others offer new forms of old favorites—repackaging.

There are no regulations to state what amount of fragrance concentration differentiates cologne from toi-let water. Manufacturers could add one or the other to a fragrance line, and repackage by changing the wording.

L'Air du Temps was modified a little, given the name Wind Song, and repackaged with an entirely different ad-vertising campaign. So were Scoundrel Musk and Charlie Naturals, both of which were promoted as new products instead of line extensions. Repackaging. "Estee Lauder once correctly described Opium as 'Youth Dew with a tassel,' " remarked (in a personal letter) Lisa Mercer, vice president for the public relations firm G.S. Schwartz and Co. Repackaging.

"Constant changes in marketing made production lines impossible to run efficiently," the manager said. "They were always coming up with new bottles that sim-ply wouldn't fit on production lines."

And guess who pays for the stops-and-starts of the production line, a cost that has nothing to do with the efficacy of the product?

Packaging can have a life of its own. The story of Ruffles, the perfume by Oscar de la Renta, is hardly un-usual: the name and the bottle design were invented long before there was even a scent. The same goes for Paloma Picasso fragrance—the samples offered at a pre-release press party were not the final perfume.

Perfumers seem to have missed a poll taken by *Ad-week*, published in its February 25, 1986 issue, that only

7 percent of women have been attracted by a nice bottle, and more than 25 percent never have considered the bottle significant.

The industry would rather people not realize that once the aroma is out of the bottle, no one sees the packaging. Unless a diehard status-seeker carries around the bottle with her, no one but her will know she paid $28.50 for a three-ounce bottle of Calvin Klein's Obsession, and not $7.50 for three ounces of Confess, the knockoff by Parfums de Coeur.

Oops, take that back about no one knowing. According to Mark Laracy, president of Parfums de Coeur, a mere 95 percent of the people tested could not tell the difference between Obsession and Confess.

One of the many methods Parfums de Coeur uses to keep prices down is to do away with expensive packaging gimmicks like fancy French bottles, cut-glass stoppers, and elegant boxes.

More proof that packaging has nothing to do with effectiveness can be found in a survey of shampoo in the September 1984 issue of *Consumer Reports*. The survey poured Colgate's Octagon dishwashing detergent into one of its unmarked bottles and name-brand shampoos into others. The female panelists liked Octagon better than Avon's New Vitality, Clairol Herbal Essence, CVS Concentrate, Faberge Brut, Jheri Redding Milk'n Honee, Jhirmack Gelave, Johnson's Baby Shampoo, and a few private-label brands.

Packaging gimmicks can cost more in other ways, too. A survey in *Consumer Reports* included soap in pump dispensers. Panelists used an average of 1 3/4 pumps of soap to clean their hands. The more pumps, the faster the soap is used up, and the consumer has to buy more, right?

Overtested, overresearched, overhyped, the packaging is probably the least relevant part of a product's effectiveness. But it also holds the most useful item for consumers. And it is not even really a part of the design.

There it lies, in tiny letters and unglamorous words, like a grudging acquiescence to government snoopervision: the list of ingredients. In the list of ingredients lies all an informed person really needs to know.

There lies the secret that the active ingredients in both Cachet Moisturizing Hand and Body Lotion and Vaseline Intensive Care are identical (glycerine, mineral oil, and lanolin). There is the proof that hydrolized animal protein is the effective ingredient in both ritzy Pantene Shampoo for Fine or Thin Hair and the supermarket Clairol Herbal Essence.

There lies the name of the one ingredient that a person is known to be allergic to, thereby saving the person the pitfall of thinking she must use only hypoallergenic products. There lies the ingredients that have been continually proven harmless but unhelpful.

Since cosmetics are by definition not able to do much, the makers have decided we must be persuaded we need them anyway. Thanks to the FDA, they cannot promote effectiveness very far. And thanks to the glut of products already, they cannot simply announce there is another product. All that is left is fantasy. The most obvious fantasy is contained in advertising. A customer can expect about ten cents of every dollar spent to go directly into the company's advertising coffers.

"The success of a product is the end result of an enterprise war," stated the ex-Revlon manager. And that means advertising. Fragrance is a dandy mien for examining the element of fantasy in the cosmetics industry.

Pity the perfumers—their market is drenched with competition. Presently, the fragrance industry is static, with growth either flat or negative. So they take the easy route through the image avenue. Selling an image works in the perfume field.

Take Charlie, developed in the 1970s to be the darling of liberated women. The current image promoted by Charlie in the 1980s is a more mellow, yet still independent woman.

Take Scoundrel, which was introduced four years before Revlon hired Joan Collins as the image, and sales took off.

"There's a certain level of the public that looks to relate to movie stars, or athletes, and want to do whatever they do," remarked the ex-Revlon manager.

What about the notion that the public is getting wiser, not so willing to blindly follow the superstars? "I don't think they will. They live in a dream world, and advertising is geared toward them. They won't raise too many questions because they love the person and want to be like them. And that's exactly who the advertisements are aimed at.

"We want to get everyone to try it once. If everyone tries it once, that's 200 million sales right there."

The fierce world of fragrance advertising just might backfire. The blatantly sexual, $15 million ad campaign for Calvin Klein's Obsession is indicative of the trend. Most companies cannot justify spending that much to launch a new fragrance, especially in light of the fact that few perfume brands survive more than three years. If $15 million in advertising is what it takes, fewer fragrances will be introduced. New fragrances might price themselves right out of the business.

The fantasy of cosmetics extends into the current trend for "scientific" formulas and claims. Ad copy can send one scurrying for a dictionary:

"microcirculation" (touted by Charles of the Ritz' Age-Zone Products)

"non-comedogenic" (a term for "anti-acne," found in Neutrogena products)

"hydroscopic" (means "retains moisture," found in

The Skin Solution from Vita-Plus Industries)

"humectants" (ingredients that attract and hold moisture, found in Discipline)

"pro-collagen" (one-upmanship on collagen, pushed by Ultima II CHR Pro-Collagen Anti-Aging Complex)

"mucopolysaccarids and glycoproteins" (synonyms for fats, found in Bio-Concentre from Stendahl)

"botanical lipid extracts" (fats, touted by Lancome Trans-Hydrix Multi-Action Hydrating Creme)

These are all fantasy ways of saying the same old things: clean skin, moisturize, unclog pores.

Another fantasy method is to connect a product with Europe. Glycel is manufactured in Switzerland, many products are developed by French scientists. The United States has weaker laws on cosmetic claims and ingredients labeling than France or Switzerland. But United States' laws are weaker than those in Chile, too. Where are the ads touting Chilean scientists?

"It seems that Americans are finally catching on to what Europeans have always known: skin care is important," opined a skin care specialist for Elizabeth Arden. EA is owned by Eli Lilly, based in the United States.

COPYING: AN ACT OF FLATTERY
AND COST CUTTING

Parfums de Coeur, dedicated to removing the mystique of prestige perfumes prices, gave in to the French mystique for its name, which translates to "perfumes of the heart." President Mark Laracy defended the choice of the name, "I believe a French name conveys authority in food, wine, cheese, fragrance, and sex."

"Would a rose really smell as sweet if it didn't get such good advertising from the poets?" an article in *Adweek* queried. "Doubtful. And marketers of fragrance and beauty products know it. In no other category is the advertising so much a part of the product."

Adweek's review of advertisements gave high marks to one pushing Neutrogena Facial Cleansing Formula, saying: "In an industry whose products have shorter and shorter life cycles, there's nothing more valuable than a mystique—a widely held belief that the stuff truly works, that it's the best around."

Fantasy, imagery, mystique—how much are you willing to pay for these?

A company's reputation is probably the most important factor in its success. But how much are you paying simply for the name on the package? How much of the price is simply the name can be realized by examining the other industries of knockoff and private-label products.

At this writing, one ounce of Opium cologne sells for $33. One ounce of Parfum de Coeur's "If you like Opium, you'll love Ninja" sells for $7.50. Two products that 95 percent of a test group could not tell apart have an 87 percent price difference.

Amitee Cosmetics, Inc., knocks off salon-brand shampoos and conditioners. "We select a product (to imitate) because of what it does," stated Maria Denzin Havey, vice president of marketing of Amitee Cosmetics, Inc. "And we believe salon products are better (than drugstore products). But the manufacturers have stringent rules to keep the prices up. And we don't believe that people should pay what they are paying for those products."

Amitee markets a Salon Image shampoo which urges consumers to compare it with a Nexxus brand. Sixteen ounces of Amitee sells for $2.79 (at my Revco down the street), fifteen ounces of the Nexxus brand costs $20. Salon brands, according to Amitee, do more for hair than mass-marketed brands because they contain a higher percentage of active ingredients (an estimated 8 to 10 percent more). Havey explained the lower-priced mass-marketed brands sold at drugstores contain a lot of inexpensive detergent. When challenged on the fact that detergent is soap, and soap is what cleans hair, she responded: "You could use Tide detergent, and it would clean anyway. But would you do that?"

Two reasons Amitee and other salon hair product knockoff manufacturers can sell their shampoos and such for less is they need few, if any, distributors since they sell their products in retail stores and they can mass-produce their wares. Salons need distributors who sell in small amounts and this results in increased manufacturing costs.

Another type of knockoff has been around for years, but can still be startling. On the shelf at Revco sits a ten-ounce bottle of Seabreeze antiseptic cleanser in its box with its distinctive design. Next to it is a ten-ounce bottle of Revco Antiseptic for Skin, in a box with the same colors as Seabreeze. Seabreeze's price is 59 percent higher than Revco's version.

Farther down the shelf is a six-ounce bottle of Phisoderm. Next to it is a six-ounce bottle of Revco PH Skin Cleanser. Phisoderm's price is 66 percent higher than Revco's version. The ingredients listed are exactly the same.

Revco brand products are manufactured by B.H. Krueger, a private-label manufacturer. According to spokesman Tal Vance, this is how Krueger works: a research-and-development laboratory of four people break down a national brand product, and try to create a product that looks, smells, and feels the same. Then they send their new product to an independent lab for a second opinion.

When Krueger is satisfied it has a good duplicate, it peddles it to Revco, or another drugstore chain such as CBS, Super-X or American. The chain buys it, packages it (Krueger does its own packaging, others contract it) and shelves it right next to the original brand.

These private labels can lower their prices for a variety of reasons: they do not have the elaborate, structured overhead that a name brand company must support; the name brand company has already tested new ingredients and effectiveness; there is not much of an advertising budget to support a private-label company; and name-brand companies may have to keep prices of old favorites up to support the cost of launching new products. Private-label companies only duplicate proven winners.

B.H. Krueger duplicates antiperspirants, after-shaves, creams and lotions. This sort of duplication is legal because a product ingredients list is public knowledge. In fact, Vance said, the only thing illegal to duplicate is the packaging. (Again, packaging seems more important than the product.)

There are a few caveats to private-label brands. First, be aware that while the ingredients list matches the original, the percentage of each ingredient may not, despite all efforts. Also, product quality varies. Vance suggested buying private-label products only if the consumer trusts the store selling them, since it is the stores that set the standards.

EXCLUSIVITY: COSMETICS WITH PRESTIGE

"I used Chanel products on my face for years," confessed an industry spokeswoman. "They made my skin feel terrific. But my skin didn't look any better. Chanel is a great merchandiser."

"Consumers have merely been programmed to think that the more they pay, the better quality product they are getting," states esthetician Regina Lynch Worthy.

Prestige and exclusivity are the slipperiest elements to examine. Spokespeople for prestigious products and prices tend to either (a) disavow such a notion that a customer pays for prestige—the high price is due to expensive research, or (b) shrug and stare blankly, as though they actually believe that prestige is imperative and can only be purchased.

"A customer can compare the ingredient label of a $10 lipstick versus the label on a $3 lipstick. Basically, the ingredients are usually the same," Worthy stated. "This holds true particularly with eyeshadows, blush, and all color items." So the only justification for high makeup prices is prestige.

Perfumers would rather the public not care that the ingredients in a prestige perfume selling for $140 an ounce may amount to a whopping $3. The rest of the cash goes to the prestige of owning the perfume.

Parfums de Coeur president Mark Laracy admits to having a role in upping the price of prestige. While an executive at Charles of the Ritz, he directed the United States introduction of Opium by Yves St. Laurent. "Opium helped start that trend (of raising fragrance prices)," he said. "Opium debuted at $25 an ounce. Before that, the highest price (for a fragrance) was $15 an ounce."

Prestige is a commodity to a degree. One thing the markup for prestige pays for is overhead. Laracy explained the overhead his company does not incur: "We use the same expensive essentials oils as the high-priced perfumes, but we don't charge the consumer for fancy 'Made in France' packaging, hugely expensive advertising campaigns, department store markups and royalties to designers with homes in Morocco or Switzerland. (Designer royalties can range from 4 to 8 percent.)

"We accept a lower gross margin—a smaller profit per dollar. The bottle and the cap are plainer; there are no cartons, no cellophane wrapping. We have fewer employees and a lower corporate overhead. Add all that stuff up and it amounts to quite a bit of money.

"Our policy is: we chisel and compromise on everything but the juice in the bottle."

Overhead includes training. The skin-care specialists

in the twelve Elizabeth Arden salons scattered across the country must endure eight forty-hour weeks of training. Then each year an instructor makes the rounds of the salons to review and update techniques. Somebody must pay for all that training.

Where companies set up shop is a factor in overhead, therefore prestige. "Department stores insist on bulk discounts, special deals, cooperative ads and such, and they have the clout to get them," explained Lisa Mercer, with G.S. Schwartz, the public relations firm for Parfums de Coeur. "And if the companies want to be in that department store badly enough, they're just going to have to play."

So a customer pays more to buy a product from a department store instead of a drugstore, pays more for the prestige and the exclusivity. Manufacturers love the game of making products sound irresistible, then keeping them out of the hands of the general public.

The story of Giorgio perfume is a real tribute to exclusivity. Giorgio sports the name of the exclusive Rodeo Drive boutique, and the yellow and white stripes on the package are reminiscent of the shop's awnings. It is prestigious to buy any item from a Rodeo Drive shop.

Giorgio was promoted through direct-mail advertisements, and initiated scratch-and-sniff magazine inserts to introduce the scent to everyone. The price was pushed up to $40 for three ounces, out of the budget of the common folk, which raised its prestige.

Then Giorgio clamped down on the number of outlets that could distribute it. For instance, Giorgio is not sold anywhere in Fort Worth, Texas. Fans must drive thirty miles to Dallas to get it.

Break down the Giorgio story into components, and find the ingredients to exclusivity: high price and elusiveness.

High price is the most direct route to exclusivity. The

106

smug idea is that if a person will not find $40 somewhere in her budget to buy Giorgio, she does not deserve it. The industry would rather cater to the equally smug people who believe themselves in the 5 percent category that can tell the difference between Giorgio and the knockoff fragrance, Primo. Never mind that no one but the wearer knows what exactly she is wearing. This smugness can lose these companies a lot of smart customers, who can find a good knockoff at a fraction of the price.

Such smugness also makes an easy target for knockoffs. The price can be a psychological as well as actual deterrent. Fragrances cannot be patented. And both Giorgio and Obsession are heavy floral scents—much easier to duplicate than, say, Joy.

Knocking off a fragrance is not illegal or new. But only in the last year or so has it become respectable. Finally, knockoffs actually do smell like the original, and the comparative advertising ("If you like Obsession, you'll love Confess") is sanctioned by the Federal Trade Commission. It is all above board, and it infuriates the original makers. But their hands are tied—unless the name or packaging is duplicated.

Elusiveness can be overcome by diverters and discount drugstores. Jane Canning, cosmetics department director for the Drug Emporium, a discount drugstore chain that offers many prestige items, explained the stores' methods to cut prices: "We buy directly from the wholesalers, get every deal we can and pass on all the savings to the customer. For instance, wholesalers will offer quantity discounts, promotions, and incentives. We also buy things like Christmas overstocks—anything we can get a deal on."

"We carry Maybelline products at 10 percent above the original cost. Maybelline offered us 8¾ percent off their price this quarter, so we asked when the next special would be, which was not (for another six months). So we bought enough to carry us until the next special.

"We buy our products overseas from duty-free shops, we buy Opium from France, which is much cheaper than buying it here. Also, we warehouse right in each store, so there are no warehouse costs."

Many prestigious companies will not sell their products directly to the Drug Emporium for the sake of exclusivity. Also, the store does not normally carry Elizabeth Arden products or Giorgio, because the store cannot get them overseas. But once the Drug Emporium did get hold of Giorgio, through a diverter.

"The story I heard—and I'm not saying this is true, because you hear all kinds of stories," said Canning, "was that some Las Vegas hotels made a big Giorgio purchase. They said they were going to give it away to clients and conventions. Then the guy who bought it turned around and sold it to retailers like us."

Needless to say, Giorgio was furious. Drug Emporium received a letter threatening to sue if Giorgio was not pulled immediately. "We disregarded it," Canning said. "The Fair Trade Law says you can buy it if it's a legitimate sale. There's nothing the companies can do because they sell their products to shops, who sell the products to diverters. About all they can do is clamp down on the shops they sell to."

Companies have tried coding their bottles to see from which outlet a diverter is buying merchandise. "Diverters take the codes right off," said Canning.

That failing, companies resort to direct tactics. "Paul Mitchell, a high-end hair care line, doesn't want its products out of beauty shops," Canning said. "Every time we get their product, company reps come in and buy all of it."

THE SELLING OF HOPE

" 'Hope in a bottle' is a very old saying in this industry," said the ex-Revlon manager.

"Yes, it's true," agreed Laracy, "but as you get older, hope gets depleted, so you replace it with what's in the bottle."

The cosmetics industry would rather hush up and lock into a dungeon this fact: hope is free. But hope can be elusive. There are other free ways a person can work towards better looks. And, as can be shown, the free way can be the best way.

Say you would like to have better-looking skin. You could rush out to some fancy store, drink in the sales pitches, and rush out with $500 worth of skin-care products. Or you can stay home and get probably the same results for free, and in some cases *save* yourself lots of money.

1. Choose your parents carefully. "I am a believer that heredity plays a 50 percent role in the conditions of our skin," states esthetician Regina Lynch Worthy. "There are some people who are going to have beautiful skin even though they are breaking all the rules."

2. Quit smoking. Nicotine robs your body and skin of oxygen and increases hormone levels that aggravate skin problems. Smokers also are prone to "accordion lips" from pursing their lips around a cigarette so much.

3. Cut down on alcohol, which can break blood capillaries in your face. It is not pure coincidence that the image of a beer-swigger includes a ruddy face.

4. Improve your diet. Skin is a body organ which can benefit immensely from proper nutrition. Paying attention to Mother's nagging (which is also free) and cutting down on junk food, caffeine, sugar, salt, and refined bleached flour can make a positive difference in your skin. Spicy food can break blood capillaries, too.

5. Cancel the tanning salon contract. Old sol is the number one culprit in the aging process. Crow's feet around the eyes can result from squinting in bright light, too.

6. Learn to deal with stress. Again, your skin is a body organ, and suffers from stress and lack of sleep along with the rest of you. Learn to puzzle over a problem without wrinkling your forehead or leaning your cheek on your hand.

7. A perfectly cared-for and made-up face can be a work of art, but mighty expensive for such a temporary work. If you have the drive to create something beautiful, take up another hobby with more lasting results.

8. A leading fashion magazine (*Vogue*) offers an article on blemishes right next to a snazzy makeup ad. The article cites a professor of dermatology, who says the best treatment for a pimple is an ice-pack, followed by sulfur-resorcinol cream twice a day. Ice can be free.

"The best skin care does not come from a bottle," Worthy said. "A lady can invest hundreds of dollars a month on skin care products, and can get facials every week, and still have skin problems if all other components aren't right. . . . The person who (follows the steps above) will actually have nicer skin than the lady who invests hundreds of dollars in her skin care, yet (ignores her health).

"The skin is a blanket to our insides. Therefore, we must take care of inside to preserve our outside. There is no miracle cream that we can run out and put on our charge card at the age of forty that will suddenly restore our skin to that of a sixteen-year-old."

All of these are common-sense suggestions, ones we have all heard ad nauseam. They are all true, but can be boring. Not many people have the patience to wait the months necessary before seeing a real change in skin from these routines. Never mind that a new skin-care regime can take just as long to show any results at all.

In order to avoid paying for any rip-off from the cosmetics industry, spend a little cash on simple soap, petroleum jelly, and the most inexpensive makeup possible. Get other benefits for free by establishing good health habits, and find romance and hope elsewhere besides in a bottle.

ONE LAST TRUTH: COSMETICS ARE FUN

A good appearance can make a good impression. Cosmetics make it so easy. You do not have to do anything hard like improve your personality or curb your terrible temper to make a good first impression. The cosmetics counters are a grown-up's circus.

"It's been proven in times of poor economy, cosmetics never match the downturn of the entire economy," stated a former Revlon manager. "Women may do without food but they'll scrape enough together for a lipstick or a rouge."

Cosmetics appeal to all the senses. The panorama of beautiful (or at least eye-catching) colors. The look of wrinkle-diminished skin and smooth cuticles, elbows and feet. The look of even-toned, blemish-free skin and shiny hair. The feel of soft hair and skin, of smooth lotions, of masks tightening, of scrubs scraping off ugly cells. The taste of flavored lipsticks. The fragrance in everything be it perfume, lotion, eyeshadow. Even the not-so-pretty odors of masks and astringents that smell like they are working. The sound of the compliments!

Applying makeup has always been fun, from Cleopatra's time through women's own childhood when they messed with Mommy's stuff. Would clowns be as funny without greasepaint? Would Joan Collins be so beautiful if her face were bare? A little color, a little shadow—wow! The same old person in the mirror looks different.

Cosmetics can be so elegant. Those who cannot afford Waterford crystal can at least find a cut-glass atomizer. Even people who can never hope to visit Paris can

111

buy a product with a French name—truffles on a mushroom budget. The oils touted in moisturizers can sport such exotic names. Those images perfumers conjure up for their advertising can be breathtaking. So what if the dream does not waft out of the bottle like a magic genie? It still smells good.

Cosmetics can soothe the spirit. Probably everyone has experienced that little lift that can come from buying a new lipstick or eyeshadow. A great deal of research is being done on cosmetic therapy, where terminally ill people experiment with cosmetics. These groups find they feel better.

Salespeople provide the opportunity to discuss in detail such a personal part of one's life—one's own body. Those who slave for others can relax and be pampered while someone else fusses over their hair, face, makeup, body massage.

A professional facial can feel so good. The skin even looks better for a while. You pay for the elegance of the salon too and it is quite enjoyable.

"For most people, it's a real getaway," confessed one skin-care specialist with Elizabeth Arden. "They come in and sit in my chair, and for an hour they're away from the kids and the phones. It's real mental relaxation—and the skin *does* look better!"

Cosmetics can boost the ego. "A lot of women bring in their children, under fifteen years old, and get them the treatment," the specialist continued. "They get the deep pore cleansing for blackheads. But the psyche is involved too, those years are tough for kids with blackheads. We get a lot of boys in here too, with a real macho drive—football and stuff—and they love it."

And most of all, it is always fun to beat business at their own games. The cosmetics empire is glutted with gimmicks and come-ons, all aimed at luring a customer to try a product once, then get hooked and buy more. As long as the customer does not feel pressured into buying more, the promotions can save money and be fun. Here are some examples:

1. Free samples are offered in hopes that the customer will enjoy it and buy more. Remember, you are under no obligation to buy more.

2. Buy one, get more: for instance, the shampoo products that include a free bottle of conditioner. It is established that any hair product will make hair seem different for a while, so go ahead and use it without being fooled into thinking it is really better.

3. Introductory packages, those $50-value-for-only-$10 types; and promotions (yours for only $10 with any purchase) allow consumers to sample products at a lower cost.

4. Free gifts sweeten the purchase. One swoop through one perfume counter in one hour at one off-price drugstore turned up these gifts: Adolfo—a quartz watch, Adolfo for Men—a pen-and-pencil set, Interlude—six lip glosses and a lip brush, Jontue—an eighteen-inch strand of faux pearls and a lace pocket square, Enjoli—free fragrance gifts worth $15 (send $1 for postage and handling), Jordache Love Musk for Women—free spray cologne of Jordache Love Musk for Men (or vice versa), and Chaz and Coty Chateau Collection—sweepstakes.

5. Free makeovers are great opportunities to learn new techniques and new colors without paying for a color that looks all wrong at home. The sales talk is fascinating too—listen closely and see just how little is actually said.

There is a method to beat the industry's game and still reap the full benefits of cosmetics.

1. Spend money on knowledge, not products. Start with an esthetician, a licensed specialist in skin care, makeup application, and facial massage. The license means an esthetician has learned much more about her field than the average company saleswoman. An esthetician takes into consideration current skin care routines, diet, health background, and allergies in formulating a skin care plan. Most of all, since an esthetician may work for herself, she is not bound to prescribing only the products made by the company who hired her.

2. Armed with explicit advice, go to the most prestigious, exclusive retail outlets and drink in the elegance (it is free). Compare your own knowledge to that of the company representatives. Compare product labels, checking for ingredients that are proven effective. Do not buy anything yet.

One caveat is that reading too many ingredient labels at one time can frazzle the mind and take the fun out of comparison shopping (the labels are not written in any language resembling English). Fortunately, some good books list ingredient names and explain what they do. If your esthetician cannot help, these books can.

3. Work down the line from most exclusive to the cheapest, comparing labels, not claims. It is possible that the most desired ingredients can only be found in expensive products—but not very likely.

4. Buy.

You have reaped all the benefits of cosmetics, without paying for a single unnecessary thing. And that is the last thing the cosmetics industry would have the public know: the price of admission to the beautiful cosmetic empire is set by the public.

FOOD

Everything in today's supermarket—from the label on a package to the intensity of the lighting and the selection of music—is planned to encourage the consumer to buy. The plan is based on rather complex facets of human behavior that have been uncovered by highly paid food industry consultants and marketing research teams whose jobs require them to constantly stay abreast of consumer's buying habits. Why? To develop new ways to help grocers manipulate shoppers.

Bright, even lighting allows the consumer to see everything equally: soothing music, wide aisles and colorful, eye-catching displays make consumers more comfortable so they will stay a little longer, stroll down a few more aisles—buy more on impulse.

What may look to be nothing more than good business sense is actually an attempt on the part of every food manufacturer and retailer to gain control of the consumer's food dollar.

The process starts with the manufacturer. Major companies, such as General Foods, Frito Lay, and other snack food and cereal manufacturers, have marketing research teams who do little else but determine precisely what will sell and then zero in on exactly which consumer will buy the product and how much he will spend for it. By doing so, each manufacturer is determining what will not sell or how the company can avoid losing money.

For instance, if a company can forecast the popularity of a particular item, it can make money off of the idea by duplicating it. One easy-to-target consumer is the three- to eight-year-old age group. It was not by coincidence that shortly after the Cabbage Patch doll and Pac-Man toy hit the market and became the hottest sellers, there were manufacturers cashing in on the idea with Cabbage Patch and Pac-Man cereals. Other times, the insertion of a tiny plastic replica of a current toy is enough to sell an otherwise fledgling cereal.

More often, the product on the shelf is the result of comprehensive consumer profiles that often involve years of testing, researching, targeting. Companies set up test market areas across the United States to conduct demographic profiles. The process typically begins with focus groups who, in the early stages, conduct surveys, and send out questionnaires to simply find out what it is the consumer wants that is not already available to him in the market. Once determined, small-scale development of the product will begin with consumer panels reviewing the product during each stage of development. Up to five years can be spent on the development of one food product.

THE SUPERSTORE PHENOMENON

The latest phenomenon in food marketing, aptly called the superstore, represents every successful marketing strategy in the history of food retailing. Practically making the standard grocery store and supermarket obsolete, the superstore aims to make the consumer's shopping a one-stop venture. Beyond that, it is also the merchant's attempt to make the entire process more comfortable so the consumer will spend more time in the store and spend more money.

The superstore offers a combination of standard supermarket items, service-oriented, and gourmet foods plus any one of a number of specialty features, such as an in-house florist, pharmacy, and liquor store.

According to a recent issue of *Consumer's Digest*, four out of every five grocery stores under construction today are superstores-in-the-making.

The Stop and Shop chain of superstores throughout New England typifies the trend. Each has 55,000 square feet (as opposed to the standard 18,000 feet of retail space in the traditional supermarket) filled with virtually everything to lure the shopper in and make him stay longer.

Each Stop and Shop has a bakery (goods are baked on the premises, as opposed to being centrally baked and sent over); pharmacy (in Connecticut and Rhode Island where it is legal); a florist with bigger, better, more spectacular flower arrangements; a bigger variety of beauty and cosmetics aids (6,200 square feet as opposed to a standard supermarket's 1,200); and a Barnes and Noble bookstore in the middle of the superstore selling books and magazines at a discounted price. There is also a Food Bazaar offering a combination of health and natural foods, imported cheeses, a variety of bulk foods; a fresh fish department which carries fish sold on ice rather than packaged frozen plus a tank of live trout; a deli featuring everything from homemade pizza and fresh pasta to hot, stuffed potatoes and barbecue; a forty-five-item salad bar; a video rental department offering some 4,000 titles; and a general merchandise department selling everything from hardware to panty hose.

Other amenities in the superstore take shape in wider aisles (8 1/2 feet wide, as opposed to 6 1/2 feet in standard supermarkets) and updated frozen food sections. "We've found that customers buy more in the frozen food sections with closed-door cases," said Dick Ponte, vice president of grocery and general merchandise sales and procurement, Stop and Shop in Boston, Massachusetts.

"The open cases were too cold and also too energy consuming. We've also begun installing misters in the refrigerated cases that spray directly onto the produce to keep the produce fresh." Studies indicate moistened produce has more than a slight tendency to naturally make consumers believe it is fresh off the vine.

"Lighting has improved over the years, in that there's more of a tendency to highlight rather than use fluorescent lighting," added Ponte. "There's more spotlighting of the product, especially in the specialty areas."

Superstores may be working to replace supermarkets (which actually replaced grocery stores sometime ago), but discount and warehouse food stores are giving both a run for their money. One of the most popular of this discount genre is Fazio's—with one store in Dallas, Texas, and another in Willowick, Ohio. Fazio's is a full-service combination food-drug-and-variety discount store that sells mostly non-perishable goods that can be offered at discount prices. "We pick up merchandise from people who are going out of business, reductions of inventory deals," said John Fazio, president of the company, "whatever lessens the price for us." Sugar, for instance, is not sold at Fazio's because they cannot pass on any sort of savings to the consumer. The concept is that the variety of merchandise found in a standard supermarket or superstore may not be offered, but the discount is there.

"Another reason we are able to offer low prices is that we're in the import business," said Fazio. "We sell to other supermarkets—items such as tuna, canned mandarin oranges." Yet another reason the prices are lower at discount stores is because these stores rarely, if ever, advertise. "We advertise very little," said Fazio. "Most of our ads run in order to collect money. A distributor says he'll give us a discount if we advertise the product." Fazio's is different from the warehouse store in that it is a full-service discount store. That is, consumers don't have to bring their own shopping carts or bag items themselves.

SAVINGS AT NO-FRILLS WAREHOUSES

The biggest savings for both the consumer and the merchant is derived from no-frills warehouse stores which offer prices from 10 percent to 20 percent lower than competitors, but often with the trade-off in services such as shoppers usually bagging their own groceries or bringing their own bags with them. These stores also compromise on aesthetics to some degree such as shelves that are stacked high, warehouse-style and merchandise that is displayed in shipping boxes or crates.

The warehouse club industry, perhaps best exemplified by the Price Company's Price Club, is expected to move into a major new phase of expansion. Price Club's enormous success has spawned clones that are systematically staking out markets across the country in an effort to be the first in each area to establish the wholesale/retail concept of distribution. Price Club got its start in 1976 in San Diego and by the end of 1982 was operating eight warehouses in Southern California and Arizona. Price Club's enormous success, the apparent—and deceptive—simplicity of the concept spurred on the rapid development of this type of format in other cities. A number of clones came about in 1983, several more in 1984. Although the assortment of merchandise and mix of wholesale/retail vary considerably, most of the newcomers have virtually adopted the warehouse layout and membership of the Price Club. Some of the newest are divisions of large retailing companies seeking their share of the pot—Sam's Wholesale Club, Price-Savers, B.J.'s Wholesale Club. Others are founded quickly by companies wanting to capitalize on the trend.

The lure of the warehouse format is its low prices

achieved through direct shipment from manufacturers. There is no middle man between the manufacturer and the wholesaler, and there are typically lower labor costs. Since there are no departments and merchandise is displayed on somewhat crude steel warehouse racks, stores do not have to hire stockers. This results in absolute minimization of costs and, therefore, prices.

Most warehouse clubs require membership dues, although this is usually a formality. The idea of restricting membership to certain employee groups, members of savings and loan associations, and credit unions is something of a farce. The $15 to $25 annual fee is charged to support the unusually low-priced items and also to supply the warehouse club with valuable membership information that can be used as a marketing tool. Twenty-five dollars a year—in interest alone—adds up to quite a bit.

There is quite often a lack of variety of brand and size assortment and usually the focus is on high turnover items in one or two key brands. (Since the wholesale club is also an import business, one of its customers is the small-grocery-store owner, and thus many products come in too-large containers. Skippy peanut butter, for instance, available in the five-pound jar is larger than most families can deal with.)

Consumers should be aware if their city has several wholesale clubs. The cyclical effect of saturation is the more clubs, the more competition among them, usually results in a larger assortment of goods which ultimately leads to a less-efficient, less-competitive outfit.

DESIGNED TO SELL

In the supermarket and superstore, of course, shoppers have to hunt down products offering the biggest savings. While warehouse clubs are sans embellishments, these stores are deliberately designed to force the shopper to cover the entire store. One study determined the greatest percentage of customers circulate around the periphery of a store. A store, therefore, is likely to have its most profitable items such as meat and produce along its edges. The standard layout in a Stop and Shop superstore, for instance, has the produce department at the front and on the opposite end of the produce department the frozen foods section (frozen dinners, ice cream). The back wall is taken up with fresh meats, fish, and dairy products—which means a consumer has to virtually cover an entire store to gather the staples on his shopping list.

"If you compare the layout of three different stores, you would find the staples—flour, bread, eggs, etc.—strategically laid out across the store so that the customer is forced to scan entire aisles," said Dr. Carol Shanklin, chairman of Nutrition and Food Sciences Department, Texas Women's University. "The placement of many products makes little sense." For instance, Campbell's soup displayed with the saltine crackers rather than the other soups. Or, Hershey's chocolate syrup displayed with marshmallows and graham crackers rather than with the other ice cream toppings. "The first exposure is the best exposure," said Ponte. "But, unfortunately, we can't lay out a store that way."

The most important department in a store, to be sure, is the one nearest the entranceway because it gets the heaviest traffic. The produce department is often here because, like other perishables, they are high-profit items frequently purchased on impulse.

At a Stop and Shop store, said Ponte, a consumer must go through its in-house florist to get to the produce. "We used to think the produce department should be last so consumers could put the items on top of other goods," said Ponte. "But now it's near one of the entrances so it will sell better." (Studies have shown that produce sales add a whopping 1 percent to 1½ percent to total store sales when displayed near the front of the store.)

Also typically at or near the front of the store is the bakery (with the aroma factor) and delicatessen (with their delectable salads and meats, they suggest ready-made old-fashioned warmth). Since frozen foods are typically purchased impulsively, they get a preferred location, often in the center of the store.

"We usually have the produce on one end and meats on the other end to balance out the shopping, to get the consumer to shop the entire store," said Liz Minyard, vice chairman of the Board, Minyard Food Stores, Inc., Dallas, Texas.

Within departments, items are often arranged to give some of them greater prominence. Island displays and displays at the end of an aisle are there to make the consumer believe the product is "on special," when many times it is not. According to designer Milton Glaser, who addressed the topic in a recent issue of *Harper's*, when one of his clients asked him to construct an in-store display called "Basics," it was important the finished product look cheap. The display ended up having cardboard on top of pressed plywood to give the appearance of three layers of corrugated cardboard. And when the supermarket decided that a bare floor would better serve the image of a store with rock-bottom prices, it spent $50,000 to tear up the tile floor to reveal concrete underneath.

Shelf position is another major bone of contention among manufacturers who vie for the best spot, which is, not surprisingly, at eye level. Consider the aisle of cereals. It is no coincidence that those with trendy names, the aforementioned Cabbage Patch and Pac-Man cereals, or with games and gimmicks are placed at the eye level of children while Corn Flakes and Raisin Bran sit on higher shelves, within eye range of adults.

The worst shelf space is at the top (if the customer cannot reach a product he is more likely to simply move on).

How does a manufacturer avoid having his product displayed on the lowest shelf? The more brands one company carries, said one food industry analyst, the more clout it has with the retailer . . . the more likely it is to get the preferred shelf space.

"Shelf space is more sophisticated today," said Ponte.

"We set up based on sales, a lot of big sellers are at eye level. But how much shelf space is given to a product depends on how much is required and on the category. We keep all of one product together. For instance, if a company has twenty-eight flavors of a certain food, we'll keep them all together." Which, of course, typically makes manufacturers come forth with more variety to dominate the shelf space.

A recent study determined that 65 percent of brand-decisions are made on impulse. "We like male shoppers, they spend more money and are more susceptible to impulse buying than females," said Minyard. "Most of the impulse items are placed at the checkout areas." Little wonder, then, that profit margins at the checkout counter, according to one study, run around 30 percent to 35 percent.

LABELS TELL THE STORY

Consumers do not always get what they think they are buying. In 1938, Congress gave the Food and Drug Administration the authority to adopt standards of identity, quality, and fill-of-container to protect consumers from being defrauded by cheap substitutes or deceptive packaging. But due to continual advances in food technology, increasing consumer demand for more information about food products, and the complexity of current food regulations, labels have become increasingly difficult to understand.

Nonetheless, many products find ways of cutting corners. For instance, how much fish is a consumer actually getting when he purchases a frozen fish food? Consumers may be surprised to learn that by law, some frozen fish products are allowed up to 40 percent of their weight in breading (according to a recent *Consumer's Digest* article).

In the case of product substitutions, deception in the following food areas have been common in the past:

1. Honey, maple syrup and sorghum products, in which fructose is substituted wholly or in part for those the manufacturer claims for the products.

2. Apple juices that have been adulterated and misbranded through the use of various sweeteners, water, apple flavoring, apple essence, and other ingredients.

3. Olive oil and sesame seed oil in which corn, soy, and cottonseed oils are used instead.

4. Breaded shrimp that is sold with less than the minimum of 50 percent shrimp material; and scallops that are not scallops at all—they consist of cheaper fish fillets cut up to resemble scallops.

5. Grated cheese that contains whey solids instead of what the label promises: Parmesan, Romano, or some other kind of cheese.

6. Products with net weights less than declared weights, often show up in these products: nuts, instant tea, instant coffee, spices, and over-glazed seafood, especially rock lobster tails.

One of the most reliable sources of information on food is the product label itself. In some instances, the information provided is required by the FDA: in other instances, it is put there voluntarily by the manufacturers.

The amount of information, to be sure, varies, but

all food labels *must* contain at least the following: the name of the product; the net contents or net weight (on canned foods the net weight includes the liquid in which the product is packed, such as water in canned vegetables, syrup in canned fruit); the name and place of business of the manufacturer, packer, or distributor; and as of July 1, 1986, the sodium content. (The FDA called for the addition of sodium information after studies showed an association between sodium intake and high blood pressure.) Surprisingly, the FDA requires nutrition labeling only for fortified or enriched foods, such as cereals and other products; foods making specific nutrition claims like "high in Vitamin C"; and foods used in special diets such as dietic cookies.

The United States Department of Agriculture regulates the labeling for all processed meat and poultry products, such as hot dogs, turkey pot pie, chili con carne, and pizza with sausage.

How long a product has been on the shelf and the date by which it must be sold are some of the other facts that must be included on the labels of many foods. For instance, all processed foods have a fixed shelf life, which generally lasts at least one year after the coded date of packing stamped onto the package.

Unfortunately, it is almost impossible to decipher many of the codes. An issue of *Consumer's Digest* recently addressed the subject: "178F2" stamped on a Progresso Food Corporation product means it was packed on June 27 (the 178th day of the year) by the F shift in 1982. This type of coding is part of the quality control programs many companies give manufacturers on exact information about where and when products were processed and packaged so that products can be recalled when necessary.

Perishable items such as milk and certain cheeses and some semi-perishables such as cereal, mayonnaise, and baked goods offer an open date that is deceptively easy to read, though not necessarily easy to understand. For instance, the "Sell By" date is the last day the product should be offered for sale, while the "Expiration Date" is the last date the item should be used at home. Many products do not make it clear whether the date shown is the "Sell By" or "Expiration" date. (The "Sell By" dates on cottage cheese and milk are least likely to be accurate, according to *Consumer Digest*.

The additives used in a product, on the other hand, are not so visible and are, thus, given ratings. While many additives get a clean slate (such as Alpha Tocopherol, the most potent form of vitamin E, which is typically found in cottonseed oil and wheat germ oil), others do not. Among the latter is Butylated Hydroxyanisole (BHA) which has been on the market since 1947. BHA is a preservative and antioxidant used in almost every processed food containing fat or oil and is known to be capable of causing allergic reactions and affecting liver and kidney functions. BHA is a good example of an unnecessary use of synthetic food additive, as demonstrated by the fact that some companies have found that it provides no improvement in the stability of their product.

PRESERVATIVES FOR PERISHABLES

The food industry has come a long way in determining new ways to preserve foods. The idea of preservation began in 1795 when Napoleon's military campaigns were sending French soldiers farther and farther afield, away from normal sources of supply. Their rations typically consisted of salt meat, salt fish, and hardtack. When French soldiers and sailors began dying from scurvy and other diseases caused by dietary deficiencies, Napoleon pleaded for better rations. The Directory (a group of five men who ran France before Napoleon took over) offered a prize of 12,000 francs to anyone who could devise a method of preserving food for transport and military campaigns.

Nicholas Appert, a Parisian pickler and winemaker, was responsible for developing and perfecting the method for canning foods. (Basically, he was able to show that meat which had been thoroughly heated in sealed flasks would not spoil.) He used the method to preserve fresh eggs, milk, cream, many vegetables and fruits, mushrooms and meat, poultry, and other low-acid foods. The French government sent samples of his preserved foods around the world on ships and, indeed, they retained their wholesomeness. Appert won the 12,000 francs for discovering "the art of making the seasons stand still."

Louis Pasteur, of course, later discovered why food spoils and an Englishman, Peter Durand, patented the tin can in 1810. Referred to as "tinned foods," English explorer William Edward Parry took tinned foods to the Arctic during the 1820s. A tin of pea soup and a tin of beef were recovered and the contents eaten with no ill effects almost 100 years later.

The latest move in food preservation, however, has been met with some trepidation. Irradiation, treating food with low levels of ionizing radiation to dramatically extend its shelf life, is the wave of the future in food preservation. It has already been FDA-approved as an effective means of killing insects on wheat, herbs, and spices and for inhibiting sprout growth on potatoes and onions.

A recent ruling by the FDA approved the use of low doses of irradiation in pork to kill the parasite that causes trichinosis, a potentially fatal disease. With this advantage comes an esthetic one: irradiated pork will not have to be cooked until well done to be safe.

When it hits the stores, it will be labeled with an international symbol, a broken circle with a small ball and two leaves in the middle and/or with the words "treated with picowave processing." The first foods bearing the symbol likely will be papayas, nectarines, peaches, strawberries, and melons. Look for these soft, perishable fruits to be slightly more expensive because of the new process.

This method has been used in the past for space shuttle astronauts and for fish, poultry, and fruit exports to other countries. Its proponents contend that the food is changed chemically only slightly and, at that, the chemical and nutritional change is minimal. One food industry source claimed irradiation alters nutrient value less than heat processing (the process used in canned foods). Furthermore, with fresh foods, nutrient losses from irradiation vary, but to meet FDA standards are kept low, too low to induce radioactivity.

Others believe it could cause cancer. There are no laws stating that any of the fruits and vegetables grown in the continental United States have to be treated with radiation or other preservatives. But some imported foods do have such restrictions, and these are the ones likely to be irradiated. The first such batch will probably be from Chile, which has to be fumigated to rid them of pests. (The Isomedix facility in Morton Grove, Illinois, now radiates herbs and spices for use in commercially processed foods such as cheese spreads and luncheon meats.)

"There is no conclusive evidence on the effects of irradiation," said Shanklin. "Besides the obvious, a longer shelf life, its use will work to stabilize prices. Since products with a short shelf life can't maintain quality, it becomes more costly not to have a long-term preservation technique."

JUDGING A PRODUCT BY ITS PACKAGE

Manufacturers learned early on that products most definitely are judged by their pretty, if not simply eye-catching, packages. What consumers are just beginning to learn, however, is that a hefty 10 to 15 percent of a product's price goes toward its packaging.

Cardboard tends to be less expensive than plastic, although plastic is typically a bit easier to handle. What consumers may not realize, according to *Consumer's Digest*, is that convenience is not the only variable in this equation. Light can cause deterioration of milk's Vitamin A and riboflavin, and cardboard tends to be the greatest shield against the light. Plus, the longer the time in the dairy case, the greater the loss, which is why milk should always be moved within twenty-four hours.

However, sometimes packaging does not tell the entire story. When it comes to deciding between national, private label (the store's brand), or generic (typically black and white packaging), the surprise may be in discovering one company typically manufactures all three.

Another surprise may be in discovering that the packaging on the generic product, in spite of its plain looks, costs just as much as the fancier looking facades of national brands. According to Glaser, the Grand Union supermarket chain's generic packaging (which Glaser designed) costs just as much to print and manufacture as the brand-name packaging. But it is designed to look as though very little time and money have gone into it.

Many times a supermarket will contract private-label manufacturers to can and package both generic and private-label goods. According to an industry source, national brands use only the "prime parts" of a product (the center of the green bean, for instance) and then contract out to another packager to use the remainder (as in, the tip of the green bean). The difference, said Minyard is in the grade. All three have the same nutritional value.

Some food products carry a grade on the label—"U. S. Grade A," for instance—which is set by the United States Department of Agriculture for meat and poultry products. The standards for grades are based on the quality levels of various characteristics of the product—its taste, texture, and appearance. USDA grades are not based on nutritional content. Milk and milk products in most states carry a Grade A label, which is based on FDA-recommended sanitary standards for milk and milk products, some of which require specific levels of vitamin A and others which permit the optional addition of vitamins A and D.

Packaging takes on an entirely new and different meaning when it is sold in bulk—the latest throwback to yesterday. The idea of selling by bulk actually goes back to the early marketing days when a customer would go to the local grocer who would scoop up a pound of this, half a pound of that. With today's larger supermarkets and superstores selling bulk foods, there are infinitely more risks many of which are only exacerbated by the fact that the area of packaging and food sales is not regulated. Although the United States Department of Health sets certain criteria—such as the container must be closed and the scoop must have an attached handle that is long enough so that the hand does not touch the product (hands are the greatest carriers of bacteria)—there are no industry-wide standards. Thus, cleanliness and sanitation are almost impossible to monitor.

A consumer can save from 10 to 25 percent, however, since he is not paying for a company brand name or the mentioned 10 to 15 percent that is tacked onto other products for packaging. From a merchant's point of view, there is considerable savings in labor since they pay less (because of the fewer manhours required) for the stocking of the shelves and bins. The savings are most dependable with staples such as beans, sugar, and flour, than with cookies or other bakery products.

PRICES, MARKUPS, AND SPECIALS

The average markup on groceries at supermarkets and superstores runs around 22 percent—a fact that makes consumers cringe, if not more pursuant of that ever-elusive "special." In spite of its obvious lure, beware the word "special," in the market, as it is often nothing more than a ploy used by supermarkets to ensure quick sale of an over-stocked item. Other specials, dubbed by food industry officials as "loss leaders," save consumers money—but only on that item. Occasionally, a store will get a special price on a large quantity of merchandise and choose to pass the savings on to the consumer. The assumption is that once the shopper is in the store he will buy other non-reduced items. Admitted Minyard: "Some items are marked at cost or below cost and that is what we call 'loss leaders'—it's what we use to get people into the store."

Other price variations have to do with demographics. Suburban shoppers are more apt to compare prices than are urban shoppers because, quite simply, it is easier for them to hop into their cars and drive to another store where prices are more competitive. Prices also may fluctuate within a chain in one given area, because of demand. Stores typically determine the food dollars one neighborhood has to spend—again, through demographics—and price their goods accordingly. Other times the manufacturer sets up promotions that look like specials. "Island displays make the consumer think he's buying a product that's on special, but often that's not the case," said Shanklin. When a new product is introduced, the manufacturer usually provides a display to the merchant. Consumers have little, if any, way of knowing if the product is really "on special." And since it is a brand-new item, it is impossible to compare prices.

Coupons are another way for manufacturers to promote a new or ailing product. Although studies show about one of every two shoppers use coupons, their value is debatable. Some food industry experts believe they are less a savings than a gimmick, designed to get the consumer to buy brand-name products that are more expensive—even with the coupon—than a comparable item by a competitor.

"The larger the amount, the newer the product and, by no coincidence, the shorter the coupon's expiration date," said Shanklin. "The small amount on other coupons is for products that are already big sellers, but could benefit from a little advertising. These usually have no expiration date."

If the new high-tech Universal Product Code (UPC) pricing system employed at most supermarkets today makes it difficult to compare prices, there is little wonder why most supermarkets use the method. This is how it works: the first five digits of the UPC identify the company, the second five identify the product, and the checkout computer is programmed with the day's prices. While supermarket executives tout its pros—the consumer gets an itemized receipt, stores are able to offer lower prices since they do not have to hire labor to do the individual marking—consumers find it a nuisance. The UPC often makes comparison shopping difficult since shelf cards are often illegible or out-of-date. Since the UPC system is not FDA-regulated it is easy for retailers to abuse the system.

SO-CALLED DIET AND NATURAL FOODS

Perhaps the most obvious example of consumer manipulation in the food industry is within the $25 billion-per-year diet foods arena. The fastest growth has been in the "light frozen entree" category. Shoppers pay a premium for these glorified TV dinners, and what are they actually getting? According to Shanklin, they are getting a lot of sodium: "These diet entrees are bought for convenience and for controlled calorie count, but if you eat light frozen entrees it's important to be aware of everything else in your diet." For the money, many of these offer little nutrition and the calorie count can be as much as 20 percent inaccurate. For instance, a product claiming to contain 100 calories could actually contain 80 calories—or worse, 120 calories.

The FDA, however, attempts to monitor the calorie count of these and other diet foods. A product that claims it has "reduced calorie," according to one official at the FDA, is one in which the calorie content has been reduced by one-third from the traditional product. "Low calorie" denotes a product that does not contain more than 40 calories per serving.

According to a recent *Newsweek* article, companies are scrambling to produce entries in this nutritious food category. Campbell's Soup, for one, has come out with a high-fiber bean-and-bacon soup, while virtually every cereal manufacturer has increased or introduced bran cereals. And, *U.S. News & World Report* reported that supermarkets are revamping to meet the consumer demand for low-caloried nutritious products, even in the dessert category. Pepperidge Farm is experiencing success with its low-cholesterol pound cake. This is ironic when one considers that in the 1970s shoppers rejected Sara Lee's line of Light and Luscious desserts.

Not to be confused with reduced and low-calorie products are those offered as "health foods." The so-called health food industry is virtually unregulated and is, as such, full of terms without meaning. The Center for Science in the Public Interest has chosen to label it "nouveau junk food." Two of the industry catch-all terms are "organic" and "natural." Organic foods have been harvested, distributed, processed, and packaged without any fertilizers, pesticides, or growth regulators. Consumers, however, have no way of being assured that organic products are actually chemical free.

Honey-laden granola bars are among the foods marketed—usually on the cereal aisle—as natural foods, giving the illusion they are good for you when they should be shelved with the cookies. Other products claiming to be natural contain artificial coloring, monosodium glutamate, processed oils, thickeners, stabilizers, or preservatives. Foods purchased in health-food stores cost, on the average, twice as much as similar items at regular markets. That is because "natural products have a shelf life that is typically half of its preservative laden equivalent," said Shanklin. "Many natural products have natural preservatives, such as Vitamin E, and if the level is sufficient, it can act as a preservative."

Natural has been loosely defined within the industry (not by the FDA) as a product in which nothing has been added, nothing taken away . . . but it does not necessarily mean the product has not been dusted with something along the way.

For additional information on labeling and food products in general, you can contact the Food Marketing Institute, 1750 K. Street N.W., Washington, D.C. 20006, (202) 452-8444.

GRAY-MARKET CARS, CAMERAS, AND COMPUTERS

There is no other time when the Latin warning "caveat emptor" (or "buyer beware") applies more appropriately than when buying merchandise on the gray market. The ill-informed and unsuspecting shopper can become easy prey for a sharp but unscrupulous dealer. Yet a careful and well thought-out purchase from a reputable dealer can save a buyer hundreds, and sometimes thousands, of dollars. Knowing where the financial landmines lie can help you decide if this is how you want to shop and, if so, how to do it.

What is the gray market? It is a marketplace made up of independent dealers who sidestep traditional corporate distribution channels. These independents sell brand-name products even though they are not factory-authorized distributors. By eliminating many of the costly middleman markups and many of the expensive after-purchase services like warranty repair work, they can sell the same merchandise to you at significant savings.

In theory the process is a win-win transaction for all participants. The shopper can purchase expensive goods at a more reasonable and affordable price and for a sum which still yields the dealer a respectable profit.

The problem is the entire transaction is a based on nothing but trust. The minute the purchaser leaves the showroom with the goods, he becomes responsible for all repairs. There is no manufacturer's warranty on any gray market goods; if there is a warranty, it usually covers only a ninety-day period. This kind of dealing can create vast opportunities for deception which can sometimes prove to be too much for even the most respectable dealer.

The horror stories abound. An investigator in the Dallas Region VI office of the Environmental Protection Agency, one of the three government agencies involved when importing a gray market car, described the agency's current investigation of Michael Kap, a gray market automobile importer whose two ventures, Cameleon Cars of Texas and Dream Rides, ended in Chapter 11 bankruptcy filings. A number of Kap's customers paid cash—up to $50,000 for hard-to-get European model Porsches. Not long after the customer received a title from the State of Texas, Kap allegedly sent a wrecker to the home of the buyer, saying the title was not good. The repo man, who also worked for Kap, then confiscated the car. The owners have sued the dealer, and have now joined the list of creditors in bankruptcy court.

In another case, explained the investigator, Kap sold a Porsche to an enthusiast in a cash sale. In less than six months the engine blew a piston, requiring a very expensive repair. The unsuspecting owner took the car to a dealer to repair the engine. The dealer noticed the engine identification number did not match other vehicle identification numbers on other parts of the car. The dealer called the police, who impounded the car. They believe the car is stolen. If the police can find the owner, the Porsche will be confiscated from the unsuspecting gray market buyer and returned to the legal owner. Only if the legal owner's insurance company has already paid for the theft will the gray market buyer get to keep the car. But he is still responsible for the cost of the major repair. Either way, the gray market buyer is out several thousand dollars.

The EPA investigator also said unscrupulous gray

market dealers will pocket the purchase price and then waffle on the title. Weeks and even months can go by. Then the original importer, who sold the car on credit to the gray market dealer and who still has possession of the title, goes to the dealer and asks for payment. The dealer sends the importer to the new car owner. In many cases, the new car owner will have to pay an additional sum to the importer to gain possession of the title if the dealer has already pocketed and spent any of the funds used to originally purchase the car. If the car owner does not pay the importer in full, the importer has the right to repossess the automobile because he is the one with the valid title.

The gray market is neither illegal nor immoral. Bypassing normal distribution channels is a fairly recent phenomenon which started in response to good old American capitalism. Restrictive federal policies left legal loopholes in the law, allowing gutsy entrepreneurs to step in and make a profit. World economics helped, too. The rise of the dollar against foreign currencies from late 1984 through most of 1985 gave gray market dealers a significant edge when importing cameras and cars from Germany and Japan.

Demographics were the third factor in giving rise to the gray market. The baby boom generation metamorphosed into the yuppie generation, producing two-income households eager to invest in snazzy Mercedes Benzes, flashy Nikon cameras, and their very own personal computers. Having grown up with the Underground Shopper®, they were accustomed to searching for name-brand bargains. The gray market seemed a perfect fit.

Purchasing gray market goods makes financial sense only if you have the time and knowledge to be able to assess whether you are indeed receiving the goods and services for which you have paid. Understanding how the market works and where the profit comes from can give you a negotiating edge. The three most popular gray market purchases are cars, cameras, and computers.

THE HIDDEN RISKS OF GRAY-MARKET CARS

Texas, California, and Florida provide the biggest market for gray market cars, according to the National New Car Dealers Association. The gray market for luxury automobiles became a major factor in the automobile import business around 1980. The EPA reported that in 1980 only 1,200 were "federalized" or structurally changed to meet the United States' clean air standards. Today Jeff Deasy of Texas Vehicle Management estimates about 65,000 cars a year are directly imported by gray market dealers. In 1984 these dealers contributed $1 billion to America's Gross National Product.

Today one industry analyst "guesstimates" 25 percent—that is one out of every four German cars—turbocharging down America's highways were purchased from gray market dealers. That number is significant. While Jaguars are indeed a popular gray market brand, the lion's share of the gray marketeer's lineup belongs to that sleek and staid symbol of status, the Mercedes Benz. BMWs and Porsches as well as exotic cars not found in ready supply elsewhere in the States comprise the gray marketeer's lineup.

What caused this sudden exponential increase? The Motor Vehicle Safety Standards Act, which Congress passed into law in 1967, and the Clean Air Standards implemented by the EPA in 1968. Until that time any consumer could easily purchase a foreign car, bring it home, and register it like any other car.

At first the new rules killed the European import market, because the law required all new cars to meet the stringent requirements. These were just too costly for European manufacturers to meet. So they confined their markets to the Common Market where the laws were much more lenient. Citroen, a French manufacturer, refused to import cars to the United States during that time period.

This made foreign car enthusiasts an unhappy but vocal lot. They organized and lobbied Congress for a change. In the mid 1970s Congress agreed to a compromise: it would license any European car if it was modified to meet all safety and emissions standards set forth in those two acts.

Until 1981 this exemption was nothing more than a way for the very rich to spend their untold wealth on souped-up toys. But that year Mercedes Benz introduced its gas guzzling big sedans. In Europe the sedans had two different engine sizes: a 5 liter V-8 engine and a smaller 3.8 liter engine.

Mercedes Benz of North America sold only the 3.8 liter engine because it, like all other automobile manufacturers, had to meet another law: the Corporate Average Fuel Economy Standards ratio. This arcane requirement averaged the fuel economy of all the manufacturer's models to see if they met federal fuel economy rules. The 5-liter engine pushed Mercedes over the line, requiring the company to pay rather hefty gas guzzler penalty fines. A good portion of this sum was passed along to the consumer, of course, producing a princely price tag for the stately 500 SEL sedans.

But real estate developers liked ferrying around clients in the roomy and plush sedans. So they turned to the direct import market to help them buy their cars. And soon they were satisfied customers. Not only could they buy the car they wanted, but also at a substantially reduced rate—anywhere from $3,000 to $7,000 was slashed off a dealer's list price.

Deasy said in 1982 a customer could buy a four-door 500 SEL for between $41,000 and $47,000. List price at that time was about $51,000.

The gray marketeers could afford to buy the cars in Europe and import the automobiles themselves because at that time the dollar rose to a singular high against the deutsche mark. One dollar equaled more than three deutsche mark between 1982 and 1985; today the exchange ratio is approximately two to one. The foreign exchange rate lowered the independent importer's buying power.

Jack Hooker, who in the 1970s owned the largest Mercedes dealership in Dallas, Texas, and later sold his interest to car import gray marketeers, explained how the finances worked during the gray market heyday.

In early 1984 Hooker would pay 31,000 deutsche mark or $10,000 for a Mercedes sedan that sold for $26,000 from a local American dealer. That gave the dealer a gross margin of $16,000. From that he had to pay shipping and duty (about $2,000) with another $5,000 needed to pay for the required conversion. That gave the gray market dealer a markup of $9,000 after an investment of $17,000.

Authorized dealers, however, had to pay $21,000 or $4,000 more than the direct importer. Thus, no matter what price he set for the automobile, the direct importer could always undercut him and still make an enviable and larger profit—usually 10 percent or more—than the authorized dealer.

The Mercedes dealership by definition has higher costs than the direct importer because it must meet all Mercedes franchise agreements. In general these include training personnel twice a year, operating a specified number of maintenance stalls, and carrying a minimum parts inventory—all of which cost the dealer money. Gray

144

marketeers, of course, are under no such obligation and can instead pocket their profits.

And in 1982 the European manufacturers were looking for new markets. Flat auto sales created an excessive inventory, leaving automobiles to languish on the lot. Swollen inventories led to depressed prices, forcing the manufacturers to seek more eager customers. And so the gray market was born.

In the beginning, the direct importers specialized in selling cars with amenities unavailable in Europe. Such extras included heated seats or orthopedically adapted seats as well as powerful engines. Today, however, these seats are available options on dealer Mercedes. They became American options in 1985 when Mercedes of North America decided to fight back and win some business from the direct importers.

Before the United States Customs Department will allow any individual to import a European car into the United States, he must promise to convert the car to meet EPA as well as Department of Transportation standards. To guarantee compliance, the government requires the importer to post a bond worth the value of the car. He then has ninety days once the car reaches the United States' shores to complete all the compliance work. If he does not comply, the United States Customs will either confiscate the car or collect the bond.

Typically cars are shipped by boat from Europe to New York, where they are either air freighted, trucked, or driven to their final destination. The importer then sends the car to a conversion center, which is not a governmental agency. (Two of Houston's busiest conversion centers are Mario's Conversion Center and Jack's Conversion Center.) Hooker said he eventually quit the gray market import business because he felt conversions tended to be "slipshod."

Gil Jordan, regional director of the United States Customs Bureau in Dallas, said currently these conversion centers are unregulated. Jordan said EPA laboratories did make spot checks of the equipment at the conversion centers to ensure correct compliance. But if one gauge is out of calibration (its proper setting) or is faulty, all vehicles that run through that center may be recalled. Jordan recalls one instance when the EPA contacted the current owners of all the cars that had been federalized at that center to be rechecked. The second round, however, was at the owner's, not the dealer's expense.

The EPA requires all cars to meet its exhaust standards. Converts must add positive crankcase ventilation valves, catalytic converters, and other exhaust inhibiting parts. DOT is concerned about safety. It requires increased bolts for added bumper strength, additional support bars for crash resistance, warning buzzers for seat belts, modifying the speedometer to record distance in miles instead of kilometers, replacing the halogen lights with sealed beam lights, and exchanging the windshield glass to meet American specifications.

Originally so few cars needed conversion the centers could handle the work load. But when the crush of cars began, manufacturers like Mercedes began to claim these gray market cars were unsafe because they were incorrectly converted.

Today the gray market is stalled, a victim of bad press, bad dealers, and a bad foreign currency exchange rate. The latter has taken away the price differential, taking the thrill of the bargain away from the less secure transaction. By 1986 the gray market cars were, on average, selling for just $3,000 less than their American version. And the American version comes with a full dealer warranty.

The gray marketeers also discovered their buyers were one-time customers. A well made 500 SEL that is well cared for can look dashing and ride smoothly for twenty years. Last year the gray market buyer comprised only less than 1 percent of the entire American car buying public. That number fell and will continue to fall as the price differential disintegrates.

Typically the gray marketeers did not have service departments, so their customers had to turn to dealers who were unhappy about servicing a gray market car. Car trouble is always a hassle, but trying to get gray market cars serviced often made the experience even more trying.

Parts for gray market cars have been a problem, particularly engine parts. Parts for European cars designed to be sold in Europe use different parts from those destined for the American market. One gray market owner of a 190 E discovered her more powerful engine compression created a big problem when she needed a new oil pan and brackets. Her local dealer did not have the European part on hand and had to special order it. Her Mercedes sat in the shop six weeks with no oil pan until the part arrived.

And some parts are not available, period. When an air condenser bracket cracked on one Mercedes, the owner learned Mercedes Benz of North America did not have the part. He called his mechanic, who had been a helicopter mechanic during the Viet Nam days. In his Navy tour of duty, the mechanic had been forced to fashion equally unavailable parts out of available parts and sheet metal. The skilled mechanic created a crude bracket—which worked—to get that Mercedes back on the road.

More often than not, the franchised dealer will not honor any warranties on a new gray market car. Authorized dealers worry that they will be held liable for converted car breakdowns once they have done service work on the car.

The dastardly deeds of the direct importer also made headlines, although such behavior is the exception, not the rule. The bad press has not helped the gray marketeer's cause, especially among the nation's conservative bankers who are now beginning to balk at making loans on those cars.

For example, Premier Bank, an independent bank in Dallas which caters to the upscale customer, has had its share of trying experiences with financing gray market cars. In one case, a professional woman was buying a car and the bank financed the down payment when the customer took possession of the car. But Kathy Pierce, a senior vice president, refused to fund the balance until the dealer delivered a pink slip, showing the title was made out in the bank's name as first lien holder and the applicable taxes had been paid. Because the gray market dealer had purchased the car from another importer and had not paid him, he could not deliver the title. Six months later, after pressure from the customer and the bank, the original importer walked into the bank with a pink slip and new license plates. Only then did the bank release the remaining funds due.

Pierce said, however, that the importer told her many of the other banks which had funded cars from the unscrupulous dealer had wired funds in their entirety without receiving a pink slip proving clear title. When he appeared at the bank to trade the balance for his title, he learned the sum he was due had already been paid to the dealer, who had long since spent the money. The customers had to come up with additional cash before they received a good and clean car title.

In a final instance, Premier Bank financed a gray market Mercedes. The customer later claimed the dealer pocketed his check without delivering the car. A check trail revealed the customer and the dealer were working in collusion. The bank immediately called the note. The borrower had thirty days in which to come up with $45,000 cash.

To combat the gray market onslaught, the franchised dealers have fought back by writing to both banks and insurance companies. Mercedes Benz of North America is said to have sent a letter to every major bank in North America. Junior loan officers have responded by refusing to finance the gray-market cars in many instances.

Even if you can finance it, you will have trouble trading it in, especially if you want another Mercedes or BMW. Doug Gibb, a spokesman for BMW, said many authorized dealers will refuse to accept a gray market vehicle on trade because they do not want final responsibility for the car. He explained that if the DOT or EPA recall the car for improper conversion, the last person in the title search is legally responsible. He estimated the resale value of gray market cars has fallen about 10 percent a year.

Lastly, there is a real possibility of outright fraud when purchasing a gray market car. Unscrupulous importers have been known to hide the true origin of the automobile. Jordan of United States Customs said a fair number of gray market cars were actually stolen in Europe and imported using faked manufacturer's paperwork. If the police discover your car is a stolen vehicle, it is shipped back to the owner regardless of what you paid for the privilege of parking it in your garage. Usually by the time the police discover the theft, the dealer has long since skipped town and all financial responsibility.

Unfortunately, there is no way to do a title search on an European car because title laws are much more lenient there. A crafty and crooked importer can sell the car to members of his family in a carefully coded series of transactions to cover his trail. Just because an individual is the last name on the title does not mean the car was not stolen.

Sometimes the odometer is set back. One dealer was jailed after a customer discovered he had purchased a car that had been pieced together from two totalled Mercedes. So, even though you may receive a clean title from the state, there is still no guarantee your gray market car has a perfectly clean title.

How do you know if you are buying a gray market car if the dealer is trying to hide the fact? Be sure you check the window sticker on the car. It should have both the make of the automobile and the manufacturer listed. It will also name the original owner. This should be an authorized dealership.

For Mercedes, Mercedes Benz of North America provides a manufacturer's certificate of origin with every new car. It also prints an import certificate. On it should be the statement "Daimler Benz (the European parent company) delivery to Mercedes Benz dealership." Be sure to ask for both documents.

Even if the dealer can provide both, it does not hurt to ask the dealer point blank where the car came from originally. If he hems and haws, you can be relatively sure it is gray and not lily white.

If the dealer you are buying your Mercedes from has no service department, that is another clue to its true origin. All Mercedes dealerships must maintain minimum service departments. Gray market importers generally do not spend much money on advertising. If they do, they typically take out a two line advertisement in the newspaper. If the copy reads, "Lowest prices. Cars meet all U.S. specifications," you know you are dealing with a gray market importer. Conversely, an authorized dealer's ad will always specify the dealership is an "authorized dealer."

If you are going to purchase a gray market car, be sure to check out the dealer with your local Better Business Bureau. Mel Palmer, president of American Auto Brokers, Inc., in Southfield, Michigan, said the BBBs "are 95 percent reliable" in separating the good from the bad. Since all auto dealers must be licensed by the state, Palmer suggested checking with the state agency that monitors auto dealers. In Dallas, the phone number is (214) 220-2000.

Lastly, take the car for a drive. If it shimmies and shakes, that might be a sign that it was improperly converted. If the car does not have a smooth glide at high speeds, be wary. And listen carefully for any unusual engine noises.

What if you answer an ad in the paper and want to know if that used Mercedes is a gray market car? If the owner will not own up to the fact, record the engine number and the vehicle identification number. Then send those numbers to Mercedes Benz of North America. The address is One Mercedes Drive, Montvale, New Jersey 07645. They can give you an accurate answer.

Is there a better way to save money on buying a luxury car? Yes, there is. Palmer recommended that shoppers check with brokers and dealers outside their immediate areas. This advice is especially sage if you live in a large, urban city. Some models and colors are just not popular and do not move in one area of the country, while they tend to be particularly in demand in others.

For example, a Dallas business woman wanted a Mercedes 240 D diesel sedan, a very popular car in her part of the world. She drove to Boulder, Colorado, to buy a 240 D there at significant savings. Diesel cars are particularly slow chugging their way up mountains, which is why that particular car was spurned in the Rockies. Thus the dealer was willing to sell her a car that was perfect for the flatlands of Texas. Palmer said a dealer might sell a car as low as factory invoice if he had a lot full of cars that did not sell in his market.

However, for those who want to venture on with a gray-market car, *How to Import a European Car: The Gray Market Guide* by Jean Duguay provides information on the step-by-step process, including sample forms.

DEEP DISCOUNTS ON REFLEX CAMERAS

As with cars, the upscale gray market cameras tend to be the most popular gray market items. Minolta, Nikon, and Ricoh, which control about 60 percent of the upscale reflex camera market, are the most heavily traded gray market brands.

Price has been the driving force behind the zooming of gray market business for cameras and their ancillary supplies. American retailers charge that foreign manufacturers tack on a higher price for their American shipments than they do on goods sent anywhere else on the globe. To fight back, the American consumer has increasingly turned to the gray market when buying camera equipment.

Dwig Gangwisch, owner of Super Tex, Inc., of Dallas, a high volume camera dealer, said Nikon U.S.A. usually sells cameras to dealers at about a 20 percent markup from their original cost. This sum includes the cost of national advertising and helps subsidize the fees necessary to translate Nikon's Japanese instruction manual into English. Finally, a portion of the money is used to pay for warranty work and service.

Because many of these costs are eliminated when a gray marketeer purchases a camera from an independent agent, the markup is only abut 10 percent of the original manufacturer's base price, Gangwisch explained. After accounting for overhead, this markup still nets the retailer a profit margin of between 2 and 5 percent.

This significantly lower markup can translate into big savings for the consumer. Gray market importers can sell their cameras for deep discounts of up to 50 percent off suggested retail price.

Like cars, cameras have a very distinct and defined distribution pattern. All authorized manufacturers sell their cameras to their authorized United States subsidiary, which then sells the goods to authorized dealers throughout America. This system is not particular to America; the manufacturer sets similar channels from Brazil to Bangladesh.

Like cars, camera equipment enters the gray market stream when it is imported by someone other than the subsidiary or the authorized dealer. Both the cameras and their accessories are the identical merchandise sold by authorized dealers. The only exception is that the various parts—lens, straps and accessories, for example—can be sold separately.

Businessmen who buy cameras abroad from authorized dealers and then come home to sell these cameras like to call themselves "parallel importers."

Parallel importers are winning market share from the authorized dealers. *Consumer Reports* recently estimated 30 percent of the single lens reflex cameras and their lens sold in this country come from the gray market.

Unlike the automobile gray market, camera parallel importers search the entire globe for the best price, depending on the currency rates. Some countries also place a lower markup on their goods than others. So a parallel importer will search for a week for currency which also has a low markup. Currently Bangladesh is very popular with gray market dealers. The country's markup is significantly low because the population of Bangladesh does not have a mad passion to possess Nikon cameras. Low demand translates into low markups.

Frequently parallel importers will establish business relationships with authorized dealers in a host of countries. That way they can be fleet of foot when currency fluctuations force them to do business elsewhere.

Typically the parallel importer will purchase the merchandise abroad, then sell it to a gray market retailer in the States. This is usually a cash transaction. The discount is deep because the importer eschews all responsibility and liability for the products once they change hands.

In the short term, consumers benefit. Foreign cameras are generally extremely well made and are particularly reliable. The retailers, who do give a ninety-day warranty, will then take care of any lemons. The consumer is banking on the fact that the discount will cover any extraneous repairs after the ninety days. More often than not, that is a well-taken risk. If the consumer is worried, however, most gray market retailers will also sell their own warranty for another $30.

Until Congress passed the Warner Trade Act in the 1940s, a buyer merely had to show a proof of purchase to get free warranty work done on any new product. Today, however, with the emergence of the gray market, some manufacturers are balking. Nikon, for example, is requiring proof of purchase from a proper United States distributor before it will reimburse service departments for work done after the ninety-first day of purchase. At the time of an authorized sale, the retailer will give the buyer a card listing the name and location of the retailer. No warranty work past the initial ninety days will be done without presenting that card, said a Nikon spokesman.

Moreover, camera lovers who buy their goods from the proper channels will find a Nikon USA card inside the camera box. This card must be mailed to the manufacturer within the first ninety days to validate the warranty.

If this is not done, the manufacturer will do no warranty work gratis.

Minolta and Cannon have also established protective procedures for their dealers. They, too, have warranty cards which they require customers to complete and mail to the company's headquarters. There they record all serial numbers. If the number matches a number sold in a country other than the United States, the company will void all warranty work.

A few gray market retailers are fighting back by establishing their own service departments with their own warranties. 47th Street Photo, one of New York's largest gray market retailers, gives its customers its own warranty card. All the gray market merchandise it sells comes with a complete warranty. (The phone number in New York City is (212) 260-4417 or toll free 1-800-221-7774 and 1-800-221-5858.

But most gray market retailers rarely have service departments, so do not plan on lugging your new purchase back to the store if the shutter locks. And do not count on the sales staff to provide much technical help. To keep the overhead down, gray market retailers tend to cut expensive training seminars from their budgets. Buyers flirting with their first 35 millimeter camera probably should pay the suggested retail prices offered by authorized camera dealers. But there are many competitive prices available. First-time buyers can usually find discount prices in their hometowns like Barry's Camera and Video, Camera King, and others in Dallas. Since these and many other retailers have service departments, they will have a helpful ear at the camera store when anything goes wrong. Those buying their third Hasselblad who already have a wealth of experience with cameras can profit by shopping at a gray market retailer.

Mail order catalogues are the predominant method

of selling gray market camera merchandise. Retailers generally run ads in popular trade magazines, consumer camera magazines like *Modern Photography*, and widely circulated general interest publications with a national distribution like the *New York Times* Sunday magazine. Usually the ads contain a list of prices and products and include an address where a consumer can send for a complete catalogue.

One of the largest concentrations of gray market mail order shops are located in the diamond district of New York City. Be wary of an operator who uses a post office box in his address. Without a street location it can be difficult for the Federal Trade Commission to track the retailer if something goes amiss.

Other discount mail order houses include the following:

AAA Camera Exchange
43 Seventh Avenue
New York, New York 10011
1-800-221-9521 (orders only)
(212) 242-5800 (New York)

B&H Foto Electronics
119 West 17th Street
New York, New York 10011
1-800-221-5662 (orders only)
(212) 807-7474 (inquiries)

Cameras West of Seattle
1908 4th Avenue
Seattle, Washington 98101
1-800-626-1111 (orders only)
(206) 622-0066 (inquiries)

Executive Photo & Supply
  Corporation
120 West 31st Street
New York, New York 10001
1-800-223-7323 (orders only)
(212) 947-5290 (New York,

Alaska, and Hawaii
  residents; inquiries)

Focus Electronics
4523 13th Avenue
Brooklyn, New York 11219
1-800-221-0828 (orders only)
(212) 871-7600 (inquiries)

Garden Camera
345 Seventh Avenue
New York, New York 10001
1-800-223-5830 (orders only)
(212) 868-1420 (inquiries)

Hirsch Photo
Dept. U.S.
699 Third Avenue
New York, New York 10017
(212) 557-1150

Olden Camera
Dept. U.S.
1265 Broadway at 32nd
  Street

New York, New York 10001
1-800-223-6311 (orders only)
(212) 725-1234 (inquiries)

Saverite Photo & Electronics
46 Canal Street
New York, New York 10002
1-800-223-4212
(212) 966-6655

Solar Cine Products, Inc.
Dept. U.S.

4247 S. Kedzie Avenue
Chicago, Illinois 60632
1-800-621-8796 (orders only)
(312) 254-8310 (inquiries)

Spiratone
Dept. U.S.
135-06 Northern Boulevard
Flushing, New York 11354
1-800-221-9695 (orders only)
(212) 886-2000 (inquiries)

Because of this intense concentration, New York has a very competitive camera market. To monitor the actions of the gray market vendors who sell Nikons on street corners in Manhattan, the New York State Attorney General's office conducted a study which was released in November, 1985. The report found most complaints filed against camera retailers were against gray market mail order vendors. The study said most customers complained about slow delivery and even slower receipt of refunds and credits for damaged or defective merchandise.

The Bureau of Consumer Frauds and Protection (2 World Trade Center, New York, New York 10047) offered this advice when dealing with a mail order marketeer:

1. Know what removable pieces come as standard equipment with your purchase by calling a camera store in your area. Most will be happy to supply a customer that type of information over the telephone. That includes lens caps, straps, and cases. In some instances, gray marketeers will take a camera apart and sell its parts separately. Know exactly what you paid for and ordered. Know the brand name, model number, and price of everything you order by phone or mail. Because gray marketeers break down camera parts, your purchase may have been put together piecemeal. Check all the

157

numbers to ensure they all came from the same "kit."

2. When you receive an order, check it right away. Make sure every part of the camera works and that all accessories function properly. Since warranties last only ninety days and you have to factor in the time spent dealing with the mail, you do not want to waste time during your limited warranty window.

3. Keep explicit records. Record the date you ordered the merchandise, the model numbers of what you ordered, and who you talked to, if you order by phone.

4. Get the mail order house's authorization and approval before you return any damaged or incomplete merchandise.

Buying cameras from gray market mail order houses comes equipped with all the problems of ordering merchandise by mail. Merchandise can arrive broken with no warranty, even from the shipper. You may not receive the exact part you wanted. You can make the mistake of ordering the wrong part. Always visit a local dealer first to find out what you need so you do not order blind.

Other sources for purchasing gray market camera goods are supermarket chains and large national drug store operations. Here you can see and touch what you are purchasing.

What if you go to a camera store and want to buy an authorized camera? How do you know if you are buying a gray market product instead?

First, look at the box. The exterior is almost always embossed with the manufacturer's name. Then check the warranty card. If there is a name other than the manufacturer's on it, this is a clue.

Check to see if the batteries are included with your purchase. All authorized dealers will sell camera equipment with its first set of batteries.

Record the model number of the camera you are

looking at and call the company's headquarters to verify if that is an United States model. Some manufacturers make two versions of the same camera—one for America, the other for the rest of the world. The Minolta Maxxum is one such model. The manufacturer can tell immediately by the model number if that camera was intended to be sold in the United States.

If the instruction book is a photocopy, or worse yet, in Japanese, you can be sure the camera entered through the gray market. Be particularly wary if the instruction book is written in Spanish. That may be a clue the camera was smuggled in illegally through Mexico. Import taxes from Mexico are about 100 percent, which adds another $400 to a $400 camera. Smuggled goods escape the import taxes, allowing a dishonest dealer to sell at a deep discount. But most importers do business legally and above board. They would prefer to bring in goods through countries where United States import taxes are low.

COMPUTERS: IBMS AND CLONES

Computers present a different story. Car buyers can choose from a half dozen popular import manufacturers who produce dozens of models. The big three camera manufacturers also sell a variety of cameras. But in the computer world, there is only one big name and that is IBM (International Business Machines). Big Blue, in the eyes of the friendly users, is the unquestioned industry standard. None of the other manufacturers carry the clout and the charisma in the consumer market that IBM does.

Today IBM products control an overwhelming 90 percent of the United States computer market. Now even its competitors—AT & T, NEC, Compaq, and Apple—are all trying to make equipment which will run on IBM compatible software.

The only IBM computers demanded on the gray

market are the personal computers. Personal computers are the machines purchased by consumers and small businessmen, usually from retail stores; mainframes are sold directly from the manufacturer to the user with no retailer in between. This distinction is chiefly due to cost. Personal computers may run from $2,000 to $7,000, almost MasterCardable; mainframes can easily cost hundreds of thousands of dollars and generally require a bank loan.

Currently the most popular IBM personal computers for gray market merchandising are the IBM PC and the IBM XT.

Because IBM has the controlling share of the market, the company has enjoyed greater success at squelching the gray market sales. IBM has taken specific steps to tighten its distribution channels to ensure its authorized dealers are not dumping IBM products on the gray market. The company has begun coding boxes in order to trace them back to the original dealer. Thus, when a consumer takes the machine to be fixed under the original warranty, the authorized dealership can immediately tell if the computer was a gray market purchase. The package clearly warns that IBM will void the warranty if the product was not purchased from an authorized dealer.

IBM can tightly control its distribution because there are only three authorized distributors of IBM PC products in the country. These distributors are authorized to sell to the approximately 2,000 retail distributors nationwide.

IBM backs up its bark with its bite. Micro Mart of Atlanta, Georgia, is a 140-store chain which repeatedly sold IBM products to gray market distributors. IBM continually warned Micro Mart, ordering it to stop the practice. In February, 1986, IBM cancelled its authorization with Micro Mart. The company, which racked up sales of

$120 million in 1985, expects sales to drop $100 million this year without IBM.

John Beaudrau, an IBM spokesman, said a dealer's contract clearly states IBM can discontinue its authorization if a dealer resells its goods on the gray market.

Before the watchdog campaign started, dealers were sorely tempted to sell their IBM products to gray market retailers because of IBM's selling terms. Authorized distributors must pay the company for its order in thirty days. That rule puts many retailers, particularly during slow economic times, under a great deal of financial pressure to unload all their inventory before the bill comes due.

If the month is coming to an end, a dealer may sell his product to a gray market dealer discounting the price sometimes down to actual cost. IBM sells its systems an average of 30 percent off list price through its dealership network, although chain retailers which order large quantities may receive between 35 and 45 percent of the list price. If the authorized dealer makes his markup on the goods he keeps, he can make a small profit and still pay his bill on time.

Dealers usually will not sell their goods below 15 percent of the actual price because they have built in payroll and overhead costs. Dealers must reorder their goods, which continues to tie-up their capital. Gray market dealers need less capital to compete as effectively.

Because gray market IBM machines are IBM machines, there is virtually no way to tell if they are gray market products. Vendors are generally not forthright about the origin of the machine. Consumers, especially first-time buyers, are generally not knowledgeable enough to even ask if the computer came from the gray market. Only the code on the exterior box will tell for sure. Check it out by calling any authorized IBM dealer in your area. They can check the serial number for you, or refer you to the IBM regional office in your area for further information.

Like cameras, gray market salesmen rarely receive training, so they generally cannot help you if you have a problem. Training and hand holding can be critical for an intimidated tyro. Some gray market resellers offer a group training session, but at an added cost. Going to a dealer who will guide you during those trying first moments can often be worth the extra 15 percent built into the purchase price.

Especially in the computer world, gray market purchases are only for those who are totally computer literate.

There is one way to purchase IBM-like goods at a significantly reduced price. But this cannot be done on the gray market. Instead, one can purchase an "IBM clone."

Unlike gray market goods, IBM clones are not made by IBM and sold at a lower price by shaving off fees caused by government regulations or company rules. Instead, independent third parties are manufacturing their own computers which are IBM compatible. That means 95 percent of the time, your clone can use peripherals (ancillary equipment like printers and modems) and software designed for IBM manufactured machines. Since most of the market uses the IBM as a standard, you can enjoy all the benefits of having an IBM machine without having to pay for the IBM name. (A computer world aphorism is that consumers pay $400 extra for each letter in IBM's name.)

Clones are much like designer knockoffs in the apparel business. But the electronic components are very similar and often exactly the same.

IBM itself manufactures very little of its own products. It has thousands of subcontractors who supply the parts which are then assembled at IBM to make an IBM machine. For example, the brains of a computer is called a mother board. IBM buys many mother boards in Taiwan. Clone manufacturers can just as easily purchase a Taiwanese mother board from the same assembly line and install it into their machines. These machines cannot be 100 percent compatible, however. To do so would be in violation of IBM's copyright.

Like gray marketeers, clone manufacturers can make a similar machine at a lower cost because they do not have to fund the hyperstructure of IBM. Their advertising costs are lower. Sales forces can be leaner and the manufacturer does not have to maintain a service department. Tom Dodson, executive vice president of Five Star Electronics Inc. in Dallas (214) 733-4100, an IBM clone manufacturer, said a typical computer retailer had to make a 20 percent markup on IBM goods to make a profit. His company only needs to earn an 8 percent markup to make money.

Clone manufacturers can compete with IBM in areas other than price. Dodson pointed out they can add features the market is demanding that are not currently built into IBM models. And they can modify and improve the computer's architecture. For example, Dodson explained IBM uses a Tanden hyper belt-driven drive to power its machine. The Tanden drive can be noisy. When Five Star builds its clones, it installs a Fujitsu manual direct drive instead. The Fujitsu drive is much quieter.

Service does not tend to be much of a problem with clones. Some offer their own warranties; Five Star's warranty extends for one year. Independent service companies have sprung up as a cottage industry to repair the equipment. They are able to fix clones because the mechanics are so similar.

If you are going to buy an IBM clone, make sure you are buying it from an established company or from a firm started by a computer pioneer with winning successes in the field before playing with mother boards. Be wary of buying a machine from a fellow assembling them in his garage. This is the image IBM is trying to project upon the entire clone market. It is true—but does not apply across the board.

Finding a local retailer who sells clones is a relatively easy task in most cities. In North Texas, for example, Lolier Electronics, Sabet Electronics, and Jade Electronics have good reputations for selling top-quality IBM clones. PCs Ltd., an Austin, Texas, company, is a national distributor of clones, placing advertisements in *PC Magazine* and other electronics trade publications.

In fact, most independent store owners sell IBM compatible components. Some national chains, Computerland for one, are selling compatibles. A look into local, regional, or national computer and electronics trade publications should supply the shopper with all the sources needed to track down a clone.

INSURANCE

In 1985, a fifty-six-year-old Texas woman lost her arm while working with an electric bandsaw. The arm was saved through a lengthy operation, but the woman had additional problems—some $30,000 in medical bills that threatened her and her husband's retirement funds.

The health insurance policy she bought in 1983, after answering a mail-order advertisement, was supposed to cover up to $200,000 in medical bills. But what she—and countless others like her—did not understand was that specific dollar limitations written into the policy could sharply curtail the payments from the insurance company.

In this case the policy she and her husband paid $1,404 for annually, covered only $7,800 of the medical bills.

Before she bought the policy, the woman told the insurance salesman that she wanted a policy to take care of a tragedy, the smaller bills they could handle. What the woman did not do was read the details of the policy. If she had, she would have noted the $3,000 limit per claim on a long list of expensive medical items including operating rooms, anesthetics, and lab work, all items, when taken cumulatively, that can quickly pass the $3,000 mark per claim.

Although the couple consulted an attorney, there was little they could do. The insurance company was bound by the written policy, not by the verbal claims of its salesman.

In 1978, shocked members of the House Select Committee on Aging heard testimony concerning a seventy-six-year-old widow who purchased seventy-one policies for health, life, and accident coverage during nine years. The widow bought five policies in a single day, at one point. The payments on the policies forced her into debt, and she had to mortgage the family farm, which was nearly paid off.

The woman's daughter testified that the benefits paid on all those policies equalled $5,781 over an eight-year period, while the premiums during the same time were at least $30,000.

At the same hearing, an agent wearing a ski mask testified about some insurance companies' tactics of coaching sales personnel to scare the elderly into purchasing duplicate coverage or coverage they do not need.

In a later hearing, the same committee explored the so-called dread disease insurance that was scamming the elderly. A subsequent report from the committee called the abuses "a national scandal."

The policies cover a very limited range of expenses and often are sold by playing off the fears of people.

As an illustration, the committee looked at a cancer insurance policy (which promised to assist with 40 percent of nonmedical costs), of a woman who was diagnosed with cervical cancer. The woman paid $100 in premiums over a two-year period. But when she was later diagnosed with cancer, how much did the policy pay of her total $2,000 in medical bills? A mere $160.

"The company may suggest that the policyholder at least got her money back and then some, but the fact is only one out of six who actually contract cancer will break even or do better," the report concluded.

Investigative reporter Ronald Kessler, in his 1985 book, *The Life Insurance Game: How the Industry Has*

Amassed Over $600 Billion at the Expense of the American Public, tells about the practice of selling life insurance to the poor to pay for funeral costs in case of the death of their children.

Kessler looked at the policies called industrial life insurance policies and found them to be two to four times more expensive than life insurance policies sold to the more affluent.

Agents collect the premiums in person, often giving no receipts. Kessler interviewed several low-income people who had no idea what they were actually purchasing or that they could purchase the insurance cheaper elsewhere. (And, indeed, most consumer experts advise against taking life insurance policies out on children.)

Not surprisingly, industrial life, though a small segment of the insurance business, is more profitable than other lines of life insurance.

HORROR STORIES ASIDE, INSURANCE IS COMPLEX

To the honest agents and brokers and the reputable insurance companies, singling out the above illustrations will no doubt seem unfair. And anyone who has experienced a tragedy, and then heard the reassuring voice of an insurance representative saying that the house the tornado just took away was fully covered, knows the necessity of a good overall insurance plan.

But the insurance industry (by its own design) is a challenge to even the best-educated. It is an industry that takes in billions of dollars each year, yet has no federal regulatory body overseeing it as other financial industries do.

It is an industry so complex, wrote Andrew Tobias in *The Invisible Bankers,* that nearly two million people are employed in the insurance industry. That is almost as many people as in the Armed Forces; twenty times as many as collect the nation's federal income and excise taxes; and three times as many as it takes to run the United States Postal Service. It is an industry so steeped in obfuscation, it is maddeningly difficult to understand and compare coverage and prices. As it is sometimes said, insurance is not bought, it is sold. And it is not bought because it is so difficult to comprehend.

"Insurance is really a simple idea made complicated," wrote Herbert S. Denenberg, former Pennsylvania insurance commissioner who is widely hailed as an insurance consumer advocate.

Insurance is indeed a simple idea—you contribute to a pool and draw from it only if you have a loss. Some people take out more than they put in, others contribute but do not receive benefits.

If we knew our problems would be limited to a fallen tree limb on our fence, a broken window, or a slightly sprained ankle, there would be no need for insurance. Most of us would elect to pay the relatively minor costs out of our pockets. We would, in effect, be self-insured. But there is no way of predicting misfortunes. Insurance is a needed protection to keep from being wiped out financially.

Yet as vital as insurance is to our health and well-being, the Insurance Information Institute, a nonprofit group supported by the insurance industry, estimated that 80 percent of Americans who buy insurance misspend some of their premiums.

It is not unusual, the institute said, for families to spend $100 a year for insurance they do not need because of duplicate coverage. Yet the same people might not have adequate coverage for a major tragedy. For example, that $100 worth of double coverage could be used to buy a $1 million umbrella liability policy to pick up where other policies, such as homeowners and auto, leave off. It can save you from being wiped out in a lawsuit.

Consumers continue to buy some types of insurance they should completely avoid, or could find cheaper in other forms, according to both insurance and consumer experts.

Examples are the cancer insurance policies; credit life insurance (unless you are sick or elderly, it is far cheaper to take out a term life insurance policy); car rental insurance (a good portion is probably covered under your regular auto insurance policy); and, except in special cases, whole life and other cash-value policies.

On the other hand, the insurance agent or broker who urges you to drastically increase your life insurance policy or encourages you to consider disability income insurance and an umbrella liability policy, may well be looking out for your interests and not just for the added commission.

The National Insurance Consumer Organization, a consumer advocacy group, recommended five basic policies: life insurance (if you have dependents); health insurance; auto insurance; homeowner's insurance; and disability income insurance.

"You probably need nothing else, if you buy these coverages properly," NICO advised.

Yet consumers are bombarded with all types of insurance offers to cover everything from sick pets to your car loan if you die.

NICO warned against buying these twelve types of policies:

1. Air travel insurance. "If you have dependents, you need to be covered for the economic consequences of your premature death from any cause, be it heart attack, auto accident or air crash. . . . Air travel insurance costs too much. (Note: This is referring to air travel only, you may need some other types of trip insurance.)

2. Life insurance if you are single.

3. Life insurance if you are married with no children and your spouse has a good job.

4. Life insurance on your children.

5. Mugging insurance. "Here is a classic example of 'junk' insurance," said NICO. "It pays if you die or are hurt in a mugging. It pays very limited benefits as well." Choose life and health insurance policies that cover all types of catastrophies, not just a particular case.

6. Contact lens insurance. "These policies pay if you lost a contact lens. The cost of the premium is about equal to the cost of a lens at a discount eyeglass store. Not catastrophic."

7. Cancer insurance.

8. Rental car insurance.

9. Mortgage insurance and credit insurance.

10. Pet insurance. This is an area garnering increasing media attention and advertising space. While some avid pet lovers might disagree, this is the official statement from NICO: "The veterinarians are jealous of the impact Blue Cross/Blue Shield has had on the income of their brethren in the human health provider network. So, they are trying to emulate the practice. Pets are dear to us, but the cost of health care is low and is limited by the fact that the absence of third-party payers has, mercifully, hindered the development of CAT scans for dogs. It is almost impossible today to spend $200 on a pet's health problem. It won't be (in the future) if the vets have their way. Non-catastrophic, and dangerous to future costs of pet health care."

11. $100 a day health insurance.

12. Rain insurance. This pays if it rains over a specified amount during your vacation. NICO suggested pocketing the premium and seek indoor entertainment in case of rain.

In general, NICO's President Robert Hunter and other consumer advocates recommended buying only insurance that "comprehensively covers you against cata-strophic dollar losses."

"To buy only specific illness coverage is like buying toothpaste a squeeze at a time—and that's expensive," warned a NICO publication.

SELECTING AND EVALUATING AN AGENT OR BROKER

How do you know when you have a gem of an insur-ance agent and a broker who is looking out for your inter-ests? Or how do you know when your insurance representative is only trying to earn higher commissions at your expense?

This is difficult to answer. The problem lies in the dynamics of the insurance industry. Companies will pay higher commissions to agents and brokers for selling more profitable lines. And more profitable lines occur when a lot more premium dollars are coming in than go-ing out in claims.

An insurance broker is supposed to be able to shop around among companies and agents to find the best cov-erage, charging a commission for the work. An indepen-dent agent, as opposed to an agent who works directly for one company, represents two or more insurance compa-nies.

This is where the dynamics come in: if the broker or independent agent has the choice between two similar policies with different premiums, will they steer you to-ward the lower-priced (and lower-commissioned) policy or urge the more expensive one? (One study, for the Na-tional Association of Insurance Commissioners, did in-deed find some independent agents steering their clients to the insurers that paid the highest commissions.)

Will the car rental agent point out that your own auto insurance might cover that collision damage waiver instead of taking out an $8-a-day policy?

Will the bank tell you that it is much cheaper to get a term life insurance policy rather than to take a credit life policy to cover that auto loan in case of your death? Guess who takes a substantial chunk of the credit-life premium? That is right, the bank.

Will the insurance representative always tell you that it is better to take term insurance over whole life if, for example, you are the breadwinner and have young children? (For the same price, term would provide a much higher death benefit for your family than whole life which combines a death benefit with a savings feature). The problem is, whole life policies have much higher commissions.

Will the person selling you a health insurance policy emphasize the dollar limitations (such as only $100 a day for a hospital room when in fact the room costs much more) or will the salesman point out it is a $250,000 policy? You may have to shell out thousands out of your own pocket to reach that level paid by the insurance company, if it is a limited coverage policy.

An insurance buyer has to be tough, cynical and unafraid to ask questions. To test your present agent or broker, here are thirteen questions to ask yourself:

1. Does your agent (or broker) do more than send you a new bill and a new policy each year? For example, does your agent give you an annual insurance checkup?

2. Does your agent explain your policies fully and completely as to what they cover?

3. Do you understand what your agent says about your policies and your insurance program?

4. Does your agent explain new insurance developments without being asked?

5. Does your agent take the time to consider your overall insurance picture before selling you individual policies?

6. Does your agent return your calls and answer your correspondence and questions promptly?

7. Has your agent ever made any suggestions that reduced the amount of your insurance premium?

8. For life and health insurance policies, is your agent a Charter Life Underwriter (CLU)? For property and casualty insurance, is your agent a Chartered Property and Casualty Underwriter (CPCU)?

9. Is your agent employed full time in the insurance business? Avoid part timers and incompetent brothers-in-law offering to get you a deal.

10. How has your agent responded to you when you have suffered a loss and needed to make a claim?

11. When it comes to life insurance, does your agent explain the difference between the premiums you pay and the actual cost of your life insurance? For example, does he show you what is called the interest-adjusted cost of life insurance that he wants to sell you?

12. Does your agent place you with insurance companies that are strong financially and show you the company's financial rating to prove it? For example, an agent can show you the company's rating in Best's Reports.

13. Is your agent a member of a professional trade association? Membership can help agents stay up-to-date on new developments and can subject them to higher standards of performance.

LIFE INSURANCE

Take two aspirins and a deep breath. Life insurance is one of the slipperiest coverages with which you may ever have to deal. Do you need it? What type of policy should you choose from the smorgasbord of coverages? In 1983, purchases of life insurance exceeded $1 trillion. There are more than 1,900 life insurance companies in the United States.

A simplistic way to deal with life insurance is to divide it into two categories—term and cash-value insurance. Term insurance is pure insurance. You pay a premium for the insurer's promise that if you die, your beneficiaries will be paid the death benefit. As you get older, your risk of dying becomes greater and the premium increases.

Consumer advocates generally say that term insurance is the best deal. It is relatively cheap and the best buy for those who need insurance the most—younger people whose premature deaths would leave dependents in financial difficulty.

But if term insurance is so great, why is nobody knocking down the door trying to sell it? Because what is known as cash-value policies (particularly whole-life policies) bring much higher commissions. Cash-value policies are those that combine a death benefit (like term) with a savings plan.

Salesmen can be more eager to sell the cash-value plans. They also will be more than happy to sell credit life and mortgage life (usually just expensive term policies) to cover outstanding loans in case you die.

Despite a push by reformers since the early 1970s, life insurance remains a very difficult industry to comprehend. For consumers who may be unwilling to invest several hours reading and learning about life insurance policies, it is impossible to compare policies. Furthermore, once you buy a policy, you may not even fully understand what you have purchased.

Joe A. Mintz is a sixty-eight-year-old editor of a financial newsletter for retirees and pre-retirees. He worked for sixteen years as a full-time life insurance agent before dropping out in 1968 to fight the insurance industry. Mintz said he came to the realization that the public was being misled by the insurance companies. Articles in such publications as the *New York Times* and *Newsweek* have quoted him over the years and placed him among reformers who pushed for better price disclosure.

Nearly two decades later, when Mintz flipped through magazines, he easily found ads he said are misleading. One ad for a cash-value policy called universal secure life promises $27,356 in cash value after twenty years if the policyholder pays $1,264 in premiums in each of those twenty years. If the policyholder dies in that time, the death benefit is $100,000. On the face of it, it sounds good. Not only do you get life insurance coverage for those twenty years, but at the end of that period you get back $27,356, more than you paid in premiums ($25,480).

But what you have to consider is what that money could have earned if invested. For example, the $1,264 invested at 5 percent for each of twenty years brings $43,884.82, Mintz calculated. That is a difference of $16,528.82 over the promised cash value.

The ad shows $27,356 would be the cash value with the premiums invested at 5 percent. That is misleading, Mintz said. What the company has failed to point out in the ad is that the interest is paid on the money after expenses have been subtracted. "They've subtracted the agent's commission. They've subtracted the president of the company's salary. They've subtracted lights, water and gas, and also the cost of the term insurance to provide the $100,000 death benefit," Mintz said.

"Why would you give up $43,884 to get back $27,356 if you are able to obtain a $100,000 death benefit and give up $16,528 or less?" he asked.

Mintz pointed to another ad, this one in a trade magazine aimed at insurance agents, to illustrate the strong incentives given to agents to sell cash-value plans. The ad promises agents up to 109 percent of first-year premiums for selling a variable universal life product called the LifeFund by Southwestern Life. The LifeFund pays a 60 percent first-year base commission but increases that percentage if more policies are sold.

That means agents not only receive 109 percent on each policy they sell after a certain point, but also they collect another 40 percent on policies already sold.

Another problem is it is impossible to compare policies, despite the adoption of interest adjusted laws in many states. The laws attempt to give a better comparison by telling the consumer the cost of a cash-value policy balanced against the type of interest those premiums could have earned if invested elsewhere.

But Mintz said it is still impossible to compare. He and others (including the National Association of Insurance Commissioners) have declared the interest-adjusted index laws failures. Even though some thirty-odd states adopted such laws, they are too weak, critics charge.

The interest-adjusted index tried to discourage salesmen from such pitches as telling you a cash-value policy really was free insurance because you got the death benefit coverage for a number of years at no cost because the amount of dividend and cash value in a long-held policy exceeded the premiums paid. What is wrong with that argument is you have to consider how that money could have been invested if it had not been tied up in an insurance policy.

"Interest-adjusted, it hasn't changed a damn thing. Even if it were right, it wouldn't make any difference because people don't shop for insurance," Mintz fumed. "People have two mistaken views about these companies whose names are household words, like New York Life, Metropolitan Life, Allstate, State Farm, the companies that advertise highly. One, they believe life insurance costs are regulated by the states. The regulation, amazingly enough, is not on the most that they can charge, but on the least the companies can charge. Two, they believe the companies whose names are household words provide the most competitive product, and that is just far from the truth."

Sales pitches for life insurance are just as confusing today as twenty years ago, and maybe worse because of all the new types of insurance.

"The real argument is, is it better to buy term insurance than cash-value insurance? And there is no consumer help for that," Mintz said. "Is the cost of term insurance more or less than a cash-value type of insurance policy? That question is not answered by the interest-adjusted method."

Mintz (whose newsletter NROCA is available for $36 a year, P.O. Box 12066, Dallas, Texas 75225) also successfully campaigned for better disclosure regulations on Individual Retirement Accounts.

Mintz said he was first inspired to question the insurance industry by a book by an Indiana University professor, Joseph M. Belth, which explained why the insurance companies' numbers did not add up. The 1966 book, *The Retail Price Structure in American Life Insurance*, called for price disclosure reform.

In his most recent book, the second edition of *Life Insurance, A Consumer's Handbook*, Belth gives advice on how to purchase life insurance. Belth also traces what has happened to information disclosure since his book was published in 1966.

"In the years since, there has been an endless succession of studies, debates, hearings, reports, proposals, bills, and regulations," Belth wrote.

In 1979, the Federal Trade Commission recommended that a "rigorous system of disclosure be adopted by the states, and that the system include a requirement for disclosing information about the rate of return on the savings component in cash-value life insurance," Belth wrote. But the report infuriated the industry so much that political pressure was put on Congress, which ordered the FTC not to investigate the insurance business unless specifically asked to do so by one of the commerce committees.

The next year, the NAIC also called for a new system of disclosure for the life insurance business. Although the plan has some "technical difficulties," Belth called the plan "extraordinary." The NAIC also called the present interest-adjusted disclosure laws "fatally flawed."

The NAIC's new proposal also was attacked by the insurance industry and Belth responded: "It now appears there will never be a rigorous system of disclosure mandated for the life insurance industry. The industry is opposed to rigorous disclosure, and has enough influence to destroy any politician or regulatory agency with the termerity to propose it."

In other words, consumers are on their own in wading through the various policies.

One excellent guide to purchasing life insurance is *Taking the Bite Out of Insurance* by James H. Hunt, a director of the National Insurance Consumer Organization and a former state insurance commissioner in Vermont.

Hunt suggested you may not need any insurance at all if you are single with no dependents (aging parents, spouses, or children) or are married without children (unless the surviving spouse would be unable to work or could not find acceptable wages).

Children do not need life insurance, NICO advised.

But if you have children or other dependents, you probably need insurance, and lots of it. NICO recommended, as a rule of thumb, for a family with two young children, enough life insurance to cover five times your annual salary.

There are other more complicated formulas to use to figure life insurance needs. The February 1980 issue of *Consumer Reports*, for example, has a formula to use.

Whatever method you use to figure it, the cheapest way to gain this protection is through term insurance.

The cash-value policies should only be considered, some advised, after the age forty and, after investments have been made in Individual Retirement Accounts. Because term becomes more expensive as a policyholder ages, the cash-value policies become more attractive in relative terms. Regardless of which type you decide to buy, ask for the nonsmoker's rates (which are lower) if you do not smoke.

As defined by the American Council of Life Insurance, here are the types of life insurance policies you are most likely to encounter:

Term insurance is protection that insures your family for a specified period of time, usually one, five, ten, or twenty years, or up to age sixty-five. A term insurance policy pays a benefit only if you die during the period covered by the policy. If you stop paying premiums, the insurance stops. At the end of the term the coverage terminates, but it can be continued for another term if you have a "renewable" policy. Under such a policy, you need not take a medical examination, but each time you renew, your premiums will be higher because you are older.

Whole life insurance (or straight life insurance) is protection that can be kept in force for as long as you live. By choosing to pay a premium that does not increase as you grow older, you average out the costs of your policy over your lifetime on a yearly basis. One important feature of whole life insurance is its cash value. This is a sum which increases over the years and which you will receive if you give up the insurance benefits.

Endowment insurance emphasizes the accumulation of money as it provides life insurance protection. After a stated number of years or a certain age, the endowment "matures," paying the amount of the policy to the policyholder. However, if the policyholder should die before that time, the full amount of the insurance limit is paid to the beneficiary.

Modified life is a variation of whole life insurance. Its premium is relatively low in the first several years but increases in the later years. It is intended for those who want whole life insurance but wish to pay lower premiums in their younger years.

Universal life is a relatively new form of insurance coverage. It is designed to permit a policyholder to pay premiums at any time, in virtually any amount, subject to certain minimums. The policyholder can also change the amount of insurance more easily than under traditional policies. In a universal life insurance policy the amount the cash value increases each year reflects the interest earned on short-term investments.

Variable life insurance, while not new, has become more widely available. Under this plan cash values fluctuate according to the yields earned by a separate fund which can be either an equity, money market, or long-term bond fund. There is a minimum guaranteed death benefit, but it can go higher, depending on the earnings of the dollars invested in the separate fund.

Adjustable life insurance allows the policyholder to change the policy as his or her needs change. For example, if you want to increase or decrease your coverage, you can either change your premium payments or change the period of coverage.

Combination plans combine term and whole life or endowment insurance in one contract. This type of policy is usually called family income plan or a family policy.

For consumers wishing to look into cash-value policies, heed a warning from NICO. Over 20 percent of cash-value policies are dropped before two years of premiums are paid and nearly one-half of such policies do not last ten years. The problem is the cash-value policies do not pay off until held for many years. So think twice before purchasing cash-value policies. Choose it carefully and then plan to stick with it.

Do you need credit life insurance coverage? Credit life is often sold as the salesman or banker is drawing up the loan papers. You are told the credit life insurance will protect your family in case you die and are unable to pay off your loan (usually a car loan).

But unless you are sick or elderly and could not qualify for a less-expensive term policy, do not buy it. Credit life varies from state to state, so ask your creditor how much the cost is per $100 of coverage. Credit life insurance in the 20-cent range per $100 would be considered low while $1 per $100 of coverage is very high. Have some estimates on term life available before you take the loan. You should not be required to take credit life, so exercise your right to refuse it.

Besides the cost, another drawback of credit life is that as your loan amount and insurance benefit is reduced, the premium you pay on your credit life remains the same. Comparing a credit life policy to purchasing a term life insurance policy for the amount of the loan shows another drawback—a lack of choice on how the death benefits should be used. It is possible your heirs would find that paying off the loan is not the best choice.

The same arguments generally apply to mortgage life insurance coverage.

HEALTH INSURANCE

Unfortunately most of us wait until we have a claim before investigating exactly what is covered in our health insurance policy, and little wonder. Wandering through a maze of confusing terms such as "hospital indemnity," "guaranteed renewable," "deductible," and "co-insurance," is about as enlightening as reading a dictionary in a foreign language. Far better, it might seem, to get an abbreviated explanation from the translator, the insurance salesman (that is, if you are not lucky enough to have group coverage through work).

But like the lesson learned by the Texas woman, who found out too late what her policy did not cover, it is better to read the policy yourself and try to understand it. At least make the insurance salesman point out the written section in the policy to back up every claim he or she makes.

Because of the frightening escalation of medical costs in recent years, it is important to know how well you are covered. Living without health insurance, or the right kind of health insurance, is a very risky business. A single illness or injury for the uninsured or underinsured can drain one's entire financial resources.

Witness the jump in health care expenses: in 1965, the Health Insurance Association of America estimated the per capita expense for health care to be $211. By 1985, an estimated $1,882 was spent for every man, woman, and child. Or look at it another way: the association estimated the cost of an average day's stay in the hospital to be $38.91 in 1963. By 1982, it had jumped to $327.40, an increase of 741 percent.

National health care expense was 4.4 percent of the Gross National Product in 1956, in 1984, it was 10.7 percent.

Yet despite increases in health care costs, many live without insurance. A study conducted for the Urban Institute of Washington D.C. found 32.7 million people who were uninsured in 1982. That is about 16 percent of the population under age sixty-five.

If you are uninsured, can you possibly afford coverage? Low-cost policies without gaping loopholes are hard to find. But can you afford not to be covered? A study by the Robert Wood Johnson Foundation in Princeton, New

Jersey, found that people without health insurance are less likely to seek needed medical treatment.

If you have health insurance (most have coverage through a group plan paid in full or part by their employers), is your policy enough? Or do you need supplemental insurance? If you qualify for Medicare, do you have the right kind of insurance to pick up where Medicare leaves off?

The biggest problems in health insurance (beyond the problem of not carrying any insurance at all) are duplicate coverage and a false sense of security in believing you are covered for major problems when in fact you are not.

To check out your existing policy, ask the following six questions of your insurance representative or the person responsible for the company's group coverage, if you cannot make sense of the written policy yourself.

1. What are the maximum benefits in this policy? Most policies will have a lifetime maximum benefit that puts a ceiling on the amount you can collect in your lifetime with the policy. It might be as low as $10,000 or as high as $1 million. The Health Insurance Association of America recommended a maximum limit of at least $250,000. Be careful though, high lifetime benefits may not mean much if payment for each illness is restricted to a low amount.

Look for dollar schedules in your policy. A red flag should go up when you see benefits such as $100 per day maximum coverage for a hospital room. Other warning signals are such phrases as "Doctor visits—limited to one visit per day." This could be expensive for policyholders who find themselves hospitalized with numerous visits per day from the doctor, one agent said. "Anesthetist—not to exceed 20 percent of surgeon's fees." Anesthesiology is expensive and this could mean an underinsured expense.

2. Some policies have a waiting period and will not pay claims if a disease is detected anywhere from three months to two years after the effective date of the policy. Two years is considered a long time for a pre-existing condition exclusion, so be wary of policies that read: "Preexisting conditions—two years."

3. What is the maximum the policy will pay per day of hospitalization? Policies expressing this in terms of dollars per day (this was common in policies written years ago, now the terminology has been updated to "reasonable and customary") may fall far short of the daily costs of being hospitalized. Compare the dollar limit to costs in your area's hospitals. For example, if the policy pays only $100 per day for a hospital room that costs $300, then you will pay the difference.

4. Are there any conditions that must be met before the policy will pay for surgery? Some policies require a second opinion from another physician or prior approval by the insurance company.

5. Does your policy have a stop-loss protection? When a medical policy has an 80 percent/20 percent coinsurance factor (coinsurance means you pay 20 percent and the insurance company pays 80 percent of eligible or covered expenses), the stop-loss protection is the limit of coinsurance payment for the insured. With a stop-loss limit of $2,500, after you have paid 20 percent of the eligible expenses up to the $2,500, then your coverage changes to 100 percent payment by the insurance company.

6. How many deductibles do you have to satisfy? If you have a family of seven, get a policy that states "not to exceed three deductibles per family per calendar year."

These questions refer to the traditional fee-for-service plans where clients choose their own doctors and the insurance company pays the bill. An alternative growing in popularity with consumers is the health maintenance organizations (HMOs). For a fixed fee, you receive complete medical care from a specified group of health care professionals. The premiums may be higher than fee-for-service, but there are almost no out-of-pocket expenses (such as deductibles and coinsurance) to pay.

From mid-1971 to January 1985, the health association reported the number of HMOs increased from 33 to 377 and the number of subscribers grew from 3.6 million to 16.7 million.

For senior citizens on Medicare, the federal program pays for about one-half of Medicare clients' expenses. Medigap insurance, to cover what Medicare will not, is widely available. However, some seniors are looking at HMOs as an alternative to the medigap coverage.

These four questions will help you shop and select insurance coverage to supplement Medicare:

1. Does this policy only cover one disease, such as cancer insurance? Does it overlap other policies?

Avoid the single-disease policy. It's usually a rip-off. One good supplemental policy is usually enough, although salesmen have been known to scare people into multiple-policy coverage that would duplicate benefits.

2. Do you have the right to renew the medigap policy? This probably is the most important consideration. The best protection is a "lifetime guarantee of renewability." A policy that can be dropped at the company's option should be avoided.

3. Have you compared it to other offerings? For example, have you checked out HMOs in your area? Have you looked at the nonprofit Blue Cross/Blue Shield offerings or policies by the American Association of Retired Persons?

4. Are the verbal promises of the salesman backed up in writing in the policy? Have the salesman show you an actual copy of the policy or coverage statement you will purchase.

If you do not have group coverage through work, the

policies you will find probably cost more and cover less. One thing to consider is group coverage through an alumni association, trade union, veterans organization, and so on. If you are self-employed (with one or more employees), you might search for a small-group policy. The next best alternative, NICO's Hunt told *Parent's Magazine* (October 1985), is an HMO, if you can find one.

If you have to look for an individual policy, be prepared to spend $1,500 to $3,000 a year for a family, in addition to any deductibles and copayments (copayments are usually 20 percent of the first $5,000, or $1,000 out of your pocket after the deductible has been met). NICO warned to stay away from the mail-order policies or those advertised on television. If it costs less than $2,000 a year, be very careful, there may be too many loopholes.

NICO advised looking into Blue Cross/Blue Shield Plan coverage for individual policies, because they offer comprehensive coverage. Additionally, the Blue Cross/Blue Shield plans boast the highest payout—giving back to subscribers about 90 cents on the premium dollar. Some companies are as low as 35 cents. A good ratio, known as loss ratio, is considered to be 65 to 75 cents. Ask your state regulatory body if it can supply you with the loss ratios.

If you prefer to shop at commercial companies, NICO suggested shopping for health insurance with major life insurance companies. Before you sign, get a copy of the policy and ask the questions listed earlier.

Losing your health insurance when you are laid off from your job is such a major problem in America that a bipartisan group of legislators, including Senator Edward Kennedy, has proposed a law requiring employers to extend health insurance coverage for four months following a layoff. Some companies voluntarily do this and some states require some sort of continuation. The costs for the four months would be split between the employer and employee.

But without such legislation, what can you do if you find yourself in that position?

1. Find out exactly how long your present group coverage will last.

2. Check to see if you can convert your group policy coverage to an individual policy. This will probably be more expensive and the benefits may not be as good, but it could be the only alternative for workers with pre-existing conditions.

3. If your spouse is employed, see if you can receive coverage through his/her plan.

4. Consider a short-term policy to tide you over until you can get another job.

5. Older workers, who might have problems with pre-existing conditions, may consider taking a job with a company that has good group coverage, even if the pay or work is not what was desired.

DISABILITY INCOME INSURANCE

Disability income insurance is an often-ignored but an essential insurance coverage. Did you know that if you are between ages thirty-five and sixty-five, your chances of being unable to work for ninety days or more because of a disabling injury or illness are far greater than your chances of dying? Furthermore, if you are over fifty, there is one chance in four that you will be disabled for six months or more before you retire.

Disability insurance provides you with income should you become sick or injured and unable to work. Some, but not all, employers provide disability income coverage. Find out if you have this coverage and, if so, what types of benefits are included.

For a detailed form to determine whether you need

disability income coverage, write to the Health Insurance Association of America, 1850 K. Street N.W., Washington, D.C. 20006, and ask for a free pamphlet titled "What You Should Know about Disability Insurance." The pamphlet explains how to figure potential benefits, such as Worker's Compensation or Social Security disability, to see what type of coverage you might need.

Only one in five workers have long-term disability coverage from their employers. Most of us cannot count on Social Security Disability Insurance either. SSDI will not be paid unless you are unable to do any substantial work—not just if you are unable to continue in your profession.

Dallas financial planner Bob Hazelbaker said it is essential, when looking at disability income policies, to find the terms "non-cancellable" and "guaranteed renewable."

This means that a company cannot change the premium rate and it cannot drop you once you have filed a claim.

Also study carefully the definition of disability. Hazelbaker said it is important the definition take into account your occupation. A nervous condition, for example, might make it impossible for you to continue your profession as an attorney, but not as a store clerk.

A good definition is as follows: "Total disability means your inability to engage in your occupation. . . ." But once benefits have been paid out for a period of two years, the definition broadens to: "Your inability to engage in any gainful occupation in which you might reasonably be expected to engage, with due regard for your education, training, experience, and prior economic status."

Small-business owners might consider checking into a Business Overhead Expense policy which is similar to a disability income policy, except it provides funds to keep the business going until you are back on your feet or can sell the business without having to unload it in a hurry and at a loss.

TRAVEL INSURANCE

Do you need travel insurance? It is important to ask that question *before* you take off on your vacation.

Check your health insurance policy to see if you are covered for medical expenses in a foreign country. If you rely solely on Medicare for health and accident protection, you will need a short-term travel policy because Medicare does not cover expenses incurred outside the United States. Make sure you check your medigap insurance, however, if you have that. Also, check with your agent to see if your homeowners policy would cover your baggage.

Travel policies will pay such things as airlifting you to a well-equipped hospital or flying you home in case of a serious accident or illness, assisting in replacement of lost or stolen luggage or documents, and insurance for trip cancellations.

A comprehensive policy is likely to duplicate your insurance coverage if you have decent policies, so it is better to buy travel insurance (if you need it at all) to cover only the needed items. Check out Access America, Inc., a subsidiary of Blue Cross and Blue Shield plans.

AUTO INSURANCE

Consumers pay $30 billion annually for auto insurance in the United States. It is a pricey but necessary (and in most states legally required) item if you want to feel safe, financially, on the road. For the uninsured, or underinsured, a simple act of falling asleep at the wheel could cause an accident that has the potential to wipe you out financially.

But there are many ways to cut your premium dollars without exposing yourself to great financial risk. Searching for ways to cut your premium, or increase your coverage for the same dollars, should become more and more important as auto premiums rise after a fairly dormant period. For example, State Farm's auto rates increased a mere 1.6 percent in 1984. But in 1985, it jumped 7.9 percent, and the prediction for industry-wide increases in 1986 is an average of 10 percent.

To understand the ways to cut costs, first look at the six basic auto insurance coverages:

Bodily Injury Liability—If the car you are driving injures or kills someone, this insurance coverage provides money to pay the claims against you. Costs could include the injured's hospital and medical bills, long-term nursing care, or, in the case of death, funeral expenses.

Property Damage Liability—If your car damages the property of others (whether it is a fence, building, or another auto), this pays the claim. One example, from the Insurance Information Institute, an industry-supported center, was a driver who sideswiped a dairy-tank truck with his car. The tanker spilled its entire cargo of fresh milk. Damage was $12,300, including the spilled milk, but the driver was only insured for the minimum amount of property liability of $5,000, and he had to pay the rest of the bill out of his pocket.

Liability limits are expressed as a single limit (such as $50,000 to pay for personal and property damage) or a split limit such as 10/25/5. This means that you have $10,000 worth of coverage for bodily injury liability per person, and a total limit of personal liability of $25,000 per accident; and $5,000 worth of property damage liability per accident. Single limits are generally considered better than the split limits because they allow the money to be spread around to where it is needed.

Medical Payments Coverage—This will pay for the doctor and hospital bills incurred by you and your passengers, regardless of who caused the accident. If it was not your fault, the insurance company can collect from the responsible party's insurance company. The exception to this is coverage in no-fault states. Benefits can be as low as $500 per person, but the Insurance Information Institute recommended more unless you have an extremely good health insurance policy. You might also be asked if you want death and disability coverage in case you die or become disabled in an auto accident. You do not need it if you have good life insurance and disability plans.

Uninsured Motorists Coverage—Pays for injuries caused by an uninsured or a hit-and-run driver. In some states, drivers may find another option, underinsured motorist's coverage. This would pay you if the other driver was at fault and had low limits in his policy. This might be a duplication of coverage if your medical and disability coverage in other policies would handle your bills. Check your policies and get your agent's advice.

Collision Insurance—This is the insurance that pays for physical damage caused by a collision to your own car. Collision coverage can account for a large part of the premium.

Comprehensive Coverage—Gives protection should something happen to your car other than a collision. For example, if your car is stolen, your insurance company will reimburse you for the value of the car. Comprehensive also covers fire, flood, and vandalism.

In states with "no-fault" insurance, personal insurance protection pays for medical bills for you and your passengers. No-fault states also put limits and restrictions on liability lawsuits.

No-fault auto insurance, generally backed by consumer advocates and opposed by personal injury lawyers, originated to eliminate long, expensive lawsuits over accidents. By not assigning fault (in most states with no fault, this only applies to injuries and death, not property damage), victims of accidents are supposed to receive speedy compensation for medical expenses.

Like other types of insurance, premiums for auto insurance vary widely, not only between companies but within the same company from market to market. Such factors such as state regulations, geographic regions (high-crime areas versus low-crime areas), age, sex, marital status, and driving records are used to determine an individual's rates.

While many of these factors are not easily changed, there are some things you can do to get the best rates and coverage possible.

Consumer experts generally agree on the following ways to save money:

1. Shop around. Prices may vary substantially from company to company, depending on state regulations. Ask a general insurance broker to obtain at least three quotes in writing for you. You can also obtain your own quotes through direct writers such as State Farm or Nationwide Mutual.

2. Practice risk management yourself. This means to take the highest deductible you can and still feel comfortable. According to Consumer's Union (publishers of *Consumer Reports*), raising your collision and comprehensive deductible from $100 to $500 can save close to half the cost of your collision and comprehensive coverages. This means you have to balance the risk of losing that $400 of coverage against the potential savings in premiums.

3. Consider dropping collision coverage altogether if you have an older car with low resale value.

4. Take advantage of discounts. Depending on the company and the state, discounts are offered for completion of driver's education training; a "good student" status for young people with high scholastic achievement; a student attending school away from home; use of a car pool; multi-car coverage; use of seat belts; anti-theft devices; a female between the ages of thirty and sixty-four who is the sole driver in a household; senior citizens; farmers; completion of defensive driving course; and non-smokers.

5. Avoid duplication. For example, if you belong to an auto club, you already have towing service. Therefore you do not need this option in an auto insurance policy.

6. Raise your liability limits. Because of the potential for lawsuits, insurance experts recommend you increase your liability coverage (insurance for when you injure somebody or destroy someone's property) above the required state limits. Most states require a total liability minimum of $25,000 or $50,000. But liability coverage of $100,000 or $300,000 is comparatively cheap. Consider using the dollars you save by raising your collision deductible to buy the higher liability coverage limits. *Consumer Reports* recommended at least 100/300/25 on a split limit or $300,000 on a single limit. Another option is to take an umbrella liability policy on your homeowners policy which takes up where other insurance leaves off, covering you usually for up to $1 million).

7. Check insurance costs before you buy a car. You may realize the fancy sports car you can barely afford is not affordable at all when insurance rates are taken into consideration.

8. Check into combining homeowner's and auto insurance policies into a single package. It is called a personal package policy, and it might save you dollars.

9. Notify your company when any changes occur, such as when a son or daughter leaves home.

10. And, very importantly, avoid insurance for rental cars. It could be a waste of money. Rest assured you will be asked by the car rental companies to take it, but they might be steering you in the wrong direction.

The insurance can cost as much as $10 a day if you take all the options. According to the Insurance Information Institute, you should be protected under your own auto insurance policy. Collision insurance is already included in the rental fee, but it usually comes with a fairly high deductible (say $3,000) and you may be asked to take out coverage on the deductible, called collision damage waiver (CDW). That is what the CDW is supposed to be about, they will tell you, to keep you from being stuck with $3,000 worth of bills. But what you probably will not hear from the car rental agent is that you would only be stuck with your own deductible on your regular policies (in most cases). That is, if you can afford a deductible when you drive your own car, why should you pay $5 to $8 per day for CDW in case of an accident on a rental car?

"It may overlap your personal auto policy and will almost certainly duplicate a corporate auto policy if you are covered by one," warned *Changing Times* magazine (March 1986). "The crucial piece of information you need is what your own policies cover and for how much. Only then can you make an intelligent judgment about what additional coverage you need, if any."

Other options on car rental insurance is the personal accident insurance (PAI), covering loss of life and medical expenses; and personal effects coverage (PEC) for damage or loss of personal property in the car.

You may already be covered for these under your auto and homeowner's or renter's policies. It is worth a quick check with your agent or broker to find out if you are covered while driving a rented car. Also, recheck the limit of your deductibles.

But regardless of how carefully you shop, what if the insurance company turns you down? Companies are not obligated to take you on as a customer and high-risk drivers (such as a young, single male with a bad driving record) may find insurance at reasonable costs very hard to find.

If you get turned down, try another company. Or, if you are using an agent who represents several companies, none of which will take you, try another agent.

But if you still come up empty-handed, you may find yourself assigned to the "shared" market as a last resort. Every state has a shared market auto insurance plan (an assigned-risk pool of insurance companies), that will give any licensed driver at least the minimum coverage required under state law. Premiums will be higher than in the voluntary market, and you probably will not get collision coverage (to cover damage to your own car). There are companies that specialize in collision coverage for high risks, but you will pay dearly.

If you feel you have been placed in the assigned-risk plan unfairly, contact your state insurance department and ask for help.

Do not give up. Keep shopping in the voluntary market for a bargain. If you can establish a good driving record for two to three years in the assigned-risk pool, you can usually return to the voluntary market.

HOMEOWNER AND RENTER INSURANCE

Homeowners insurance policies are really a package of different types of insurance that insure your home and can cover you and your belongings even when you are not at home. In 1984, homeowners spent some $13 billion on these coverages.

Beyond what we usually think of as homeowners insurance—protection against fires, tornadoes, and theft—the policy also gives you liability protection (for when you cause injury or damage) and covers your personal goods.

These examples show how broad this coverage can be:

Your son accidentally knocks out another softball player's front tooth while swinging the bat at practice. A homeowners policy could pay for the damages.

Vandals pull out your flowering shrubs while you are away on vacation. You return to find the bushes dead. Your homeowners policy will pay for at least part of the damages.

Your clothes and briefcase are stolen from your hotel room while you are on a business trip. Put in a claim. You should be covered.

There are many potential claims that never get filed because policyholders fail to realize the extent of their coverage. What if your toddler spills chocolate milk on your friend's expensive wool rug while you are visiting? Check your coverage, it may pay for damages.

But beyond the smaller claims, a homeowners policy can mean the difference between a financial disaster for you and the satisfaction of total replacement of everything you might lose when disaster strikes.

However, it is not enough to have a homeowners policy: you must update it regularly, both consumer and insurance experts advise. You must have your house insured for at least 80 percent of the replacement cost. Otherwise you will not be fully reimbursed for losses, even when it is only a partial loss. It is vital to check your policy and discuss your needs with your agent or broker. Do it once a year.

To choose the best homeowners policy, or to decide whether you have the right coverage, look at the different types of coverage. Premiums can vary markedly, but what is covered in the homeowners policies is fairly standard. Policies include insurance to cover repairs or replacement of your house and its contents (non-maintenance); claims against you and members of your household for injury or property damage you cause; and living expenses if you are forced to relocate while repairs are being made.

The four standard forms (there is a special policy, too, for older homes with irreplaceable features as well as policies for condominium owners and renters) are HO-1, (basic); HO-2, (broad); HO-3, (special); and HO-5, (comprehensive).

The policies range from the basic, which covers eleven specified perils, to comprehensive, which covers almost anything except flood, earthquakes, war and nuclear accidents.

If you choose the comprehensive form, you will pay more in premiums, but it will cover more than the less expensive policies.

Here are three actual cases, provided by the Insurance Information Institute, where damages would be covered by the comprehensive or "all-risk" policy (HO-5) but not under the HO-1 or HO-2 policies.

1. A man was walking on floor joists in his attic, when he missed his footing and fell through the ceiling. "All-risk" covered the damages.

2. A man laid a fresh cement driveway, which his wife drove over. Covered by the "all-risk" policy.

3. Expensive out-of-season clothes in storage were inadvertently given to a charity clothing drive. Covered under "all-risk" policy.

Beyond the type of insurance form of coverage to select, consumers should choose a "replacement cost" policy over an actual cash value policy that will pay only for the depreciated cost of your home and belongings.

It is also important to note that the policies place limits on some valuable items such as furs, silver, coin collections, and jewelry. Most policies, for example, place a limit of $1,000 for "unscheduled" (meaning not listed separately) jewelry, watches, furs, and precious and semi-precious stones. Unless you have such valuables listed separately on a schedule with estimated value, you can collect only up to $1,000 regardless of the value of what is stolen or lost.

To insure more costly jewelry and other valuables, you can take out a personal articles floater (the coverage floats or follows the items wherever they are taken) as a rider on your homeowners policy. An appraisal or receipt of each item usually must be furnished to get this coverage.

One thing to be wary of is a common type of floater containing a clause that allows insurers to offer comparable replacement articles (often bought at some of our best "underground" discount stores). If the customer refuses the replacement, however, the insured can offer a cash value for replacement. This price may or may not be what is listed as the estimated value of the jewelry or other covered items. The price, instead, could be what the insurer could expect to pay for a "discounted" replacement item.

If this bothers you, check out a "valued contract" policy. This policy guarantees to pay claims in cash according to the value listed on the schedule.

These seven consumer tips help you get the best value:

1. Again, as with other types of insurance, shop around for price comparison and take the largest deductible you can to save premium dollars.

2. Shop for a policy that offers premium discounts for installation of burglar alarms and smoke detectors, and for using marking devices to identify theft-prone items such as stereos, televisions, and typewriters.

3. Compare your policy's coverage to the current replacement value of your home. Your agent or broker should have a replacement cost guide. Or, you can hire an appraiser or do the estimate yourself by measuring your square footage and getting a cost-per-square-foot estimate from your county builder's association.

4. Check into special coverage for valuable items such as furs, jewelry, antiques, coin and stamp collections, and computer equipment.

5. Buy insurance from a company with an A+ or A rating from Best's Insurance Reports, which should be available at your public library. Best's is an independent rating organization that uses information from state regulatory agencies to rate companies' financial stability.

6. Pay annually, as opposed to semiannually or quarterly. This way you can avoid a finance charge.

7. If you have a claim, notify your agent or broker as soon as possible after the damage occurs. Do not make any permanent repairs until the insurance company adjuster makes an inspection. The company can refuse reimbursement for repairs made prior to inspection, and it is legal for them to do so. Also, it will help if you keep receipts for major purchases in a safe-deposit box away from your home. You should photograph òr inventory your household contents from time to time.

You should consider hiring an independent adjuster to represent you if the damage is extensive. The adjuster represents you in dealing with the insurance company. The fee is about 10 percent of the claim but an adjuster might point out damage that would otherwise be overlooked. Make sure the adjuster is licensed by the state or is a member of the National Association of Public Insurance Adjusters. Ask for references from former clients.

Consumer Reports asked subscribers to tell how they were treated by their insurance companies. The magazine, in August 1985, rated twenty-three companies based on responses from more than two-hundred-thousand people. Companies were rated only if there was a report on at least two hundred resolved claims.

Unfortunately, it is difficult for most consumers to get a policy from the two companies that were rated the best—Amica Mutual and United Services Auto Association (USAA). USAA limits its policies mainly to former and present military officers and their families. Likewise, the majority of new customers for Amica are referred by present policyholders.

The next highest-rated were Erie, U.S. Fidelity & Guaranty, and State Farm, the largest writer of homeowners insurance. (These companies rated third, fourth and fifth, respectively out of the twenty-three companies.)

The second-largest company, Allstate, however, was fourth from the bottom (number twenty out of twenty-three), followed by Metropolitan Property, Prudential, and Geico at the bottom of the list.

You may choose a company, but what happens if that insurance company decides not to choose you? A common reason for denying (or terminating) a contract is that too many claims have been filed. Another reason might be that you live in a high-crime area. Insurance companies have been known to stop issuing policies in certain "high-risk" neighborhoods. The practice, known as redlining, is illegal. Complain to your state regulatory body if you suspect that is what is happening.

If you cannot get insurance after contacting several insurance representatives (again, ask an independent agent or broker for several quotes), see if your state has a FAIR plan. This is a Fair Access to Insurance Requirements plan formed by a pool of private insurers who do business in the state. Ask your insurance agent or contact your state insurance office.

A federal program, to protect residents of high-crime areas from losses due to burglary or robbery, also is available. The program, Federal Crime Insurance Program, requires certain locks and security devices before a resident can qualify. Ask your agent or call the program's toll-free number at 1-800-638-8780.

While about nine out of ten homeowners have insurance, only three out of ten renters carry insurance on their personal possessions, by some estimates. Renters insurance generally covers the same potential losses as a homeowners basic or broad coverage on personal belongings and liability exposures, without covering physical damages on the actual building.

According to *Changing Times* magazine (November 1985), premiums of about $80 to $100 a year would pay for $8,000 worth of coverage and would give $25,000 worth of liability coverage to pay for legal expenses and damages in case you, a member of your family, or pet, causes injuries or damages.

What most renters might not realize is that the landlord, unless proven negligent, is not responsible for damage to the contents of the rental unit.

Without insurance, fire, theft, smoke damage, and a host of other potential disasters could leave the tenant holding the bag (and little else).

LEGAL INSURANCE

Legal services plans are tapping into the vast middle class that is neither rich enough to afford private attorneys, nor poor enough to qualify for free legal assistance. The legal plans—whether in group plans or individually sold, prepaid policies—are giving people who might otherwise hesitate to contact attorneys access to a legal network.

William Bolger, executive director of the National Resource Center for Consumers of Legal Services in Washington D.C. (an industry-supported research center), said some 15 million Americans now participate in legal plans. But that is 15 million out of a potential 165 million members of the middle class. The top 10 percent of Americans, Bolger said, can readily afford legal help. Another 20 percent, because of income, are eligible for legal aid.

Most of those in legal service plans are involved

as part of an employee benefit or other group, such as unions. Only 1.5 million are estimated to have purchased plans individually through insurance companies. But the individual plan is garnering increasing interest. Bolger said the biggest advantage of any legal plan is "preventive law for the middle class."

What can you expect from the plans? Services are limited. Do not expect help with a murder charge, for example. But common problems, such as consumer complaints when your newly purchased auto is full of defects, or estate-planning matters, are covered.

Most problems (Bolger estimates 70 to 80 percent) that could be helped with the aid of an attorney, are cleared up through a telephone call. Bolger cited an American Bar Association legal-needs study: "Only one-third of Americans had used a lawyer more than once in their lifetime despite the fact people are faced with five to six matters a year where legal advice can be helpful."

"Legal services plans help solve the two major difficulties that average middle-class individuals have—they don't know when to go to a lawyer and they don't know how to choose a lawyer. The arrangements are made in advance of the need so that when a situation comes up, people don't procrastinate," Bolger added.

Group-plan participants include most of the nation's schoolteachers and auto workers. The United Auto Workers has nearly 2 million participants, for example, when covered family members are included in the count.

Other group plans involve credit unions and professional organizations. In some plans, enrollment is voluntary and only those choosing to use the service pay the membership costs. Others, called true-group plans, automatically include all persons eligible because of their employment or membership in the organization.

Bolger likes what he called a "no-cost" plan. This involves a group, such as university students or church congregations, which pre-screens and selects lawyers. These lawyers agree to give free initial consultations and give set rates, usually discounted, for more involved work. This way, attorneys are able to "drum up business," and group members have a readily accessible lawyer or group of lawyers to turn to, Bolger explained.

Only a few companies sell prepaid legal insurance for individuals. One, considered a pioneer in the field, Pre-Paid Legal Services, of Ada, Oaklahoma, allows you to choose your own lawyer for a variety of services, for about $100 a year.

The plan (1-800-654-7757) is sold in about twenty states. It gives covered members and their families free, thirty-minute consultations for each personal (note the word "personal," business matters are excluded) legal problem. There is a unlimited number of subjects, but each subject may be repeated every ninety days.

In addition to the half-hour consultations, the plan gives more coverage, but only for a limited number of problems. For example, the plan will cover you for court representation for traffic tickets and some criminal auto-related charges not covered under your auto liability policy. Drug and alcohol-related charges and appeals of convictions are excluded. It also provides up to $250 for attorney fees to help reinstate your driver's license and up to $250 for legal assistance to help collect damages when your auto, private boat, or motorcycle is involved in an accident.

Additionally, it pays $5,000 in attorney's fees the first year, and up to $25,000 by the fifth year of coverage, for a "legal defense benefit," to cover some specific problems.

Divorce, for example, would only be covered under the free half-hour consultation, not the legal defense benefit. But a job-related criminal charge could be covered under the legal defense benefit.

Examples of benefits paid listed in the Pre-Paid Legal Services company literature:

Pre-Paid paid $130 on an Oklahoma City member's claim covering four separate one-half hour consultations at one time: what to do about defective merchandise, considerations in selling his home, the consequences of bringing suit against someone, and provisions for his will.

Pre-Paid paid an attorney $240 to represent a member in Midwest City, Oklahoma, in the recovery of damages done to her automobile.

Pre-Paid paid a Colorado Springs attorney $340 to defend a member on a criminal suit charging him with assault while removing an irate customer from his store.

Pre-Paid paid $2,500 in defense of a Muskogee man on a manslaughter charge.

THE INSURANCE CONTROVERSY

Not only do consumers have to worry about getting the best value for their insurance dollars, but they are also affected by insurance on all levels. The cost restaurants must pay for liability coverage will, in part, be reflected in the price of your dinner entree. Liability insurance for day-care centers (horror stories abound about policy cancellations and sky-rocketing insurance costs for operators) are paid for by mothers and fathers who leave their children at such centers. Malpractice insurance also shows up in your doctor bills.

At the eye of the current storm of controversy is the so-called tort-reform movement. It began in 1985 with a multi-million dollar public relations campaign by the insurance industry.

The insurance industry, aided by manufacturers, professionals, medical specialists, and their trade associations, is fighting for limits on awards in lawsuits such as medical malpractice suits.

The opponents of this movement charge that the industry is trying to create panic by widespread cancellation of insurance coverage in some industries and professions. Opposing the tort reform are groups like NICO, Ralph Nader's Public Citizen, trial lawyers, trade unions, and other consumer groups.

The insurance industry, through such groups as the Insurance Information Institute, charges that high-dollar jury awards have driven the cost of insurance to impossible levels.

The consumer groups are crying foul. They charge that the industry dug its own grave through vicious price-cutting in the 1970s. The idea is that interest rates were so high in the late 1970s, that companies would violate sound underwriting practices (taking on higher and higher risks) in order to draw the premium dollar to be invested. When interest rates dropped and claims came in, the bottom fell out.

Consumer advocate Ralph Nader said: "The goal of both the business policyholders and the insurance industry is to take it out of the common law, take it away from the jury and the judge, and put it into a codified system in a formula of compensation rates which then can be changed in accordance with political action committee money and all the regular influence peddling that reaches the ears and pockets of legislators. They cannot stand a system they cannot control. They cannot stand a system they cannot totally predict, budget in as a cost of doing business, and then pass on to the consumer."

Laws and regulations governing insurance vary widely from state to state. Each state has a commissioner or other officials designated to enforce these laws and regulations. A consumer should contact the state authority if a problem cannot be solved with an insurance company. Also, many insurance departments will give guidance on how to choose insurance. They can provide you with vital information such as the loss-ratio of a particular company, which will give you an idea of the consumer track record by telling you how much of every $1 in insurance premiums is paid back to the consumer as a whole.

Write or call them.

ALABAMA
Tharpe Forrester
Acting Commissioner of
   Insurance
135 South Union Street
Montgomery, Alabama 36130
(205) 269-3550

ALASKA
John George
Director of Insurance
Pouch D
Juneau, Alaska 99811
(907) 465-2515

ARIZONA
S. David Childers
Director of Insurance
1601 West Jefferson
Phoenix, Arizona 85007
(602) 255-4862

ARKANSAS
Robert Eubanks III
Insurance Commissioner
400–18 University Tower
   Building
Little Rock, Arkansas 72204
(501) 371-1325

CALIFORNIA
Bruce Bunner
Insurance Commissioner
600 South Commonwealth
14th Floor
Los Angeles, California
   90005

(213) 736-2551

COLORADO
John Kezer
Commissioner of Insurance
303 West Colfax, 5th Floor
Denver, Colorado 80204
(303) 573-3410

CONNECTICUT
Peter W. Gillies
Insurance Commissioner
165 Capitol Avenue
Room 425
State Office Building
Hartford, Connecticut 06106
(203) 566-2810

DELAWARE
David N. Levinson
Insurance Commissioner
21 The Green
Dover, Delaware 19901
(302) 736-4251

DISTRICT OF COLUMBIA
Marguerite C. Stokes
Acting Superintendent of
   Insurance
614 H Street N.W.
Suite 512
Washington, D.C. 20001
(202) 727-7419

FLORIDA
Bill Gunter
Insurance Commissioner

State Capitol Building
Plaza Level 11
Tallahassee, Florida 32301
(904) 488-3440

GEORGIA
Johnnie Caldwell
Insurance Commissioner
West Tower Floyd Building
Suite 716
#2 Martin Luther King, Jr.
  Drive
Atlanta, Georgia 30334
(404) 656-2056

HAWAII
Mario R. Ramil
Insurance Commissioner
1010 Richards Street
Honolulu, Hawaii 96813
(808) 548-7505

IDAHO
Wayne Soward
Director of Insurance
700 West State Street
Boise, Idaho 83720
(208) 334-2250

ILLINOIS
John Washburn
Director of Insurance
320 West Washington Street
Fourth Floor
Springfield, Illinois 62701
(217) 782-4515

INDIANA
Harry E. Eakin
Commissioner of Insurance
509 State Office Building
Indianapolis, Indiana 46204
(317) 232-2386

IOWA

Bruce W. Foudree
Commissioner of Insurance
State Office Building, G23
Ground Floor
Des Moines, Iowa 50319
(515) 281-5705

KANSAS
Fletcher Bell
Commissioner of Insurance
420 Southwest 9th Street
Topeka, Kansas 66612
(913) 296-3071

KENTUCKY
Gilbert McCarty
Insurance Commissioner
229 West Main Street
P.O. Box 517
Frankfort, Kentucky 40602
(502) 564-3630

LOUISIANA
Sherman A. Bernard
Commissioner of Insurance
P.O. Box 94214
Baton Rouge, Louisiana
  70804
(504) 342-5328

MAINE
Theodore T. Briggs
Superintendent of Insurance
Hollowell Annex
State House, Station #34
Augusta, Maine 04333
(207) 289-3101

MARYLAND
Edward J. Muhl
Insurance Commissioner
501 St. Paul Place
7th Floor South
Baltimore, Maryland 21202
(301) 659-6300

MASSACHUSETTS
Peter Hiam
Commissioner of Insurance
100 Cambridge Street
Boston, Massachusetts
 02202
(617) 727-3333

MICHIGAN
Nancy A. Baerwaldt
Commissioner of Insurance
P.O. Box 30220
Lansing, Michigan 48909
(517) 373-0220

MINNESOTA
Michael A. Hatch
Deputy Commissioner of
 Commerce
500 Metro Square Building
Fifth Floor
St. Paul, Minnesota 55101
(612) 296-6907

MISSISSIPPI
George Dale
Commissioner of Insurance
1804 Walter Sillers Building
P.O. Box 79
Jackson, Mississippi 39205
(601) 359-3569

MISSOURI
C. Donald Ainsworth
Director of Insurance
301 West High, Route 630
P.O. Box 690
Jefferson City, Missouri
 65102
(314) 751-2451

MONTANA
Andrea Bennett
Commissioner of Insurance
Mitchell Building

P.O. Box 4009
Helena, Montana 59604
(406) 444-2996

NEBRASKA
Michael J. Dugan
Director of Insurance
301 Centennial Mall South
State Office Building
P.O. Box 94699
Lincoln, Nebraska 68509
(402) 471-2201

NEVADA
David Gates
Commissioner of Insurance
Nye Building
201 South Falls Street
Carson City, Nevada 89710
(702) 885-4270

NEW HAMPSHIRE
Louis E. Bergeron
Insurance Commissioner
169 Manchester Street
Concord, New Hampshire
 03301
(603) 271-2261

NEW JERSEY
Hazel Gluck
Commissioner of Insurance
201 East State Street
Box CN 325
Trenton, New Jersey 08625
(609) 292-5363

NEW MEXICO
Vincente B. Jasso
Superintendent of Insurance
PERA Building
P.O. Drawer 1269
Santa Fe, New Mexico
 87504-1269
(505) 827-4535

NEW YORK
James P. Corcoran
Superintendent of Insurance
160 West Broadway
New York, New York 10013
(212) 602-0429
1-800-342-3736 (toll free)

NORTH CAROLINA
James E. Long
Commissioner of Insurance
Dobbs Building
P.O. Box 26387
Raleigh, North Carolina
27611
(919) 733-7343
1-800-662-7777 (toll
free—North Carolina only)

NORTH DAKOTA
Earl R. Pomeroy
Commissioner of Insurance
Capitol Building, Fifth Floor
Bismarck, North Dakota
58505
(701) 224-2444

OHIO
George Fabe
Director of Insurance
2100 Stella Court
Columbus, Ohio 43215
(614) 466-3584

OKLAHOMA
Gerald Grimes
Insurance Commissioner
408 Will Rogers Memorial
Building
Oklahoma City, Oklahoma
73105
(405) 521-2828

OREGON
Josephine M. Driscoll

Insurance Commissioner
Insurance Division,
Commerce Building
Salem, Oregon 97310
(503) 378-4271

PENNSYLVANIA
William R. Muir, Jr.
Commissioner of Insurance
Strawberry Square
13th Floor
Harrisburg, Pennsylvania
17120
(717) 787-5173

RHODE ISLAND
Clifton A. Moore
Insurance Commissioner
100 North Maine Street
Providence, Rhode Island
02903
(401) 277-2223

SOUTH CAROLINA
John G. Richards
Chief Insurance
Commissioner
2711 Middleburg Drive
P.O. Box 4067
Columbia, South Carolina
29204
(803) 758-3266

SOUTH DAKOTA
Susan L. Walker
Director of Insurance
Insurance Building
320 North Nicollet
Pierre, South Dakota 57501
(605) 773-3563

TENNESSEE
John C. Neff
Commissioner of Commerce
and Insurance

211

114 State Office Building
Nashville, Tennessee 37219
(615) 741-2241

TEXAS
Lyndon Olson, Jr.
Chairman, State Board of
  Insurance
1110 San Jacinto Boulevard
Austin, Texas 78786
(512) 475-3726

UTAH
Roger C. Day
Commissioner of Insurance
160 East 300 South
Salt Lake City, Utah 84145
(801) 530-6400

VERMONT
David T. Bard
Commissioner of Banking
  and Insurance
State Office Building
Montpelier, Vermont 05602
(802) 828-3301

VIRGINIA
James M. Thomson
Commissioner of Insurance
700 Jefferson Building
P.O. Box 1157
Richmond, Virginia 23209
(804) 786-3741

WASHINGTON
Dick Marquardt
Insurance Commissioner
Insurance Building AQ21
Olympia, Washington 98504
(206) 753-7301

WEST VIRGINIA
Fred Wright
Insurance Commissioner

2100 Washington Street,
  East
Charleston, West Virginia
  25305
(304) 348-3386

WISCONSIN
Thomas P. Fox
Commissioner of Insurance
P.O. Box 7873
Madison, Wisconsin 53707
(608) 266-3585

WYOMING
Robert W. Schrader
Insurance Commissioner
122 West 25th Street,
  Herschler Building
Cheyenne, Wyoming 82002
(307) 777-7401

AMERICAN SAMOA
Lyle L. Richmond
Counsel to the Governor
Office of the Governor
Pago Pago, American Samoa
  96797
(written complaints only)

GUAM
Dave Fantos
Insurance Commissioner
West Marine Drive
855 West Marine Drive
Agana, Guam 96910
(written complaints only)

PUERTO RICO
Juan Antonio Garcia
Commissioner of Insurance
P.O. Box 8330
Fernandez Juntos Station
Santurce, Puerto Rico 00910
(809) 724-6565

VIRGIN ISLANDS
Julio A. Brady
Commissioner of Insurance
Office of Lieutenant
  Governor

P.O. Box 450
Charlotte Amalie
St. Thomas, Virgin Islands
  00801
(809) 744-2991

KNOWLEDGE IS POWER

Insurance is such a sticky, complicated matter that many of us just ignore the subject altogether. This is a mistake. Knowledge is power.

A basic understanding of insurance and how it works can help avoid sucker pitches from salesmen. Always be suspicious of any insurance that covers a specific item, incident, or illness. Look for broad, comprehensive coverage. Always, always compare prices and policies with the offerings of other companies. Shop around.

Once you have checked your coverage and updated it, stay informed on happenings in the insurance industry. *Consumer Reports* and *Changing Times* magazines both have excellent, regular features on insurance.

A basic understanding of insurance deflates the mystique of the business. It could help you save thousands of dollars over your lifetime, or save you financially when disaster strikes.

For further information, one of the best books around explaining the workings of the insurance industry (from a critical viewpoint) is *The Invisible Bankers*, by Andrew Tobias (The Linden Press, Simon & Schuster, New York 1982).

The National Insurance Consumer Organization is also a good source for information (they will give you a copy of Tobias' book free with your $25 annual membership fee). To join, write to 344 Commerce Street, Alexandria, Virginia 22314. Membership also entitles you to the consumer alert series. *Taking the Bite Out of Insurance* is available for $7.25.

Joe A. Mintz' newsletter, The NROCA (that is acorn spelled backwards) is available for $36 a year, P.O. Box 12066, Dallas, Texas 75225.

The American Council of Life Insurance and the Health Insurance Association of America operate a toll-free hot line to answer questions concerning life and health insurance. The number is 1-800-423-8000.

The Insurance Information Institute also offers a hot line to answer questions pertaining to property and liability insurance (1-800-221-4954). Ask these two groups for a list of free publications available.

JEWELRY

There is an axiom in the appraisal world: the value of a piece of goods—be it diamonds or real estate—is only worth what a willing buyer will pay to an unpressured seller. This is a particularly important point to remember when purchasing a precious gem. Since no two stones are alike, there is really no benchmark a shopper can rely on to compare price and quality. The ultimate price of a piece of jewelry is determined by how much markup you, the shopper, are willing to pay.

Henry Kostman, one of Dallas' leading discount jewelers, trenchantly observed: "Customers are charged what the market will bear."

Because price is very much in the eye of the beholder, true discounts are almost impossible to determine. Just because a jeweler advertises that some of his merchandise is on sale for 50 percent off does not guarantee a bargain. The consumer has no way of knowing whether the original list price was inflated before the sale began. Such misleading—though not illegal—advertising is common in the industry, maintain observers.

America's jewelers have another advantage over consumers star-struck with love and looking for an engagement ring or eager to outdo the Jones's with this year's anniversary present. The science of gemology is as technical as engineering the space shuttle. The uninitiated and the uneducated can easily become the unwitting dupe of a greedy jeweler using his superior knowledge to his advantage.

The wise consumer should always ask to see a loose diamond under the harsh glare of a high-powered microscope before ever pulling out the checkbook. Jewelers can easily hide flaws under prongs. Most jewelers will appraise a piece for a fee, either charging a flat fee ranging from $25 to $50 or on a percentage cost basis. Even though "14 k" is engraved on the inside of the ring, this does not ensure that an unscrupulous jeweler isn't trying to pass off 12 karat goods instead.

Fortunately, a shopper does not need a graduate degree from the Gemological Institute of America (the Harvard for jewelers) to learn how to be a wise shopper. Kostman suggests researching your diamond purchase as thoroughly and carefully as you do the selection of your automobiles. If you research your purchase properly, you can enjoy your gem knowing you paid a fair price for what you bought.

There is one way to generate significant savings, and that is to shop at a discount jeweler. These jewelers are sometimes called "upstairs" jewelers because they are frequently located in office parks instead of glitzy malls.

All the rules of being a wary consumer apply here, of course. But discount jewelers can afford to charge less for their goods and still earn a tidy profit. They lease space in office buildings instead of malls, which means they enjoy much lower rental rates. Their inventory is a fraction of a retail jeweler's, which lowers both their carrying costs as well as their vulnerability to theft. And they rarely advertise (a large expense passed on to consumers), relying almost solely on word-of-mouth referrals. Because of these economic advantages, a reputable discount jeweler can share his savings with his customers.

Each gemstone has different characteristics and different considerations. Here's what to watch for in each category.

DIAMONDS

Five and a half tons of earth are needed to produce 4.5 carats of cuttable diamonds. The circuitous route from Africa to your local jewelry store greatly influences the price tag placed on your purchase.

South Africa, Zaire, and Sierra Leone are the major diamond producing lands. Machines dig up the blue earth and dump the soil into a mechanized sieve. The rocks, dirt, and minerals fall through the mesh, leaving the diamonds entrapped, stuck to an oiled wheel. (Diamonds have an affinity for oil.) The diamond miners plunge the rough stones into an acid bath for their first cleaning. Then experienced cutters cut a small window in the crystal. A trained cutter evaluates and grades the stone and places it in an appropriate parcel. Most mines. assemble parcels with stones of varying quality.

De Beers Ltd., the mammoth South African company, virtually controls the world diamond market. Ten times a year De Beers sells its sorted stones to sight holders and cutters. A sight holder is a businessman authorized by De Beers who receives the first cut in the selection. Sight holders select the best of the diamonds available. They then sell them to cutters.

About a dozen large U.S. retailers have their own sight holders. Zales, for example, is one. Employing a sight holder allows the retailer or manufacturer to maintain tighter controls over the cost and quality of his goods.

Cutters perform the first magic on the diamond, transforming it from a rough crystal into the familiar cut stone. It is not unusual for ten different processes and ten different people to work on one diamond to achieve a specific effect. While these diamond cutters can be located anywhere in the world, the lion's share of the work is done in either Antwerp, Belguim, or New York City.

The cutter can then sell the diamond to either a rough diamond broker who continues to work his wizardry or to a polished diamond broker. The latter typically sells the finished stone to the retailer.

Until the stone reaches the retailer, the markup has been relatively modest, given the number of hands that have worked on the diamond. When the stone surfaces at a retail jewelry store, the markup is generally no more than 50 percent from the original price. Typically each person who works on the stone takes a 10 percent markup. Steven Schwarz, owner of Diamond Insurance Appraisers, a Dallas appraiser and jeweler, said this 50 percent markup over the original rough crystal price is well worth the money given the cost of the specialized equipment needed to cut diamonds and the skill and training required to correctly cut one.

Diamonds, unlike all other precious stones, have four set characteristics which consumers can use as a yardstick when researching their purchases. The Gemological Institute of America, located in Santa Monica, California, has developed these standards. They are called the "four Cs": clarity, color, cut and carat weight.

Donna Dirlam, a spokesperson for the Institute, explained these four categories and described what consumers should consider when choosing a diamond.

Color—The GIA color system assigns a letter designation to each stone depending on the quality of its color. The letter scale ranges from D, the finest, purest stone, to Z, the least desirable. D stones are white or almost colorless. E, F, and G stones begin to have a yellowish tint. As a stone moves further down the alphabet, the color becomes gray. Dirlam said the untrained eye can have great difficulty determining the different gradations of color because the shades are subtle.

Clarity—This measure describes the amount and kinds of flaws in the stone. Scratches, nicks, and chips lower the value of a diamond. The diamond may also have particles inside the stone which are called inclusions. Diamonds may have a host of different mineral deposits within their crystals. Garnet, for example, is commonly found within diamonds. Imperfections close to the surface of the diamond can affect the stone's ultimate durability, making it much earlier to crack.

Carat—This is the measurement used to weigh the stone. There are 100 points in a carat.

Cut—This refers to the precise measurements and angles etched into the stone to allow light to cast brilliantly within it, not the overall shape of the stone—such as an oval. Diamonds are cut in facets which are in direct proportions to ensure the proper refraction of light.

Jewelers insist color and clarity are the two most important considerations when purchasing a diamond. "The biggest mistake most consumers make when purchasing a diamond is they prefer to buy a large stone," observed Schwarz. "They have mistaken carat weight for beauty. The average buyer purchases a diamond which weighs between one and two carats. Most buyers would buy a two carat stone with a lot of flaws. What they should be buying is a one carat stone that is cleaner and clearer."

Today technology allows jewelers to calculate the exact proportions of all angles of the cut of a diamond needed to provide the maximum amount of reflection and refraction. Light is reflected in the diamond when it bounces off its outer surfaces. When light enters the stone, it bounces around inside the stone and then leaps out. This is called refraction. When a stone is cut improperly, it loses the ability to reflect and refract light. Reflection and refraction give diamonds their luster and their shimmering glitter.

If a diamond is cut incorrectly, light will get lost in the crystalline abyss and never bounce back to the viewer's eye. If the pavilion or bottom part of the diamond is cut too shallow, light leaks out the bottom, instead of bouncing around inside the stone. If the pavilion is cut too deep, light leaks out the side. Either way, the faulty cut chisels away the beauty inherent in that stone. That is why cut is so critical.

Technology has determined the ideal cut for diamonds. These proportions are called Tolkowsky's proportions, named after the gentleman who discovered them. Since there is no such thing as perfection in the world, there is no stone that is cut exactly according to Tolkowsky's proportions. But you can use them to see how close to perfect your prospective stone is.

The table or top plane of the diamond should be no more than 53 percent of the width of the stone. The crown, or space fanning out under the table, should be no more than 16.2 percent of the length of the stone. The girdle, or widest expanse of diamond, should be no more than 1 to 2 percent of the length of the stone. The pavilion, or lower triangle, of the diamond should comprise 43.1 percent of the length of the gem. A diamond cut to these proportions will return the maximum amount of light to the eye.

Jewelers can "chisel" unsuspecting consumers by cutting the pavilion too deep. That adds weight—and cost—to the diamond but takes away from the sheen by robbing the diamond of light. The same goes for jewelers selling diamonds with girdles too thick. Once again, that adds weight and cost, but nothing else, to the stone. If you are going to pay for weight, buy weight that is proportionally correct.

Jewelers can easily hide flaws in a diamond by covering the imperfection with a prong. If you are buying a stone, examine it before the jeweler locks it into a setting.

Schwarz recommended looking at the stone under a microscope with a 10-power magnification. Microscopes are easy to use (everybody had to take biology in high school) and have an internal light source to provide more accurate viewing.

Even if the jeweler offers you his jeweler's loop, don't think it can protect you from an unfair purchase. Schwarz said most novices hold the loop away from their bodies, rendering it ineffective. The loop is a technical instrument which requires training and experience to use accurately. Your stone might have flaws and you might not know how to see them. If you want to trust a loop, ask for an allochromatic loop. This one has three lens.

Always look at a diamond sitting on a white background. Never judge the color of a diamond if the background is black. Rennie Ellen, a diamond wholesaler and manufacturer in the diamond district in New York City, said that a dark backdrop will make the diamond reflect a rainbow of colors, even though it could be very flawed in cut or composition.

Unlike Shakespeare's rose (is a rose is a rose), an industrial diamond is a cut below a diamond destined for a precious setting. Some unscrupulous jewelers set industrial grade diamonds in the same mount as their high ticket counterparts. The naked eye and an inexperienced consumer cannot tell the difference. Only an expert who can distinguish the difference in cut can separate the commercial from the industrial.

Ellen said consumers can be easily taken in by jewelers selling painted diamonds and precious stones, which can be passed on to shoppers as purer in content or value than they really are. Some jewelers use various dyes, rosins, and plastics to doctor gems and make them more appealing to the naked eye. The paint comes off in a low grade acid bath. Have an expert do the dunking, if you are worried about the stone.

Maxine Bennett, part owner of Castle Cap Jewelry in Dallas, said turquoise can be altered through "stabilization" processes, for example. The texture and strength of the stone can be changed by applying rosin to the stone. Though an expert jeweler can uncover the truth through observation, Bennett said it is almost impossible for the average shopper to know anything has been done to the stone. One popular misconception is that lighting a match to turquoise will cause an altered stone to become pliable and exhibit a loss of hues, according to Bennett. However, there are some methods to spot the real from the phony, the valuable from the valueless.

So is the case of cubic zirconia, a synthetic copy of a diamond. "It has no flaws inside it whatsoever," said Bennett. "A cubic zirconia (simply called cz's among jewelers) is very, very white . . . only investment quality diamonds worth $10,000 or more would be so clear to the naked eye. Ninety percent of the time, you can tell a cz from a diamond by using a simple test. Place the stone over a book or a line of copy in a magazine or newspaper. If you can read the copy, or the line is unbroken, nine times out of ten you're looking at a cz."

Ellen also sells cubic zirconia through her wholesale establishment in New York City, using separate offices for working with and displaying the cz's. The reason is though it is easy for a trained jeweler, upon observation, to differentiate between the two, mistakes can happen. Being an artificially manufactured stone, cz's can splinter under a cutting tool far easier than a diamond. Cz's also can melt. However, they also have hues and colors just like real diamonds.

"For your own protection, always ask for a detailed bill of sale. This document should list the size and weight of the diamond and the weight and type of gold," said Ellen.

Make sure the information—especially the weight—

of the diamond is listed separately. And insist that the jeweler clearly designate the color of the gold by letter. White gold is not descriptive enough. Your invoice should read something like "14 karat white gold grade g."

Once you leave the store, the invoice stands as is. If there is a dispute later and the bill of sale is not detailed enough, it is your problem.

COLORED STONES

While diamonds are without question the stone of choice for America's newly engaged brides, that is not the case elsewhere in the world. In Europe sapphires and rubies—in combination with diamonds—are equally popular. American jewelers say these two colored stones found their allure rising when Prince Charles gave Princess Diana a sapphire and diamond engagement ring before their nuptials. And Prince Andrew purposely selected a ruby as his engagement stone for Sarah Ferguson to complement her red hair.

Unlike diamonds, colored stones do not have a scientific yardstick like Tolkowsky's proportions to technically measure quality. Consequently, very few jewelers can accurately assess the quality of a colored stone. The most famous example of professional ignorance of colored stones concerns the British crown jewels. For centuries, one of the most famous stones was the Ballis ruby. Only in the twentieth century did jewelers have enough tools to discover the stone was not a ruby at all but a red spinel, an even rarer stone. It turned out to be the largest red spinel ever found. But a ruby it was not.

The roster of colored stones includes emerald, beryl emerald, ruby, sapphire, garnet, tourmaline, topaz, cat's eye, onyx, aquamarine, and opal. All the birth stones are colored stones.

Since colored stones are far softer a material than the steely diamond, they can be cut on less sophisticated machines. The direction of the polish of the facets can all be in the same direction. With a diamond, each facet must be polished in a different direction. "That means diamond cutters must be much more skilled than cutters of colored stones," said Schwarz.

Diamonds have a uniformity and consistency of construction that colored stones lack. While diamonds come out of the ground with the same physical properties, the characteristics of colored gems can vary widely. For example, the gradations in a diamond's color are quite difficult to ascertain with the naked eye. But the color of rubies can range from a light red to a dark purplish red.

It is very hard for man to manufacture a diamond without it looking fake. That is not so with colored stones. It is quite easy to fabricate a fake with synthetic materials. Also, these stones can be treated to enhance their color and thus falsely boost their value.

Some unscrupulous cutters in foreign countries use nuclear radiation to alter the color of a colored stone before it ever gets to the jeweler's hands. They place the stones in a Van deGraaff generator which bombards the gems with radiation. Only a spectroscope can determine whether a machine has altered the color of a stone. Spectroscopes are effective in protecting consumers against irradiated stones in all categories except topaz.

Spectroscopes can be purchased from chemistry supply stores or jewelry supply houses, although the easiest and cheapest way for a consumer to check authenticity can be attained in a visit to most retail jewelry stores.

The spectroscope under an expert eye can determine if opals have been boiled in sugar-treated water. Opals can also be baked in a bag of manure to give them a smoked look. This technique can transform a pedestrian white opal into a rare looking and much sought after black opal. A look through a microscope can reveal if opals have been treated.

Matrix opals, which flash a whirlwind of colors in the stone, are also very rare. Greg Sherman, owner of Sherman Opals in Syndey, Australia, said a real matrix will have its colors very sharply defined. If the colors are fuzzy, beware.

Often the blue in an aquamarine has a faded hue. Some jewelers will buy a dime store magic marker and color the girdle. This trick will intensify the color throughout the stone.

Jade can be dyed. Lapis lazuli is an opaque, deep-blue colored mineral which is sometimes sold as a gemstone. The rock is porous and can be dipped in grape juice, then hot wax applied, and lightly polished to resemble true jade. Once again a microscopic exam should reveal whether the stone has been tampered with.

Jewelers say smart consumers will always ask them if the stone they are considering has been treated. If the jeweler says no, get the denial in writing. If, after your third party appraiser breaks the bad news that the stone has indeed been tampered with, you can take the jeweler to court. Just remember, it is up to you and your appraiser to bring the microscope into the courtroom to prove it.

Most likely, you are going to place your gemstone in some kind of setting. Schwarz said, "Settings provide a jeweler with many opportunities to rip off a consumer." One of the easiest ways to be cheated is to not receive the karat weight of gold for which you have paid. An acid test is the only way to know for sure.

The term "karat gold jewelry" when used by itself refers to pure gold and the percentage of the pure gold within a piece of jewelry. It is a measure of purity. Pure gold, however, is soft and pliable and unsuitable for the hard knocks of everyday jewelry wear. So base metals are added for hardness. The designation 14 karat gold means 14 parts of the mixture represent gold; the other 10 parts are made of metal, meaning 58 percent of the item is made of pure gold. Likewise, 18 karat gold represents 18 parts pure gold and 10 parts base metal. The higher the karat rating, the more gold is in the jewelry.

There is a way to keep your jeweler honest and test the actual proportions of gold in your jewelry. Your jeweler should own a scratch block and a series of wands. The end of each wand is dipped with a specific karat purity of gold. If you are buying a setting made of 14 karat, have the jeweler take the 14 karat wand and draw a line across the block. Then take a sample of the setting you are about to buy and draw a parallel line. The jeweler then grabs an eye dropper and applies acid to both lines.

If your setting is indeed 14 karat gold, the acid will eat its line at the same pace as your jeweler's stripe. The test measures how quickly the materials other than gold are consumed by the acid. If your line disappears faster than the 14 karat line, start growing angry. That proves you are not buying 14 karat goods. A honest jeweler should agree to perform this acid test cheerfully.

Most major retailers who do not manufacture their own goods do not have the opportunity to add non-gold filler to their settings. But the smaller jeweler who makes all his pieces himself can alter the karat weight of gold. Never be ashamed to ask the jeweler to test the gold in front of you.

When dealing with gold, you have the power of the federal government behind you. The Federal Trade Commission enforces very strict rules on gold. The government requires gold to be 58 percent pure. The law states within that parameter, if you alloy gold and stamp in 14 k, it had better measure up to 14 karat.

If you suspect a jeweler is gypping you on the gold content, you can report him to the FTC or the Federal Bureau of Weights and Measures. They have the authority to demand a core assay of the jeweler's entire inventory.

This entails drilling a tiny hole through the entire piece and then testing the samples for gold content. If the inventory fails the test, the FTC can either fine the jeweler or close his shop and put him out of business.

WATCHES

None of the above applies to watches. While jewelers are trained to fashion by hand all or part of their inventory, they have not a clue how to assemble all the intricate inner workings of a watch. The Swiss watchmakers are masters of their craft; they do nothing but make watches. The original factory product is nonpareil.

If you want to buy a Rolex or other highbrow Swiss watch, go to an authorized distributor of the watch and nowhere else. There are a limited number of these annointed sales outlets. In the Dallas-Fort Worth area, for example, there are only five authorized Rolex dealers: Linz Jewelers; Black, Starr & Frost; Corrigan's; Fred Joaillier; and Tiffany & Co.

Real Rolexes are expensive. The two-toned gold and stainless steel watch costs about $2,600 new. A man's 14 karat gold datejust president's watch has a suggested retail price of about $8,850. If you are buying a new Rolex at significantly lower prices, be wary.

One way to tell is by the box. All men's president watches are sold in a leather box. The ladies' president comes in a needlepoint box. (The boxes add $60 and $55 to the price of the watch, respectively.) If you buy a watch and it comes in the box, you still cannot be sure the Rolex is real. Fort Worth Gold and Silver Exchange Inc., a company sued by Rolex and eventually put out of business, ran extensive classified ads in the newspaper soliciting watches from consumers and jewelers as well as selling Rolexes at substantial discounts. The company would purchase the watches including the boxes and then sell its fake Rolexes in the real box.

Learning how Fort Worth Gold and Silver Exchange did business will teach you how to spot an adulterated Rolex. The company, which declared bankruptcy in January, 1986, was substituting cheaper parts on the bands, dials, and faces of both new and used Rolexes, according to John Flarity, attorney for Gibney, Anthony & Flarity in Manhattan, the law firm handling legal matters for Rolex Inc. Flarity said the Texas company may have also purchased and sold watches that were smuggled into the United States. In this way, importers could escape import duties, which account for approximately 14 percent of the watch's base price.

Flarity said the best test to determine if a Rolex watch has been tampered with is to submerge it in water. Every Rolex is waterproof. If a jeweler has replaced parts, the adulterated watch frequently leaks when plunged into a pool.

The attorney also suggested checking for scratches around the face of the watch. Also, the hands might be bent slightly from unskilled hands tampering with the movement.

Another trick is to change the bands. Because of the mountains of gold that comprise the band, here is where the real expense of the watch lies. Some unscrupulous jewelers will substitute the Swiss band for a cheaper copy from Italy or Hong Kong. These bands generally do not have the same amount of gold and do not have the precision of the factory craftsmanship.

Flarity warned consumers to never buy expensive watches from mail-order catalogues. Fort Worth Gold and Silver Exchange enjoyed a healthy mail-order business. When the company started to fail, he said it cashed its customers' checks but never mailed the goods. Today they stand in a long line of other creditors at the bankruptcy court.

Finally, Flarity said consumers should beware of discounted prices. He said 25 percent off listed price is possible if a dealer wants to move his inventory faster. But if goods are marked 50 percent below suggested retail, he said to question the watch's authenticity.

Despite Flarity's warnings, a shopper can get a replica of a genuine Rolex from non-authorized retailers such as Walnut Coin and Jewelry Exchange of Dallas. Elliot Cashdon said he can sell the same watch going for $10,000 at a mall jewelry store for about half the price. While an authorized warranty may not be available with a facsimile, he said his own store offers a two year warranty.

Although replicas abound, there also are pure facsimiles manufactured overseas and in the United States which have the look of fine quality, but are instead cheap imitations of their high-priced cousins. The age-old adage "you get what you pay for" certainly applies, for a fake priced under $50 usually comes without a warranty and is more subject to breakage under normal wear than a finely crafted timekeeper.

Such is the chance the shopper is taking when purchasing a replica—they may be able to save a lot of money, but they are banking that their seller will still be there if the watch becomes defective during the warranty period, if a warranty is offered at all.

UPSTAIRS JEWELERS

Discount jewelers can offer consumers the same quality of goods for a much reduced price. Their lowered cost of doing business produces their significant savings.

Kostman, an upstairs jeweler, said "the overhead expense strangles" the typical retailer. All key overhead expenses are greatly reduced for a discount jeweler. The store's square foot rental costs are much lower. Mall rates rise upward from about $20 per square foot, but rent in an outlet mall or office building can be as low as $10 a square foot. The $10 per square foot price differential becomes readily apparent in the cost of merchandise.

Mall owners also receive a portion of every tenant's monthly earnings. At the Galleria in Dallas, for example, every retailer pays 7 percent of his monthly gross sales to his landlord. These percentages range from a low of 3 percent to a high of 7 percent in upscale space like the Galleria.

"Someone has to pay these costs," said Kostman. "They are factored into the price of the merchandise."

Mall stores generally have more inventory on hand and, therefore, spend more money for protection and insurance. Rapael Alfandary, owner of Rapael's, a discount jewelry store in Austin, said the cost of insurance alone runs into the thousands of dollars in annual premiums.

Insurance is expensive. But jewelers are also required to have an insurance block policy, which translates into more operating expenses. To meet the qualifications to get the policy, jewelers must have a fireproof safe and install sophisticated electronic alarm systems. Alfandary said his alarm system costs him $5,000 a year to operate. Coupled with monthly rental costs of about $3,000, it is easy to see the large financial outlays mall owners must endure—and the prices they must charge customers to cover them.

Kostman said he saves his customers money by assembling the pieces himself. He buys the mounting blanks for rings, necklaces, and earrings from jewelry designers, frequently the same blanks his retail competitors are also purchasing. He buys the stones for the blanks and then manufactures the goods himself. Many retailers and most department stores purchase the same goods already assembled. The discounter said he can save his customers a lot of dollars by cutting out the assemblers' markups.

A discounter's typical markup is between 25 and 50 percent over cost, though in some extreme cases where a jeweler is glutted with a number of fashion pieces suddenly out of vogue, the markup can drop as low as 10 percent.

Price is not the only advantage discounters can offer a shopper. Speed is another plus. Discounters can order and set a large and costly stone in a shorter period of time than a retail store. "If a mall store wants to sell a 3 carat diamond, the manager must call the home office to receive approval. But buyers want their stones, now, and often will refuse to wait a week to make their purchase," said one discounter. Discounters, on the other hand, will jump to make that sale.

Chuck Fazio, owner of Fazio's Grocery in Mesquite, Texas, is one of Dallas' leading discounters. He added jewelry to the goods in his grocery store in 1983. Fazio is known for discounting his jewelry less than one keystone. (A keystone is a jeweler's term meaning doubling the price or receiving a 100 percent markup.)

Fazio said he purchases his jewelry directly from its manufacturers. He is not a full-service jeweler with a wide range of inventory. Instead, he sells only what he can discount, period.

"We'll purchase direct from the manufacturers, be it a fella making custom jewelry in his garage or a large operation like Zales, which does sell some jewelry to independents," said Fazio. "We follow the gold prices, so the savings to the shopper really remain constant throughout the year."

Advertising is another major component in a retailer's cost of doing business. Major chains can spend between 5 and 10 percent of their gross sales on advertising.

They also must contribute to general mall advertising. Discounters, on the other hand, rely on word-of-mouth marketing from satisfied customers.

Discounters have one disadvantage, though. You usually have to surrender a check for the entire sum when you pick up your goods. Most do not have credit cards or financing plans. Financing can be an important consideration, given the costly price tags of precious gems.

WHAT TO DO IF YOU GET BURNED

To prevent consumers from getting burned by an irreputable jeweler, many have taken it upon themselves to educate the public about jewelry purchases. Wholesaler Rennie Ellen is one who has testified before governmental committees on the subject, and is a sought-after speaker on the jewelry lecture circuit.

"A place like Tiffany's is outrageously expensive for a buyer," she said. "It's very difficult for the average shopper to know what they're getting, too. There are so many ways stones can be altered . . . it really takes an expert opinion to get the true value of a gem."

Ellen, along with other wholesalers and retailers alike, offer the following advise if you think you are not getting what you paid for.

First, ascertain that you have a problem. A third-party appraisal will provide an unbiased view of the value of your purchase. Try to find a reputable appraiser who will charge a flat fee for his work, rather than a per-centage fee.

If you are dissatisfied, call the jeweler and threaten to write a letter to the Better Business Bureau and the Jewelry Vigilance Committee, an industry association. (Address: 1180 Avenue of the Americas, 8th floor, New York, New York 10036.) Give the jeweler ten working days

234

to right your wrong. Then on the eleventh day, if he does not repent, write your letter. Reputations are precious to jewelers. Most will try to appease and please you to keep you from besmirching their good name.

MAIL-ORDER
SHOPPING

Beyond a doubt, the people at Sears, Roebuck & Company never envisioned the wide array of mail-order companies that would evolve in the future. When the retailer first distributed its famed catalogues in the 1920s, country-folk who had never seen the new-fangled appliances for the kitchen, mechanically stitched overalls, or the latest in "Sunday meeting" clothes quickly joined their urban cousins and placed their orders with the big-city department store.

From its beginnings as a method for regular retailers to reach out and capture a share of the virgin rural consumer market, mail order soon blossomed into an industry unto its own—with companies springing up across the country touting their ability to discount their goods below those garnered by the department store down the street.

In the 1980s, mail order represents more than a billion dollars in sales annually. And as with any retail industry which can attract that much money, unscrupulous business people who see the opportunity to make a quick buck at the shopper's expense await the unsavvy consumer, perhaps one step ahead of the postal inspector as they ship out their wares.

Hucksters of baldness remedies and cancer-curing ointments aside, the vast majority of mail-order houses are reputable dealers of goods and often at discount prices. Although the Federal Trade Commission, the Food and Drug Administration, the state and federal attorney general's office, and other various regulatory groups and agencies have worked to curtail the number of fraudulent claims and companies, the emergence of a more sophisticated shopper has had the most impact in cleaning up the industry.

"The majority of consumers were afraid of using the mail-order system for a long time," said Richey Levitt, president of LVT, a large mail-order distributor of household appliances based just outside New York City in Commack, New York. "But in the last ten years, I've seen a definite shift in consumers' attitudes. They've gotten more sophisticated in their approach to this method of shopping, and I think this has forced the industry to respond with more safeguards for the customer."

As more shoppers become more knowledgeable in their quest for a dependable mail-order resource, they have likewise increased their understanding of comparative shopping in their search for elusive bargains within their respective communities.

This is where the true beauty in mail-order shopping lies. Not only can shoppers buy goods from jewelry to pet supplies at discounts ranging from 20 to 60 percent, they can also do so from the convenience of their armchair. No more fighting for parking spaces at the mall, no more credit card approvals at the checkout counter and an end to helping retailers at the local shopping center pay top dollar for rental fees and high-tech decors.

Don Ball, president of Imoco, one of the largest housewares mail-order companies in the United States, said, "The ease with which people can shop through the mail has especially been good for the elderly. A lot of them aren't able to get around like they once could. With the large crowds you usually experience at department stores, it can be a real hassle for the elderly to get out and shop around for what they need."

Along with older shoppers, Ball said the yuppie generation of young, upwardly mobile professionals are finding mail-order shopping can mean more leisure time activities as opposed to spending hours driving around town for that inexpensive piece of furniture for the den or the new stereo and video equipment for the family room.

Despite the pitfalls which may come with the mail-order method of shopping, more average consumers are trying it and enjoying saving money for the first time. For those who have not, take heed—with a little patience and a little extra time, you may find putting a check in the mail or giving a credit card number over the phone can save money on everything needed for the home or the office, and the time saved may make it worth waiting for the delivery.

THE WIDE VARIETY OF MAIL-ORDER MERCHANDISE

Anything you can imagine, and some things you could not possibily imagine, is available through mail-order shopping these days—requiring only a simple phone call or an envelope through the mail to bring products to your doorstep.

Most mail-order outlets have catalogues available, usually charging a small fee of $2 or $3. The amount generally covers the cost of publishing and postage and also is meant to limit the number of requests from shoppers who really intend on ordering products.

Other companies use a less expensive mode of operation—quoting prices to customers who query by phone or mail. Though using this system may be a new experience, shoppers need not be wary. Price quotes allow mail-order companies to avoid costly catalogue updates, thus passing along a larger discount to the buyer. By giving style numbers, size, and quantity requirements over the telephone, the shopper can find out immediately if the item is available and amount of the discount price. When getting a price quote by mail, supply the same information, using a self-addressed, stamped envelope to ensure quick response.

The emergence of the price quote system, computerized mail-order distribution, and the availability of in-house credit are only a few examples of how sophisticated the mail-order industry has become. As more companies have entered the business, general merchandise mail-order firms have fallen in number compared with the volume of specialized mail distributors which sell particular types of products.

There are at least one thousand companies in the United States doing business as mail-order discounters. Each has its own niche of wares: housewares, appliances and electronics, shoes, apparel, office supplies, or cameras, just to name a few. Some sell lingerie, some vitamins, others just deal in sportswear or bass fishing equipment.

In Fountain Valley, California, the Hobby Shack sells toy-size radio-controlled cars, boats, and planes, along with other accessories for the hobbyist. Though some will not, the Hobby Shack will accept a personal check for an order. Discounts can go as high as 50 percent on accessories, tools, and other supplies for the expensive toys. On the opposite shores of the United States, Hobby Surplus Sales in New Britain, Connecticut, concentrates on toys. The mail-order house advertises having the best selection of toy trains on the East Coast, offering discounts from 25 to 30 percent on all items for the toy enthusiast.

At the other end of the shopping spectrum, A. Benjamin & Co. of New York sells discounted china, silverware, and crystal at savings from 25 to 30 percent off the regular retail price. The company gives price quotes over the phone and by mail, stocking only top-name lines like Gorham, Wallace, and Wedgwood. A minimum order of $100 is required, and if the item is in stock, it will arrive within three to four weeks after the order is received.

The bargains on fine china are not limited to the big cities. Locator's Incorporated in Little Rock, Arkansas, carries more than one thousand pieces of discontinued Lenox china for shoppers looking to replace their lost or cracked patterns. A Seattle, Washington, company, Patterns Unlimited, advertises itself as a pattern-matching service. If the company finds it does not have the shopper's requested pattern in stock, it will keep the name and order in the files until it locates the china.

Although most discount mail-order companies which sell china also have crystal and expensive cutlery, some do not. Rogers Sterling Matching Service only sells silver—refinished pieces and new stainless steel, silver-plate and holloware manufactured by Oneida, Gorham, Towle, and International. Rogers, based in Mansfield, Ohio, offers the restored pieces at one-third off current silver prices and new brands are available at as much as one-half off suggested retail.

For Waterford crystal, almost identical pieces are available through The Irish Crystal Co., which operates a mail-order business along with its retail stores. Leonard McDonald, the sole United States distributor for the company, said his pieces come from the same smelting pots and blow pipes used by Waterford.

"A parish priest named Father Austin Eutuse founded the company in the late seventies," said McDonald. "The father went to the McGrath family, owners of the Waterford company, and asked for their help in putting parish children to work at the craft. The family agreed, giving him the same equipment they used to produce their crystal."

Eutuse was not able to raise the funds to start the

243

smelting and cutting operation, said McDonald, so he journeyed to Cleveland, Ohio, where his search for investors was successful. That founding has been good for smart shoppers, who can get everything from crystal wine glasses to ice trays from one-third to one-half off the price of a comparable piece of Waterford. McDonald said Irish Crystal Co. pieces are identical in lead content to Waterford and the cutting styles are also comparable.

Not only can fine china and crystal be acquired at a good discount, but also can daily household items and consumable goods be garnered at reduced prices by the mail-order bargain hunter.

Beauty Buy Books in Chicago, Illinois, issues catalogues three times a year, advertising toiletries and cosmetics, from Polo and English Leather colognes to Max Factor makeup and Vidal Sassoon hairspray, at discounts as high as 70 percent off store prices. As an additional bonus, shoppers get a free gift with each total order.

And mail-order food? Well, do not expect lobsters at a discount, but you can get close. Caviarteria in New York has the fixings for your next party—caviar, Scotch salmon, truffles, and pates available at discounts of about 50 percent. If it is cheese that you need, Cheeses Of All Nations or Cheeselovers International, both in New York, have delectable Brie, Cheddar, Muenster, and French goat cheeses available through their mail-order catalogues.

To get the best idea of what is out there waiting for you in mail-order shopping, check your local book store or library for store guides. You may find there is a company in your city or state, which can lessen the delivery period considerably in most cases. *The 2nd Underground Shopper's® Guide to Discount Mail Order Shopping*, published in 1985, lists almost eight hundred companies, what they sell, the method of payment they will accept, and the discounts you can expect from each.

Also, keep an eye on your mailbox for that trash mail most of us tend to throw away without a thought. A great many of the larger mail-order companies use direct mail to solicit new customers. If you spot a potential seller, check for a mention of the discounts you can expect. Not all mail-order outlets sell at reduced prices. A well-known and highly respected company, Horchow, sells specialty items and provides more personal service to its customers. Goods may sell for as much or more than the same piece of luggage you saw at the department store. However, Horchow's two discount catalogues, Grand Finale and SGF, offer similar quality products to those in their full-price catalogue, but at savings of up to 70 percent or more.

THE DISCOUNTS AVAILABLE

Mail-order companies do not have many of the encumbrances that plague the average strip-shopping center or mall retailer. Not only must a shop owner pay rent, utilities, and taxes like other property owners, but also they must pay employees to provide service to their customers, costs for advertising and promotion, and costs for enticing and aesthetically appealing displays.

Department store chains and independent shops alike incur the same operating expenses to keep customers coming in. They both must price their goods to cover the costs of doing business, while also including their percentage of profit on the price tag.

According to Imoco's Ball, these operating expenses force retailers to charge an average 25 to 30 percent more for an item compared to a mail-order company. Currently, Ball said, American Tourister Luggage is one of their company's best-selling products, and the markup on this item offers a good example of what shoppers can expect to save.

"Right now, we're selling a five-piece set for

$99.95," he said. "At a retail store, you can expect to pay about $99 for one piece in the set. We buy in large volumes, which reduces the price we have to pay for the goods, and we also set prices using a dollar markup as opposed to a percentage markup used by most retail stores."

Unlike the average retailer, mail-order companies usually pay suppliers in advance. Coupled with volume discounts already enjoyed, this gives the consumer greater buying power for their dollars. Department stores usually require suppliers to give them a ninety-day credit advance, an advertising allowance from 5 to 7 percent, and may ask for manufacturers' representatives to help out during special sales periods at the store.

Since mail-order companies do not ask for these services from suppliers, and pay manufacturers cash up front, they generally get more merchandise for the dollar, and you can do the same.

Industry sources agree that the bigger the purchase, the bigger the discount shoppers tend to receive. Since refrigerators, washers and dryers, or box springs and mattresses may take the department store one to two weeks to order and deliver, why not go an additional twelve days and save $200 or $300 on your purchase.

That is not to say shoppers cannot save money on their small purchases. Even consumable goods like vitamins are available at discounts of 30 percent off suggested retail prices asked at the corner drugstore. In fact, the health-conscious consumer of the 1980s can find these types of savings and buy specialty vitamins manufactured with specific dietary formulas from Freeda Vitamins, a mail-order manufacturer at 36 E. 41st Street in New York City.

A fifty-eight-year-old vitamin manufacturing company, Freeda Vitamins makes all of its vitamins salt- and sugar-free. Dr. Phillip Zimmerman, vice president of

Freeda for seven years, said none of their products contain starch, dyes, or artificial colors and flavors. Besides the strict dietary formulas, Freeda vitamins are also kosher.

Zimmerman said shoppers can save an average of 30 percent off the price of multi-vitamins, minerals, and other daily nutritional supplements. "We don't spend money on expensive promotional campaigns. We don't have an extensive sales force or the middlemen required for distribution from store to store . . . that's why we can ask a lower price for our products."

By limiting the distribution process, Zimmerman stated that he believes Freeda provides consumers with a safer product. With media reports of cyanide tampering growing in frequency each year, it is easy to see the benefit of controlling the manufacturing process and shipping directly to the end-user.

"Everything comes from our own facility," he said. "Since we ship products direct, nobody has the opportunity to sneak around and mess with our products while they're sitting on a store shelf someplace." He added that all products are dated, so the shopper is assured the vitamins are fresh and in their most potent state.

Like most mail-order companies, Freeda accepts personal checks, money orders, Visa, MasterCard, and cash-on-delivery. Many of their frequent shoppers are provided house-credit, which can speed up processing orders and the delivery time required. For customers in New York, New Jersey, and Pennsylvania, shipping usually takes only one or two days. With the standard mail order, Freeda does not guarantee the number of days you can expect to wait for an order, but the company will provide next day delivery if you pay an additional charge.

A one-hundred-count box of Theragram-M multivitamins at a grocery store or pharmacy sells for $10 or more, while Freeda's comparable Quintab-M sells for

$7.15 per one hundred tablets. For the savvy mail-order shopper, the savings can make the delivery lag an easy pill to swallow.

THE PITFALLS OF MAIL-ORDER SHOPPING

"If it sounds too good to be true, it usually is." In cities across the country, postal inspectors, FTC investigators, and vice-squad officers use this often-quoted saying each year as a warning to consumers. Be it a flimflam artist or a felonious mail-order operator, hundreds of undiscerning shoppers are taken in by false representation each year.

One fraudulent mail-order operator in New York advertised "solid copper" Panama ceiling fans in the early 1980s when the items were in great demand across the country. It turned out that only one screw in the entire fan unit was made of solid copper—the blades and remaining parts were made of just cheap plastic. At $50 an order, this operator made plenty of money before moving on to another scam.

This same flimflam artist advertised marine binoculars for $50, supposedly one-half off the regular price. The glasses turned out to be $1.98 toys which quickly fell apart once in the shopper's hands. He also advertised Le-France cookware at prices well below regular retail prices, again, cheap imitations of the real McCoy. Even after authorities caught up with him and subsequently threw him in jail, he operated a mail-order business from a post office box, using outside partners to continue his rip-off schemes.

Although one sweepstakes company in Texas is still continuing to operate freely, they are currently being investigated for mail-order fraud by federal authorities. The company, another sweepstakes clearing house similar to many legitimate businesses like Publisher's Clearing House, operates in the same manner as above-board businesses, with one major difference—this company has advertised giving away a $10 million prize if the shopper purchases goods at a discount of $200. For the last two years, the company has yet to find a winner, and sources said that is because the company has never had enough money to give away a $100 prize, much less a $10 million prize.

Diamonds for $20, opals for $5, or an ounce of 14 karat gold for $15—-the bottom line is "you get what you pay for," or so said a spokesperson for the Direct Marketing Association. Sharon O'Sullivan, editor for the organization's publications, said the majority of mail-order companies are not out to rip off consumers. But if you are a first-time user of this mode of shopping, she advised contacting DMA and ordering some of their consumer publications before you start sending your checks or credit card numbers. *Make Knowledge Your Partner in Mail Order Shopping, Guidelines for the Telephone Shopper,* and *The World in Your Mailbox* are three consumer publications DMA offers free-of-charge upon request.

DMA also has a Monthly Action Line Report which enumerates companies in the industry which have less-than-admirable records of shipping, advertising, and product quality. The report also states which companies have legitimate reasons for delivery lags, maybe a manufacturer in India that is experiencing a delay in production or parts, and even lists bankruptcy filings reported by companies throughout the United States.

Although fraudulent or deceptive mail-order operators are not as prominent in the industry now as they were in the past, there are still enough of them to warrant consumers to be cautious when buying through the mail for the first time. Advertisements still abound which claim to increase bust size and decrease weight. There are no miracle cures available not already in the hands of nutritionists and physicians, yet these claims continue to

249

attract money from undiscerning shoppers.

Federal and local regulations offer shoppers some protection. An FTC spokesman said mail-order companies are required to deliver your item within thirty days after they receive your order or advise you there will be some delay. To avoid these demands, mail-order companies are required to note the specific delivery period in its catalogues. If the company cannot get your shipment out in thirty days, it is required to offer you a refund and a cost-free method of stopping your order—typically a toll-free number or a collect call.

Mail-order sources indicated the Better Business Bureaus vary in treatment of consumer complaints. It was suggested BBB offices in the southwest tend to be harder on mail-order companies than other area offices. A call to the BBB would still be well advised before you make your payment.

The attorney general's office in your state is the most effective governmental agency involved in mail-order fraud. As consumers have become more sophisticated, so have regulatory agencies. Along with the Postmaster General, these agencies are most prominent in dealing with an unreceptive mail-order company.

The DMA trade organization will intervene on a customer's behalf. Located at 6 E. 43rd Street, New York, New York 10017, a DMA official can be contacted by phone at (212) 689-4977. The DMA will either provide its own clout to make the situation right, or refer you to agencies which can assist you.

Consumer magazines such as *Consumer Reports* occasionally publish articles on how different areas of the mail-order business relate to shoppers, and consumer advocates such as Ralph Nader sometimes take certain companies to task on their business ethics.

One such advocate, David Horowitz, took on Imoco during an episode of his syndicated television program

"Fight Back." Spurred by an Imoco advertisement stating a line of stainless-steel cookware sold by the company was "virtually indestructible," Horowitz challenged Imoco to put the claim to the test. Don Ball said Imoco was only too happy to oblige.

"They tested it severely," Ball said. "They ran a tractor over the top of it, it survived. Then Horowitz took the pan to an auto-wrecking yard, got a car on a large crane, and dropped the car on the pan—still, nothing happened. They dropped the car upon it a second time. They ended up putting the cookware through the auto-yard's car compacting machine." The cookware made it, and Imoco's reputation survived the experience, too.

Short of calling Horowitz to investigate your potential seller, there are some precautions perceptive first-time shoppers can take themselves.

1. If you order from a catalogue, flyer, or a price-list, retain a copy of the advertisement. Retaining a record of the mail-order company you are dealing with not only makes good bookkeeping sense, but also gives you some physical evidence should your order become "lost in the mail."

2. Whether it is a check, money order, or credit card payment, keep a copy or receipt in your records. If you use a personal check, be cognizant of when it clears your account.

3. Never send cash.

4. Scan the catalogue or ask the company representative about additional shipping charges. Some mail-order companies require what is called a "restocking charge," a labor fee the company charges when it has to take a return on an item. No fees are charged if the product is damaged in shipment, but if a shopper has second thoughts about the purchase it could mean a cash penalty to the pocketbook. Restocking charges can be as much as 25 percent of the total product's price.

5. Know what you want and know what you are ordering: the two are not always the same. To save on operating expenses, some companies give only price quotes instead of relying on catalogues. Read product descriptions carefully if ordering from a catalogue—weight, size, color, and contents warrant close attention, and this information is crucial when getting a price quote over the phone. If ordering a name-brand product, check for style or model numbers with a local department store or the manufacturer's area warranty service center. Taking these steps can prevent any surprises when your package arrives.

6. Take note of the company's return policy. You need to know your rights should a problem develop. Remember that the proximity of your address to the company's can speed delivery in most cases, but if the company advertises that shipments may take more than thirty days, the shopper has no recourse under FTC regulations.

7. The method of payment can often affect the amount of time the shipment in en route. Using a personal check can mean a delay of two or three weeks while the company waits for your local bank to process the payment. Credit cards are the fastest method of payment, followed by money orders and cashier's checks. Avoid using COD as a method of payment. Most mail-order companies include an additional charge for COD customers, ranging from $5 to $10.

8. When completing an order form, follow minimum order requirements. Some companies offer higher discounts on quantity purchases. Print all information legibly, including code or model numbers for the items you are buying. If you have a second choice or substitution you will accept, specify it on the form. Do not forget to include shipping charges when you total the bill, and always request insurance if it is not automatically provided. Finally, you only pay a sales tax if you are purchasing from a mail-order company which operates in your state. The order form should explain the company's tax requirements.

By following these guidelines, shoppers can dodge most of the potential pitfalls of the mail-order system. But there are a few more tidbits of information useful in navigating the mail-order experience error-free.

Some mail-order companies are operated out of office buildings, with one or two people manning telephones. Although some telemarketing operations are legitimate, others use this method of soliciting customers because of the ease at which the one- or two-man office can be moved to another location, dodging their responsibility to previous customers. These operations are sometimes called "sweat-boxes" or "boiler room operations," which is an apt description among employees—and sometimes an apt description of the shopper whose order is not filled once the operation is shut down.

Industry sources advised that if the mail-order company uses only a post office box as its address, call or write for a street address. Most reputable companies will advertise both. Since an order sent to a box is routed quicker by the postman, a company using a post office box can get your order to you faster. But if a post office box is the only address used by the company, it may be a warning sign you should not ignore.

Not all television advertising is deceptive, but it can be, and shoppers need to be vigilant. When you see a commercial, check the "qualifiers" which run across the bottom of the screen during the advertisement. Many times an item is enlarged or visually enhanced in ways to make the item look bigger or better than it really is. Also, many television commercials advertise that the goods can be ordered COD. Cash on delivery usually means the item is priced three or four times over the shipper's price to make up for the undeliverable CODs, and the subsequent costs the shipper has to absorb.

There are also many good bargains available through overseas mail-order companies, but beware of shipping duties and other hidden costs. When reading the company's catalogue, check for such things as insurance duty (with each item taxed at a different rate), the return policy, and delivery information. You will pay more for air mail shipments, but the alternative is delivery by surface mail, and the delay can make you feel you have shipped your item by raft.

If the method of payment is not spelled out in the catalogue, verify the method before sending any money. Plan to pay for the goods at the foreign country's rate of exchange—another reason ordering by credit card can circumvent some of the foreign currency hassles. However, Deak-Perera, a currency brokerage company, can supply a current conversion chart. The company is located at 29 Broadway, New York, New York 10006.

If the item arrives and it is not what you wanted, ask the company for instructions on returning goods. Not getting instructions prior to your return shipment may mean paying duty twice on the item.

Anything purchased outside the United States is subject to examination by the United States Customs Service, in addition to a duty charge which is levied by the government. The duty represents a set percentage of the appraised value of the item. Duties vary depending on the item and the country it is purchased from.

Although all items are inspected when they enter the country, not all are subject to duty charges. Some three thousand items which originate from 140 underdeveloped nations are classified as "duty-free" under the Generalized System of Preferences (GSP). To not be levied a duty depends on where the article was grown, manufactured, or produced. To learn about customs' duties and other charges related to overseas purchases, contact the

United States Customs Service at Box 7118, Washington, D.C. 20044.

The rewards of mail-order shopping, above all, are well worth the risk. Like any travel to a new area, one needs only to have a well-defined road map to make the trip both safe and productive.

RESIDENTIAL
REAL ESTATE
AND
MORTGAGES

While banking is the most regulated industry in America, the real estate industry ranks as number two. A host of watchdog agencies from the Federal Home Loan Bank Board to your city's board of realtors closely monitor real estate transactions. These groups have the power to swiftly and permanently revoke the licenses and permits of all nefarious practioners. Brokers and bankers cannot afford to cheat you; it could easily cost them their careers.

That does not mean that consumers do not need to be on guard when buying or selling their homes. On the contrary, real estate transactions have the built-in potential for big-bucks mistakes. Because the purchase price of homes in America is so high—the median price is over $100,000—even the slightest error can cost you hundreds, if not thousands, of dollars. The magnitude of money makes it imperative to be all the more watchful.

Ignorance and error on the part of honest real estate personnel can cost you money. But very often you are your own worst enemy. Misinformation makes you a willing target for those in the know. Sharp sellers can take advantage of first-time buyers who do not know the ins and outs of real estate transactions. And experienced buyers can easily—and legally—bully a worried and panicked seller. Only when you fully comprehend the nuances of this very black and white process can you protect your pocketbook.

The residential real estate boom of the late 1970s was historic, according to Kermit Baker, a building and construction analyst in the economics department of Cahners Publishing Company. Newlyweds could buy a starter home and three years later, after the home doubled in price, sell it to buy a mansion larger than their parents' abode. Home prices rising $10,000 or more a year were the rule rather than the exception during the period of what he called "rampant inflation."

In today's deflationary environment a house should be viewed as a homeowner's haven and habitat rather than an easy ticket to a higher tax bracket. Today a buyer must know what he is buying before he signs a binding real estate contract because inflation will not bail a buyer out of a major mistake, pointed out Paul Getman, senior economist at Chase Econometrics in Bala Cynwyd, Pennsylvania. "Inflation is no longer a homeowner's saving grace," he said. Knowing what you are doing is particularly important when making the single most expensive investment of a lifetime.

Residential real estate is a cyclical business. Prices rise and fall, mirroring the workings of the local economy. However, over the long haul, real estate prices have always gone up, maintained R.E. Moore, a professor of real estate at the Real Estate Institute in Dallas. After every cycle, the trough or bottom of the following cycle is always higher than the trough of a previous cycle, he explained. In the past homeowners have always made money if they have had deep enough pockets to hold on to and maintain their residences during a down cycle. It is only those who have to sell who get hurt.

Detroit and Houston are good examples. In the late 1970s Detroit was languishing. Home prices fell precipitously; people walked away from their houses and drove to Houston where home prices were rising up 17 percent a year, according to Getman. Today housing prices have stabilized in Detroit as the city enters a new economic boom cycle. But plunging oil prices have caused Houston to harbor one of the highest foreclosure rates in America. Smart money with staying power would be purchasing real estate in Houston now just as it bought homes in Detroit in 1978.

Buying real estate and selling real estate are two totally different transactions. Because the transfer of fee simple property—which means owning both the land and the structure and which is the most complete form of ownership—is governed by a host of legal restrictions, it can seem a very esoteric process. However, it behooves you to know how to read a closing statement and understand the terms of various types of mortgages. This technical knowledge can save buyers and sellers significant sums of money. A simple addition error can cost the uneducated thousands of dollars.

HOW MUCH HOUSE CAN YOU AFFORD?

About 65 percent of American households own their homes. The first step when you want to join this group, before you ever look at a single piece of property, is to know how much house you can afford. Lenders have very strict guidelines which are cast in stone, explained Michael Zerlin, a loan originator for B.F. Saul Mortgage, a Chevy Chase, Maryland, mortgage banker. "It is a rare occasion when underwriters will look the other way and approve a loan that does not meet national guidelines," said Zerlin. These guidelines are set by the Federal National Mortgage Association, better known as Fannie Mae. Fannie Mae has two ratios and loan applicants must pass both of them before a loan can be approved.

The front ratio is a ratio between your mortgage payment—here viewed only as principal and interest—and your total monthly income. The mortgage payment may not exceed between 25 and 28 percent of that income. The back ratio computes the ratio of your mortgage payment to your total debt. You must calculate all installment and line of credit debt. Mortgage bankers add this number to the mortgage payment and then see how it compares to your overall income. If the ratio is higher than 35 to 38 percent, you will not qualify for a mortgage loan. Generally it is this back ratio which kills a mortgage deal. "One new car loan payment and a sizable Mastercard balance is all it takes," observed Zerlin.

Zerlin suggested prospective homebuyers pick up Fannie Mae mortgage loan applications which are available at most mortgage companies. By filling out the form, they can easily calculate the amount of house payment for which they qualify. One of the most common mistakes neophytes in the home buying world make is assuming they can qualify for more house than the numbers allow. More often than not, buyers are shocked when they see how little house they can really afford.

The reason for prequalifying yourself before you start the house hunt is to save time and effort. A $100,000 house with a fixed thirty year loan at 10.5 percent will have a principal and interest payment of $915 per month. Taxes and insurance, which depend on the local taxing authorities and the amount of insurance coverage the mortgage company requires, are extra. They can easily add another $150 per month to the payment. If the buyer does not earn over $4,000 a month, he will not qualify for that $100,000. It is senseless to look at every $100,000 house in the marketplace if the buyer can only qualify for an $80,000 purchase.

SELECTING A REALTOR

Should buyers use a realtor when making a purchase or should they try to find a house themselves? In most instances, buyers without extensive experience in the real estate world should always use a good realtor.

Buying a house is one of the few instances in business where you can spend hours of time enjoying the expertise of an expert at the other party's expense. That is because in a real estate transaction, the SELLER ONLY is responsible for paying the realtor's fee, called a commission. The buyer contributes nothing, unless the homeowner has inflated the sales price to include the realtor's fee. Then, of course, the buyer pays the fee, albeit indirectly.

Realtors must be licensed by the state in which they practice their profession. Many states require additional educational hours for renewal. In Texas, for example, an agent must attend thirty hours per year of additional training in approved real estate courses for the first three annual renewals. If the agent does not go to school, the license is immediately revoked. These rules ensure that realtors have achieved a basic knowledge of their profession.

Knowledge is critical because the real estate market, unlike the stock market, is an imperfect market. That means an undervalued stock can be readily seen by all; its price will rise as the market corrects itself. Steals really do not exist in the world of stocks and bonds.

But in the real estate market, there are bargains because the human element intervenes. People are transferred and must sell their homes; a divorce court orders the property sold; heirs need the equity to settle a will. When disaster strikes, homeowners are more willing to bargain. Realtors are more likely than not to know of such situations.

The real estate market is also a fluid one. The price of a house can vary from month to month. Only a professional who specializes in a particular area can be aware of these economic undulations. They can tell you what the average price of a house is in the area you are considering and prevent you from paying much too much for the house of your dreams.

On a more pragmatic note, realtors have the requisite forms needed to begin the real estate process. Buyers must complete an earnest money contract which the realtor typically presents to either the seller or the seller's realtor. Usually the state bar association and the state real estate commission have produced an accepted and legally binding contract document. This is important because only attorneys who have passed the bar can practice law. Realtors, however, are entitled to complete these contracts if they are licensed.

Realtors also perform the many irritating tasks associated with buying a home. They will wait at the house for the appraiser to come so you do not have to leave work. They will do the unemotional negotiating with the sellers. They should know the ins and outs of financing. And they can peruse the closing statements to ensure a careless typist did not add an extra point on the other party's behalf.

Lastly, only realtors have access to the Multiple Listing Service reports. These are computerized listings of all the homes in your area currently for sale. The computer screen has everything you wanted to know about the house, but did not know who to ask. The computer can also spew out a printout of all the houses listed with the criteria you want. The computer can easily let your fingers do the walking so you do not have to spend days traipsing through homes. Most MLS groups also print a book with all the homes available: this hundred page document can be quite useful for a prospective buyer.

How do you know which realtor to use? Twenty percent of the realtors sell 80 percent of the houses. With the industry changing so rapidly, many agents have not kept up with the brave new world. Realtors generally are honest and upright. Their big problem is ignorance. "Most real estate agents are not dishonest or deceptive," said Zerlin. "When it appears they are, it is usually because they are not knowledgeable about their job. They just don't keep up with the industry," he added.

Real estate agents only get paid when a house actually sells. The title company distributes the proceeds of the sale to the broker, who then pays the agent. If the deal does not close, the agent, who may have spent weeks with a client, does not get paid. Because of this commission method of payment, the industry is plagued with a high turnover rate. According to an article in *Real Estate Today*, the national magazine of the National Association of Realtors, brokers across the country are constantly grappling with the problems of poor performance by salespeople. They are trying to cope with the disastrously high turnover that is endemic to the industry,

Be sure you select an agent who has been selling houses for awhile. If the agent has survived at least one real estate downturn, you can be assured he or she knows the business.

If you know what area you want to live in, drive around that area and note which real estate company—called a brokerage—has the most signs in the area. Also note which agent's name is on the most signs. These are clues as to which company is the most knowledgeable about that area. Agents are salespeople who work for the broker. The broker is legally liable for any actions taken by his salespeople as well as the expenses of keeping the office running.

If you do not want to call the name on a For Sale sign, call your area's board of realtors. Every year they list the top twenty-five salespeople. Local newspapers frequently print that list. You have a great chance of success if you call a name on that roster of success.

Once you meet an agent, ask her (a majority of realtors are women) for the names and numbers of her former clients. All real estate transactions are studded with disasters. It is a miracle most of them ever get consummated at all. Ask to see how your agent worked under pressure. Ask the former client to list the agent's strengths and weaknesses. Close the conversation by asking if the former client would use that agent again in another transaction. The nation's most successful realtors have built their business with repeat clientele.

The most important characteristic of a real estate agent is her knowledge of financing. Anybody with a driver's license can show you houses. Financing is the key to a real estate purchase. Whatever you decide then, you will be paying for the next thirty years. Financing is also the trickiest part of the transaction. Find someone who knows what she is doing.

Next, look for someone with good negotiating skills. Bargaining sessions can get heated. Engage a realtor who has tactical poise yet who is flexible and firm.

Once you find your realtor, finding the house is usually the easiest part. If you know what you want (there must be three bathrooms, a two-car garage, hardwood floors) and how much house you can afford, the computer can easily list all the houses for sale in the areas of your choice that fit your needs. If you also read the largest circulation newspaper's classified real estate ads, you will include For Sale by Owners or FSBOs.

If you have determined in advance how much house you can afford, you will automatically circumvent a realtor's trick of showing you only the most expensive houses possible. Realtors generally get paid a set percentage of the purchase price as a commission. (Half the sum normally goes to the selling realtor and with the other half going to the realtor representing the buyer. Each broker then takes half of their agent's percentage. So the agent working with you nets one quarter of the purchase price of the house she sells you for her efforts. For example, if the commission was 6 percent, the buying and selling brokers would receive 3 percent each. The agent who worked with you would net 1.5 percent of the sales price.) If you can only afford a mid-priced home, you will have avoided this expensive ruse.

If you are a savvy investor and have a good feel for the market, you can find a home without the help of a realtor. Scour the classified ads in the daily papers, when the ad begins "Must Sell" get ready to make a call. Driving around your target area is another prime way to find a home. FSBOS always have their signs in the yard.

If you have the time and want to expend the effort, you can subscribe to a foreclosure listing service. These companies list all the residential foreclosures posted each month. They usually include the amount of the loan outstanding as well as the name of the lender who is taking back the property. However, it takes hours to drive around town examining house after house. If the home is being foreclosed on, you can be sure it will have some deferred maintainence.

WRITING A CONTRACT

Once you have found the house, the hard work begins. Realtors sit down with their clients to fill in the blanks on the standard earnest money contract. At this time the buyer must decide how much he will initially offer as well as how much he will actually pay for the house. Deciding the bottom line is critical before the heat of the negotiations start. At that time, too often tempers rather than reason control judgment. If you, the buyer, remember you can always find another house if the seller is not amenable to selling this one to you, you will always make the right decisions at the bargaining table.

The buyer signs the contract, which should include a property addendum if the home is not new. These are called pre-owned homes. This contract states that if the repairs cost more than the sum stated in the addendum, the buyer is not legally obligated to purchase the house.

This addendum protects the buyer from major disasters—assuming he can find them before he closes or signs all the papers to make the home his.

Generally buyers do not have to worry about foundations or roofs. Fannie Mae guidelines require both to be in acceptable condition before the bank can fund a loan using the home as collateral. Repairs to either—which can be major—are always the responsibility of the seller. Paying for other repairs is generally negotiable.

The best time to look for homes is the day after a bad rain. If the roof leaks, you will know it. It is hard for an inspector to tell if the roof leaks in the midst of a summer drought.

Most standard contracts require the buyer to have an inspector visit the pre-owned home within five working days after the seller and buyer agree on the price. If there are major problems to break the agreement, everyone wants to know right away. Len Grossman, president of Technihouse Inspections in Bloomfield Hills, Michigan, pointed out inspectors should be licensed in a building related trade.

Inspections cost between $75 and $500, depending on the depth and the dirtiness of the examination. Getting under pier and beam foundations always costs more than walking around the exterior of the house checking a post tension slab. If the home has a swimming pool or spa, it is best to hire an established pool service to check out the equipment.

Most states require inspectors to be licensed. Choose an inspector who specializes in the residential end of the building business; examining a high rise office building is different from knowing what to look for in the attic.

Always ask the inspector if he guarantees his findings. Ask what happens if he misses the faulty wiring in the attic. Most respectable inspectors will promise to fix anything—except roofs—they miss. If a problem turns up two months after you move in, they should be happy to either fix the mistake or refund your inspection fee.

The final purchase price of the home is dependent on its physical condition. If the sellers have perfectly redone a 1933 Victorian mansion, the price will be higher than their neighbor's 1932 wreck. The best bargains in the market are sold "as is."

There are general guidelines which you, as the potential buyer, can use to determine the general physical condition of the home. The Texas Real Estate Research Center at Texas A & M University recommends buyers look for:

Noticeable exterior cracks in the foundation.

Unusual settling of the driveway and sidewalks.

Bricks, including chimneys, that pull away from the home.

Condition of the interior and exterior paint.

Insulation: does the home have double paned windows, weatherstripping, and acceptable caulking?

Age of the air conditioner. (If it works today, it will pass inspection. If it fails tomorrow, it is your problem.)

NEW VERSUS PRE-OWNED

Many buyers prefer pre-owned homes because the landscaping and shrubbery are in place. It is rare to buy a new home with three story trees already shading the lot. Establishing a lawn is an expensive and time-consuming process. Pre-owned homes usually sell at a discount price because most people prefer to buy new houses.

New houses do have their advantages. Buyers can pick the wallpaper and the living room paint they like. Theoretically they do not have to worry about home repairs in the beginning. Most new homes come with a Home Owners Warranty. This guarantee pays for the cost of all structural repairs for ten years. Since all the appliances are new and should have their own warranties, homeowners should not have to worry about expensive repairs at the outset.

There are other risks in buying a new home, however. The financial stability of the home builder is the most critical concern. If the builder suffers a financial setback or goes bankrupt, it is almost impossible for homeowners to seek satisfaction. Check out the legitimacy of the home builder with the Better Business Bureau, the local home builder's association, and past clients before you hand over any money.

Zerlin advised it was a bad idea to buy a home from a builder who had gone out of business. "You're getting in the middle of a tug of war between the builder and the banker who financed the house. The lender usually wants to recoup the full amount of the loan. If the builder can't sell the house for that amount, the lender will foreclose," explained the banker.

The typical way custom home builders cheat buyers is by not paying their subcontractors, pointed out Daniel Phillips, president of Lion Funding Corp., a mortgage lender with offices stretching from Boston to Sacramento. "If you pay the contractor and he runs off to Mexico without paying the carpenter and the plumber, those workmen can put a mechanic's lien on your house. That lien clouds the title which means you cannot sell the house (no title company will issue a new title policy without a clean title) until you pay those workmen. Just because you've already paid the general contractor does not free you from paying his subs," he said. When custom building a home, devise a system so that you, not the general contractor, pay the subs. You can even demand to pay for all the materials directly, too. Then all you owe him is his contracting fee.

Phillips told the sad story of one customer who lost close to $20,000 because his builder did not pay his subcontractors. When the builder realized he was not going to finish the house under budget, he disappeared to Canada. The homeowner had to pay the plumber, the carpenter, and the painter again so he could finally mortgage the house.

Unless you know a great deal about construction, it is a good idea to invest $100 and hire an inspector to check the quality of that new home you had your eye on. During times of financial trouble, builders have been known to cut corners to stave off their creditors. Zerlin said it was not uncommon for a builder to promise you one material but substitute a cheaper one. Inspectors can spot trouble spots before your name is on the warranty deed, the legal document that makes that house yours.

When buying a new home, everything is negotiable. If you want a fence, add it to the contract and see what happens.

Employ the same psychology when writing a contract for a pre-owned home. Use the condition of the home as a consideration in setting the price you offer the seller. If you feel the carpet needs to be replaced, include a decorator's allowance in the contract equal to the cost of newly installed carpet. In the beginning, ask for everything. Of course you will not get it. Usually after two passes both sides have either agreed to agree or agreed to disagree. Everyone, however, will have to give up something if the house is going to change hands.

Phillips said it was important to include in the contract how and when the seller or escrow agent would return your deposit if you were unable to secure funding. Also make sure the exact time you take possession of the home is clearly stated. He said possession can become a major issue if the seller needs to stay because the construction of his new home is running late but the landlord has already rented the buyer's apartment.

Once the seller agrees to your price and conditions,

he signs and dates the contract. Then both of you have a binding legal contract. Be sure you read the fine print in these contracts. When the title attorney says you owe money according to the contract, it is too late to argue.

Now it's time to shop for financing.

FINANCING YOUR HOME

Most buyers do not have $100,000 in their checkbook to buy a home. So they have to pledge the property as collateral for a loan needed to pay the seller. The mortgage is the legal instrument which pledges the property in return for a loan, which is documented in a note or loan covenant. The note usually does not mention the property. If the noteholder does not pay according to the terms of the note, the lender can foreclose by taking the pledged collateral—the house. Buyers must sign both documents to purchase a home without paying all cash.

Buyers can turn to three different sources for funding. Savings and loans are the historic source of home mortgages. Mortgage banking companies, which do nothing other than provide financing for real estate, are another source. Today other financial institutions, including retail banks and credit unions, are now offering mortgage financing.

When selecting a mortgage company, ask the banker taking your application if he is on commission. Some companies pay only salaries; others pay a small base salary and then a commission, generally in the 0.01 percent range. The loan officers only receive that commission if the loan closes. Human emotions of greed generally cause commissioned mortgage officers to work harder for you than noncommissioned bankers.

Phillips said all prospective mortgagors should ask their mortgage companies these basic four questions:

1. Am I required to carry life or disability insurance? Must I obtain it from a special company (i.e. yours)?

2. Is there a prepayment penalty if I pay off the loan before maturity? If so, how much?

3. Will the loan be assumable? Will the lender release me from personal liability if the loan is assumed by the buyer of my house?

4. Will I be required to set up an escrow fund to pay insurance premiums and taxes. If so, how much?

William Brueggeman, head of the Costa Institute of Real Estate at Southern Methodist University, warned consumers about the "bait and switch" schemes mortgage bankers use in their print advertising. "The ads in the newspaper never tell you what qualifications you need in order to get the attractive advertised rate," he said. "The ads imply the rates apply to everyone, but they don't. Rates vary depending on a person's income bracket."

While advertising may be deceptive, the fees bankers and title attorneys charge must be clearly stated to you according to the federal government's uniform disclosure rules. "You can't hide fees," said Brueggeman.

There are a plethora of options to chose from when financing a home. A major advantage of purchasing a home from a builder is ready financing. In times of soaring interest rates, builders chip in some cash to help their customers qualify so they can lower their inventory of homes. The builder typically pays the lender a sum of money so that the lender can charge a lower interest rate in the first few years of the mortgage. Lower interest rates make it easier for the customer to qualify.

Buy downs can only be had through the one mortgage company with which the builder has chosen to deal. Often the points and the closing costs are higher than the market. Shop around at other shops to compare total costs before selecting the builder's buy downs. It is quite possible the lower interest rate has associated with it such high closing costs it may be cheaper to get your own financing elsewhere.

Even though the mortgage payments inch up over a three to four year period, builder buy downs are not graduated payment mortgages. GPMs are sometimes called "gyp-ems" because they are negative amortization mortgages. With a negative amortization mortgage, you do NOT build up any equity in the home until the later years. Here is how a GPM works.

The mortgage company typically sets a rate for the home, which includes principal which is your equity, interest which is the bank's reward for lending you the money, taxes to pay for city services and insurance to pay your annual insurance premium. Taken together, they are called your PITI, for principal, interest, taxes and insurance.

With a fixed rate loan and later during a GPM, a portion of your monthly check goes to all four beneficiaries in a fixed, predetermined amount. But with GPM, the payments are low because most or all of the principal is not paid and a portion of the interest is deferred. For example, say you owed the bank $900 a month principal and interest. But the first year of your GPM you only paid $600 per month. The $300 per month you owe the bank is added to your loan balance. That means the balance grows larger, instead of slowly reducing.

State laws vary, but most will only allow a GPM to grow to 110 percent of the original loan. Thus you know exactly how much can be added to the mortgage in the worst case. GPMs work well in specific cases. They are often the only resort for first-time buyers trying to qualify for a home in today's market. They can qualify at the deferred interest rate, but not the actual one. For the same reason it allows all buyers to purchase more house than they can otherwise qualify.

GPMs are also perfect for rent properties. They allow a rent house to cash flow from day one, which does not happen in the real world. That means the investor has less money out of his pocket each month. In return, however, he will not make that much money when he finally sells the home.

GPMs are also good for people with wildly fluctuating incomes. Homeowners with these mortgages always have the option of paying the deferred interest on December 31. Those looking for instant tax deductions with a lot of clout can pay the interest at year end and shelter other, unexpected income.

GPMs only cause trouble when the homeowner gets in trouble and has to sell the home. If it has not appreciated, he will have to pay the mortgage company out of his pocket if the sales price does not cover his new, higher loan balance.

Adjustable rate mortgages are another new financing type which were created during the credit crunch of 1980 when interest rates reached new heights of 20 percent. These mortgages have their interest rates adjusted periodically according to a set financial benchmark.
Usually the rate is some kind of government security like the six month treasury bills. The mortgage company then adds a profit margin to that number. It usually is an additional 1 or 2 percent.

Adjustable rate mortgages do not always go up. If interest rates fall, so do mortgage payments. The borrower shares the risks of rising interest rates with the lender, in return for enjoying the benefits of decreasing payments when rates fall.

Like graduated payment mortgages, the first year's interest rate is significantly below market. That means lower, easier qualifying ratios. In times of outrageously high rates, ARMs were just about the only way most Americans could get into a home.

Never select an ARM without circumscribed increases and caps. Most ARMs set a maximum increase which the rate can jump. Usually the increase is no more than 2 percent a year. Thus, if your current rate is 11 percent and interest rates jump to 19, your ARM can only increase to 13 percent.

Caps describe how far the loan can rise and fall. They set floors and ceilings on your interest rate. Generally caps span about 5 percentage points. Caps of $9^1/_2$ and 14 tell the borrower his best and worst case scenarios.

America's most popular mortgage is the standard mortgage, a thirty year, fixed rate note. Homeowners like this repayment plan because they can budget accurately, since the principal and interest amounts never change. Mortgage payments, however, do change as insurance becomes more expensive and taxes ratchet up.

In addition to deciding what kind of mortgage to select, home buyers must also decide who is going to issue the mortgage. The Federal Housing Administration, which was created in 1934 in the wake of massive foreclosures, does not make loans. Instead, it insures loans made by private lenders like your mortgage company. If the loan meets all FHA's insurance requirements, it will issue an insurance policy. If the homeowner does not make his mortgage payments and the loan goes into default, the FHA will foreclose on the property and then pay off the lender in either cash or government securities.

For this service the FHA charges a fee called the mortgage insurance premium. It is either an annual fee of one half of one percent of the unpaid balance or a one-time lump sum which can be financed as part of the loan.

FHA loans are in high demand because its loans are assumable. That means the people you sell your house to do NOT have to qualify for the loan. Instead, they assume your payments. Waiving those requirements make it possible for a much larger subset of people to buy your home. Assumable mortgages are manna from heaven for investors, who are required to put down a 20 percent down payment on a conventional loan. View assumable loans as a sales marketing tool.

If the house has appreciated in value and your buyer wants to assume your loan, he either has to get a second mortgage to pay you the difference at closing or he has to convince you, the owner, to finance the difference. If you choose to do that, the buyer makes the larger mortgage payment to you. Then you continue to make your mortgage payment, pocketing the difference.

Veterans Administration insured loans are also assumable, even by buyers who are not veterans. While the FHA insures 100 percent of the loan, the VA guarantees a part of the loan. Like the FHA, the VA does NOT lend money.

What is even better, buyers of homes may not even have to come up with a down payment. Currently the VA can guarantee up to 60 percent of the loan or $27,500, whichever is less. Private lenders do not want to be liable for more than 75 percent of the amount of the loan. If the VA will guarantee $27,500 of the loan, a mortgage banker will lend the veteran the remaining 75 percent. That means a veteran can buy a home with a purchase price of up to $110,000 (four times $27,500) without having to make a cash down payment. The VA in essence makes that down payment for him by guaranteeing his money. Of course, a veteran could buy a $300,000 house. He will have to make up the difference between what he owes and the VA's guarantee as a cash down payment.

Veterans must not only meet the VA's loan eligibility standards, but also must be eligible according to the length of time they served in the armed forces. Any veteran who wants a no cash down payment VA loan must present a certificate of eligibility to his private mortgage lender. The VA will send the vet this form when requested. The back of the form keeps a running total of the amount the vet has borrowed. He may buy as many houses as he wants as long as his guaranteed sum does not exceed $27,500. If a vet sells his house and totally pays off his loan, his $27,500 entitlement is restored. He can then go ahead and buy another house with no cash down if he qualifies. If a buyer assumes his loan, his entitlement is still tied up. The VA will not guarantee a loan on his new house.

Veterans can also use their entitlement money to guarantee home improvement loans. If you have been honorably discharged from the armed services, call your local VA office and learn about your real estate benefits. They are substantial.

If you are not a veteran or are buying a house with a purchase price of more than $90,000, the FHA limit, you will have to apply for a conventional mortgage. A conventional mortgage is neither insured nor guaranteed by any governmental agency. It is you, the mortgagor, who must buy that insurance if you are borrowing more than 90 percent of the purchase price. This insurance is called private mortgage insurance. This insurance policy protects the lender, guaranteeing him the insurance company will reimburse him for between 20 percent and 25 percent of the loan if the homeowner defaults. The insurance company forecloses on the house and tries to sell it to recoup its money.

Private mortgage insurance usually costs about 1 percent of the outstanding balance of the loan. But Zerlin said the policy may cost more if the lender perceives the loan to be a higher risk than most. Homeowners pay the annual premium monthly in their monthly mortgage payments. Once the outstanding balance reaches 20 percent of the purchase price, the lenders do not requires PMI.

If you want to refinance your home, just read this section over again. Refinancing is nothing more than applying for a new loan on your home. Instead of paying off the seller, your new mortgage company will pay off your old mortgage company. The new mortgage company goes through the same procedure before it will approve your new loan. The fact that you have lived in the house and made payments for five years is irrelevant. If you added a pool or bought a Mercedes, increasing your back ratios, it is quite conceivable you may NOT qualify for your current house.

Mortgage companies will only refinance 80 percent of the current appraised value of the home. If you originally got a 95 percent loan and the house has not appreciated in value significantly, then you will have to come up with additional equity to close the loan. This is in addition to all the closing costs you must pay.

How do you know if it is cost effective to refinance? The industry rule of thumb is to make back the costs of refinancing in two years or less in reduced mortgage payments. Say your current rate is 13 percent and your payment is $900 a month. Say closings costs are $4,000. Your new mortgage payments will be $750 per month, a savings of $150. In two years you will have only saved $3600. It will take twenty-seven months to get back your money. Here refinancing does not make economic sense. If the reduced mortgage payments had equaled $650 a month, refinancing would have been wise.

When you refinance a home, there is only one area where you do save money. That is on title insurance. Title companies have sliding scales on premiums one to five years old. If you refinance a home purchased less than five years ago, be sure to ask for your discount on your new title insurance policy. State boards of insurance set rates, so be sure to check with your board about possible discounts.

When you apply for a loan, the loan officer will give you a sheet with estimates for your closing costs. Lenders usually charge 1 percent of the amount you are borrowing as a loan origination fee. This covers their costs of processing the loan as well as their profit for doing so.

In addition, you must pay discount points, which are also 1 percent of the loan value. The lender does not keep the discount points. They go to the investor—generally Fannie Mae or private investors like insurance companies who buy the loan from your mortgage banker on the day you close. It is the investor who gives the mortgage banker the money to pay off your seller. And it is the investor who keeps the interest you mail in every month. Discount points plus the interest you send in during the first year equal the yield the investor wants to earn on his money. This is why lower interest rates require more points to be paid at closing.

Home buyers must pay the loan origination fee. Discount points, however, are totally negotiable. Usually the buyer and seller split them evenly, unless one party has used them as leverage for something else in the contract.

On a pre-owned home, the seller must pay for the title policy, which costs upwards of $500. Home builders, however, have traditionally refused to pay this fee, said Zerlin. Buyers of new homes usually pay the title policy premium at closing.

Phillips said many of these settlement fees are not applicable on government insured loans. "Be certain the closing agent is aware of what legally can be charged to a borrower and still obtain the federal guarantee," he said.

Mortgage lending is so heavily regulated it is almost impossible for a lender to cheat a consumer if he wants to stay in business. If the lender makes a mistake, it is usually due purely to ignorance or carelessness.

Phillips said federal law requires all mortgage lenders to give applicants a good faith estimate of what the closing costs will be three days after you apply for a loan. They must also give you a booklet prepared by the United States Department of Housing and Urban Development called "Settlement Costs and You." Read this thirty page booklet from cover to cover. There is no way you can get cheated if you take the time to read the book.

CLOSING ON YOUR HOME PURCHASE

Closing is done at a title company by a title attorney. Generally buyers and sellers do not see a Uniform Settlement Statement until they reach the closing statement. But Phillips said the law requires the title company to let the buyer and seller see the statement one business day before closing if requested in advance. Smart buyers do this so they can compare figures in advance. For example, if the PMI premium is more than 1 percent of the loan, find out why.

Never show up to a closing without a certified check. After that, all you need is a pen to sign the half dozen documents necessary to transfer title and make that home yours.

Remember, closings should take no more than thirty minutes. They are not the place to argue about who pays what. That is done during the contract negotiation stage. Once you sign the contract, the terms are written in stone.

You should drive home from the title company in good spirits. Since mortgage payments are made in arrears, you get to live in the house for the first month "free." You do not have to make the first payment until the second month you are there.

SELLING A HOUSE

The biggest question for homeowners when they decide to sell their home is to determine whether they should hire a realtor or try to do it themselves, at least at the outset. This is a most difficult choice. Here is what to consider.

Commissions paid to the realtor are the seller's responsibility. These are negotiable, but the standard practice is 6 percent. Realtors do work hard for their money, however.

They pay for all the advertising on your home. They pay the fee to get your home listed in the MLS computer. This is an invaluable marketing advantage. If there are three thousand real estate agents in your town, you have really hired all of them to work for you selling your house. Each one knows her commission is guaranteed if she sells your house. You cannot achieve any broader exposure than the MLS network.

Realtors are also professionals who have an intimate knowledge of the market. This is crucial when setting a market value for your home. What you want for the house is a virtually irrelevant consideration. Realtors can help you select a fair price. If you want to sell the house, only a market price will move it.

If you work, you almost certainly need a realtor. Couples looking for houses usually do it during the day during business hours when you are at work. When an interested buyer wants to see your house, someone better be able to be there and let him in. Realtors are the ones chained to the house during open houses on beautiful Sunday afternoons when you would rather be playing tennis. The realtor is also there when the appraiser comes or when the termite man arrives. These people need access to the house during business hours.

Realtors are also unemotional negotiators. It is hard to be unbiased about your home sweet home. The realtor, however, can keep her sang-froid and usually negotiate a better deal for you.

However, you can be a FSBO and do it yourself. Many cities now are forming FSBO networks which list all the FSBOs for a set fee, about $100. Buy a large For Sale sign and stick it in your yard. Then advertise in the classified section of all your local papers. Usually four or five lines will do. Be sure to put the price and the approximate location. Do not hyperbolize. Adequate classified ads cost about $50 for ten days.

If you have priced the home properly, it should sell. Listing agreements with a realtor generally run six months. Be patient. Homes sell because they are priced right.

How much should you fix up your house before you sell it? You really have two options. You can sell it "as is" and take a lesser price than the house next door. Or you can spend money—which is currently deductible from your taxable gains—fixing it up. Painting inside and out is cost effective, said Al Carrell, who has a syndicated national radio program called "The Handyman." He advised that planting flowers is a must. But he does not suggest purchasing new carpet unless yours is worn to the pad.

Carrell suggested collecting all the items you have been meaning to sell for years and have a garage sale. "Clutter turns buyers off. And whatever you do, clean up the front door. That's a buyer's all important first impression," he said.

Once you find a buyer, have a real estate lawyer draw up an earnest money contract. Or go to a title company. A title officer may be able to give you, its customer, the Board of Realtors contract; all you have to do is fill in the blanks. Be sure to ask the buyer for an earnest money check made out to the title attorney which is placed in escrow until the transaction closes. Take the check and the signed contract to your title company and let its processors handle it from there.

All you have to do is show up at closing, sign the documents and pocket your check. What makes things complicated is that you probably are also buying a house at the same time. Being on both sides of the closing table can get harry, just stay cool.

BUYING FORECLOSURES AND REOS

For savvy, experienced real estate investors, buying foreclosures and properties in the Real Estate Owned portfolio of lending institutions presents a wealth of opportunity. Those in the know can add profitable properties to their portfolios at firesale prices.

But do not believe the slick spiels you hear on late night television. "If those guys could make easy money buying foreclosures, they certainly wouldn't be telling you about it. They're just good at selling books and videotapes," scoffed Zerlin.

A homeowner is in default when he does not pay his principal and interest. When a homeowner gets behind, the lender can send out a foreclosure notice. This gives the homeowner one month to make the back payments current. At the same time the lender informs the homeowner of the pending foreclosure, he must also post the information in a public place. Historically this list is posted at the courthouse in the county where the property is located.

Foreclosure sales are held the first Tuesday of every month at the county courthouse. Lenders usually try to sell the home for at least the value of their loan. If they cannot sell it for that price, they add it to their REO or Real Estate Owned portfolios. Lending institutions do not like having REOs on their books and usually are willing to negotiate.

Buying a REO from a lender "is the cleanest, safest way to purchase distressed property," said Terry Letteer, a vice president and title attorney for Safeco Land Title

Company in Dallas, Texas. Lenders usually list their REOs with realtors. Call various real estate offices and ask about their bank REO listings. Generally REOs can be bought with a small down payment and no closing costs, which slash the cost of completing a real estate transaction in half. Buyers must meet Fannie Mae qualifying standards and have enough cash to pay for the "pre-paids" which include property taxes and the annual insurance policy which are always paid at closing.

Both Fannie Mae and the VA have REOs which they call "acquired properties." These organizations have hired specific brokers in each community to sell these properties. Call the local district offices of these agencies to find out which brokers are selling their acquired properties.

The VA, for example, has its new REO list ready the first Thursday of every month, according to George Jackson, one of the VA brokers handling acquired properties in North Texas. "That's the day to call the broker. One week later and the good homes are gone," he said.

The VA will guarantee a VA loan on its REOs even though the buyer is not a veteran. It requires little money down at closing.

Do not go to the courthouse to buy property unless you are an experienced investor. First of all, you have to have the entire purchase price available. Unless you have a ready amount of cash, this is not the procedure for you. "In reality, most people do not buy foreclosed properties because they do not have the cash it takes," said Zerlin.

Also remember that all liens run with the land. That means if the buyer did not pay his income tax, the friendly Internal Revenue Service can put a federal tax lien on the house. That means whoever owns the house must pay for that tax lien. If you buy a house out of foreclosure and did not check the federal tax records beforehand, you are legally liable for the money.

Investors planning to buy a home at a foreclosure sale should notify the IRS 25 days before the sale date if they do not want the lien to run with the land. After the sale the IRS still has 120 days to scrutinize the purchase to determine if the purchase price was fair market value. If not, it has the right to sell that property for a greater amount to pay off the tax lien.

While you are checking taxes, make sure the homeowner has paid his county, school, city, hospital, and ad valorem taxes. If not, they are your problem.

Also, be sure to pay at least 70 percent of the true market value of the house. If you do not and the buyer declares bankruptcy within twelve months after you purchased the house, a bankruptcy judge can order the house sold to pay off creditors. If you paid more than 70 percent, the judge cannot touch your purchase.

Mary Pfaff of the Mortgage Bankers Association, the Washington, D.C. based industry trade group, said foreclosures are always a problem. They can hurt the earnings of a mortgage company that has to add REOs to the list. And they are even worse for the homeowner because a foreclosure destroys his credit rating for seven years.

"The problem with discussing foreclosure is it is such a complication of laws," Pfaff said. Explaining the details and exceptions to the laws would be more than the average consumer could take. Basically, states follow one of four methods of foreclosure:

1. Strict foreclosure—This takes place in a civil court, similar to a judicial foreclosure, but there is no public sale. The decree or judgment of foreclosure frees the mortgage holder of title to the property and it goes directly to the lender. The procedure usually requires a finding by the court that the property is not sufficient collateral for the debt. States that use it include Connecticut, New Hampshire, and Vermont.

2. Foreclosure by entry and possession—The lender enters the premises and takes peaceful possession of the property with witnesses present. However, if the mortgage holder does not relinquish possession of the property peacefully, the lender may have to foreclose judicially. Legal counsel should be consulted on the applicability of this procedure in states where it is used; presently only Maine follows this method of foreclosure.

3. Foreclosure by sale in a judicial proceeding—The first step is filing a complaint to determine the identity of all parties who may have interest in the property. The complaint states the terms of the mortgage, cites the nature and extent of the mortgage holder's default, and petitions the court for a decree or judgment of foreclosure and sale. Each person connected with the mortgage has a certain period of time to file an answer. After all answers have been filed, a hearing is set to resolve any disputes. The court then enters a decree of judgment to establish the amount of the debt, orders the mortgage holder to pay the debt in a certain period of time, and specifies that the property be sold at public auction if not paid in that time period. The proceeds of this sale of property go to the lender. The auction is conducted under the direction of the court. In theory, a third party buys the property and the lender is paid the amount of indebtedness. States that use this method are Arkansas, Delaware, Florida, Hawaii, Idaho, Illinois, Indiana, Iowa, Kansas, Kentucky, Louisiana, Nebraska, New Jersey, New Mexico, New York, North Dakota, Oklahoma, Pennsylvania, South Carolina, South Dakota, and Utah.

4. Foreclosure by power of sale—This is the most popular method used by twenty-five states. In this case the security instrument for mortgage gives the lenders or trustee the power to sell the property without court-supervised action. The mortgage deed usually states that a notice of sale must be published in a local newspaper or posted in a public place (usually in the courthouse). Foreclosure by power of sale is less expensive and much quicker than judicial foreclosure. Property could be sold quickly if the mortgage holder is not careful in states that use this method. Some states with this require that a notice of default be sent to the borrower to correct the default—if it is not corrected, the property is sold by public auction. States that use this method are Alabama, Alaska, Arizona, California, Colorado, District of Columbia, Georgia, Maryland, Massachusetts, Michigan, Minnesota, Mississippi, Missouri, Montana, Nevada, North Carolina, Oregon, Rhode Island, Tennessee, Texas, Virginia, Washington, West Virginia, Wisconsin, and Wyoming.

"Buying foreclosures can be very lucrative," said Letteer. "But they definitely have their downsides. It is not an area for the uninitiated," he warned.

Buying real estate is a very complex transaction. Being uninformed can cause consumers to make costly mistakes. Fortunately, the real estate industry is so heavily regulated and supervised by city, state, and federal agencies that real estate providers cannot take the economic risk of cheating the consumer. A realtor can lose her license; a mortgage banker can lose its federal funding approval.

However, consumers can lose significant amounts of money by being unaware of the nuances of buying and selling real estate. Knowing what is negotiable and how the process works is the best protection for any consumer embarking on a residential real estate transaction.